This is a great read. It is an engaging account of the motives, struggles and joys of one of the early Free Reformed families to settle in the Perth area after World War II. The author has a real historian's gift for marshalling an amazing amount of detailed historical material while maintaining a comfortable flow of the story – I always wanted to know what happens next.

In today's society where we have so much and yet complain so often, it is both inspiring and humbling to read this story in which a pioneering family contentedly built lives for themselves and their children from a position where they had very little apart from their faith, their church community and their industry. Buy it and read it, even if (like me) you're not related to any of the people in it. You'll have a greater appreciation for your own blessings.

Professor Nic Groenewold
Senior Honorary Research Fellow, UWA Business School

I highly recommend this book.

It is a gripping story of one family's journey through pre-war Holland, the German occupation and their migration to Australia. A real family, honestly and empathetically drawn, and this makes for a beautiful read!

But it is more than just a personal story of one family. The storytelling is skilfully woven into the much broader context of the world changing events of the twentieth century. It is a real history book – thoroughly researched.

Finally, this book is a wonderful testimony of God's faithfulness. In the life of this family through good times and difficulties, through the generations. And also in directing all of history for His purposes, in the gathering and preservation of His church in Australia.

Geraldine Plug
History Teacher, John Calvin Christian College

My Father's Journey

From Tragedy, War and New Hope in Australia, a Story of Inspiring Faith in God Through It All

By Harry Kleyn

IngramSpark
Australia

Copyright © 2022 Harry Kleyn

All rights reserved.

Scripture taken from the New King James Version®. Copyright © 1982 by Thomas Nelson, Inc. Used by permission. All rights reserved.

Cover design: Edwin Visser

Cover photo: 1919 image of my father with his two sisters

ISBN: 978-0-6453842-1-5 (Paperback)

ISBN: 978-0-6453842-0-8 (Hardcover)

Contents

Preface — x
Author's Note — xiv
Map of Ablasserwaard — xv
Map of Armadale (1950s) — xvi
Family Tree of the Kleijns — xvii
Family Tree of the Verhoefs — xviii
Family Tree of the Kleijn / Schutte — xix

1. Hometown — 1
2. Dad's Parents — 8
3. Dad's arrival — 11
4. That fateful Day — 20
5. The Aftermath — 25
6. Klaas Kleijn: Ward of the State — 31
7. Life at the St Joris Gasthuis — 37
8. Dad's Formative Years — 47
9. In the Work Force — 57
10. Army Life — 62
11. Back in the Work Force — 66
12. Dad Finds his Future Wife — 70
13. The Schutte Family — 73
14. Mum's Early Years — 86
15. The Happy Couple — 95
16. Sickness Strikes — 99
17. Charting a Life's Path — 105
18. The First Years of Marriage — 114
19. The Spectre of War — 121
20. Called up for Service — 128
21. Fears for Dad's Safety — 134

22.	Living Under German Occupation	138
23.	The Germans Tighten their Grip	143
24.	In Hiding	148
25.	Staying Undercover	153
26.	The Final Gasp	159
27.	Towards Freedom	166
28.	The Cost of Freedom	171
29.	The Call of a Glorious Gospel: Rev. Boodt	178
30.	Church Life	183
31.	The Liberation: Seeds Sown for the Free Reformed Churches	188
32.	The Post-War Years	194
33.	Preparation and Departure	204
34.	On the Ocean	217
35.	Australia in 1952	224
36.	The First Days in Australia	232
37.	A Home and Work	242
38.	Another Child and Another House	250
39.	Finding a Place to Call Home	257
40.	Church Life	266
41.	Tragedy in the Netherlands	273
42.	Settling in at Fallon's Place	277
43.	A Growing Family	284
44.	Building our Own Home	292
45.	A Church in Strife	302
46.	The Union Struggle	310
47.	New Directions	319
48.	Towards Self-employment	326
49.	Changing Dynamics in the Family	336
50.	The Dutch Family	343
51.	Working from Home: A Dream Realised	349
52.	Reunification with the Old Country and Barriers with the New	354
53.	Towards Retirement	358

54.	Sickness and Death	362
55.	The Early Years of Retirement	369
56.	More Travel, Celebrations and Visitors	375
57.	A Wedding – More Visitors and a Move	380
58.	Serious Illnesses	384
59.	Dad's Final Weeks	389
60.	Postscript	398

Preface

The idea of this book has been simmering since I worked on a family booklet in 2003 to commemorate the 50th anniversary of our family migrating to Australia. Doing the work on that booklet uncovered a wealth of material and highlighted there was a bigger story of my parents' life to discover. Also, as time went on, I became acutely aware that the heritage and culture of my parents was being lost and forgotten. There is so much we can learn and appreciate from our forefathers – particularly from the era of my parents who lived through the depression, the Second World War and then migration to a new country. They were able to enjoy just three years of their married life before Dad was called to join the army due to the threat of war which then broke out nine months later. How did they cope with all the various trials that were placed on their path?

Their story is a powerful witness of their faith and trust in God. Despite a difficult start in life, which was followed by decades of hardship and challenges, their strength of faith helped carry them through these situations. In this, they left a legacy, an example for all their descendants who can give thanks to God for what He gave them all through them. It is also for this reason that this story is told – so that their heritage and simple faith is not lost for future generations. Knowing their story through the lens of the times also gives us some perspective on how richly blessed we are now, living in this wonderful free country, Australia, where we have access to the best services and medical attention regardless of class or distinction. What a contrast to the era when my parents were growing up. Let us not take all this for granted but strive to maintain what we have. It can so easily be lost through neglect and ignorance.

In 2016, and then again in 2019, I had the privilege to spend three months in the Netherlands with my wife, Rita. This gave us the opportunity to meet and talk to many of our extended family as well as spend time researching in relevant libraries and historical archives. Only one auntie from my mother's side was then alive but, unfortunately, she suffered from dementia so was not able to give us any information about times past. While there, the descendants from my mother's parents had a reunion so we were able to connect and learn a lot about the past from the thirty or so Schutte cousins in attendance.

My cousins were extremely helpful in providing me with information, including old letters, booklets, photos and other material of historical interest. I would particularly like to acknowledge Johan Schutte, Jenny van der Toorn-Schutte, Wim Schutte, Jan Smit, Jenny Smit, Nico Smit, Henk Bultman and son Dick, Gerry and Goof de Boer and Huig and Atie de Haan for their committed assistance and advice.

I was also able to speak to two of Dad's half-cousins, Arie Jan Verhoef and Kees Verhoef, both then 90, who gave valuable information about Dad's youth and the war years.

The staff at the Noord Holland Archives, Dordrecht National Archives and the Historisch St. Joris Museum respectively were all very helpful, assisting me in finding the files and information about my grandfather, Klaas Kleijn. Despite being over 100 years old, my grandfather's records were meticulously stored and I was given unlimited access to them.

My siblings were supportive and helpful in the process of producing this book by providing information, advice and proof reading. Particularly my two sisters living in the Netherlands, Jenny and Mary, were able to provide additional assistance with introductions and contacts as well as giving access to letters they themselves had received over the years from my parents.

When my Dad's youngest sister, Auntie Marie, died in 2008 I received a lot of the correspondence that she had with her adopted mother, Miek, and my dad. These provided a treasure chest of information and insights. My appreciation goes to my sister, Mary, who collected the material and put it aside for me.

Another source was my Mum's diaries and scrapbooks. She handed them over to me just prior to her and Dad moving into the Fair Haven Village in 1997. Her scrapbooks had been meticulously kept and updated over many decades and in them were newspaper cuttings, articles, and photos of anything relating to family, friends or acquaintances. Her diaries, while not done daily and having some big gaps, particularly during the war years, were nevertheless started when she was just 12 and provide insight into her feelings and experiences over the years.

Work on this book has stretched over nearly three years. It has been a mammoth but rewarding task. I am particularly grateful to my wife, Rita, who was with me on the whole journey, participating in many of the interviews and discussions and gave sage advice when necessary. She also had to tolerate my absence many days and evenings as I was absorbed reading and researching in my study. Thank you my dear – you are the love of my life.

Thanks to my editor, Gerry Huizinga, who meticulously went through the draft copy line by line to make the material flow better for you, the reader. She not only edited but gave advice on structure, layout, and content. Thank you for your dedication and commitment to ensure the best outcome possible.

Thanks also to son Gary and daughter Natalie, both of whom have been on the journey in providing feedback, editing the final copy and, in the case of Natalie, doing the layout and design in preparation for the printer.

Thanks also to granddaughter Celeste Dykstra who was given an early draft copy to provide valuable feedback from the view of the younger generation. Some of her insights have been incorporated into this final edition.

Leo Schoof, my brother-in-law, read the final copy and with his attention to detail was able to still find hundreds of errors despite the meticulous work of previous editors. Thank you.

Finally, I give thanks to my heavenly Father who gave health and everything I needed to complete this book.

AUTHOR'S NOTE

Since the book takes place in both the Netherlands and Australia, I had to make some decisions on which spellings and names to use to assist in readability.

The surname Kleijn has been changed to Kleyn by most of the families in Australia and America, but I have chosen to use the original Dutch spelling throughout the book.

In Holland it is common for a child to be given a 'birth name', and then a 'roep naam', or a name by which they were commonly known. Since many of my siblings spent most of their lives in Australia, I have chosen to refer to them by the name by which they are known in Australia.

Map of Alblasserwaard

Map of Armadale (1950s)

Kleijn Family Tree

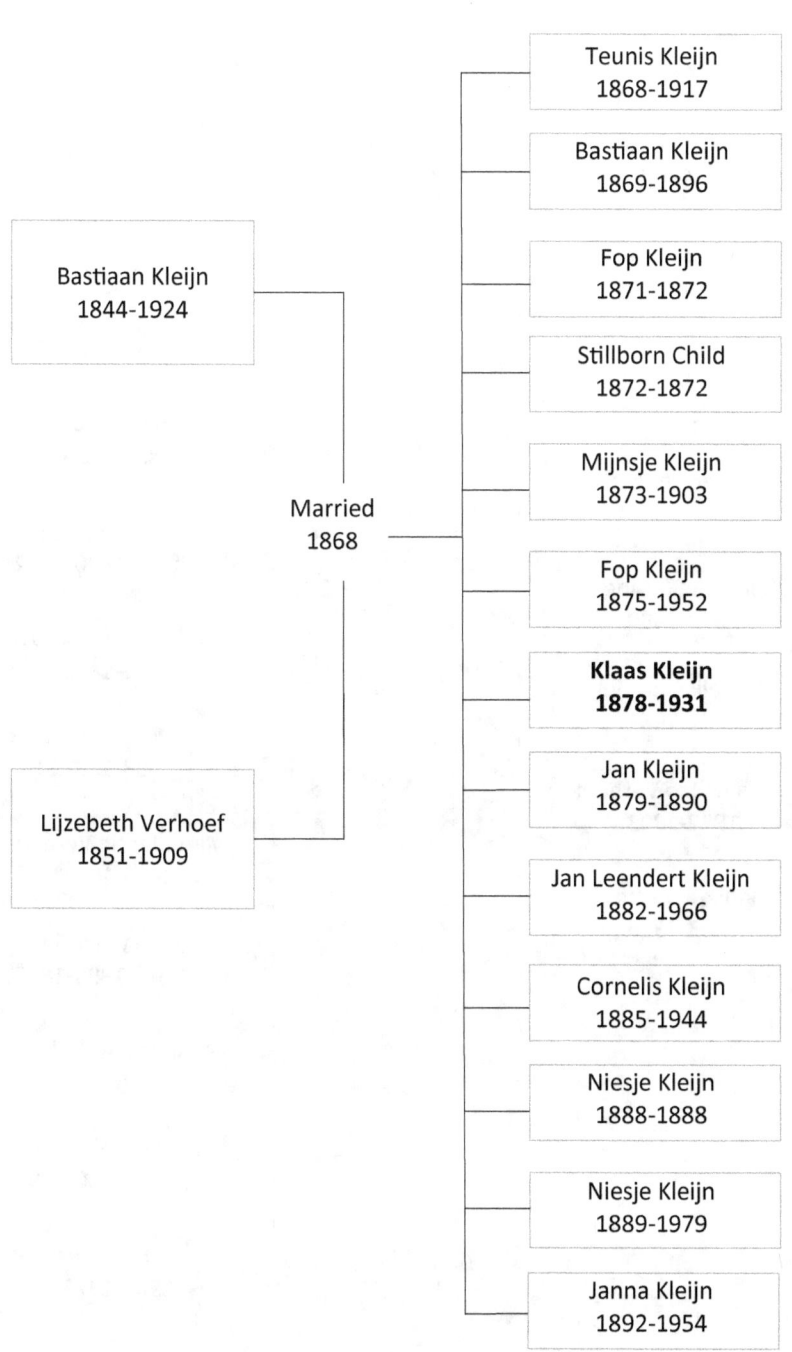

Verhoef Family Tree

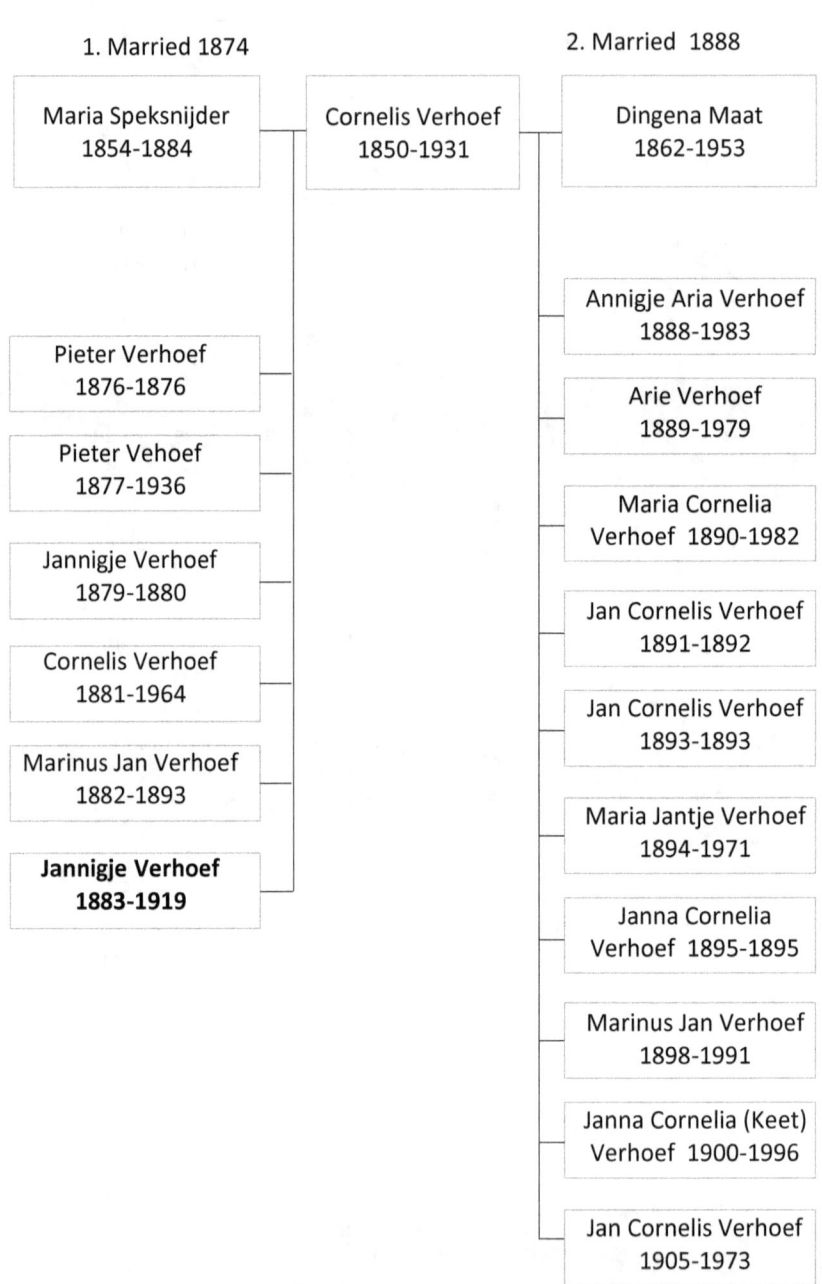

Kleijn/Schutte Family Tree

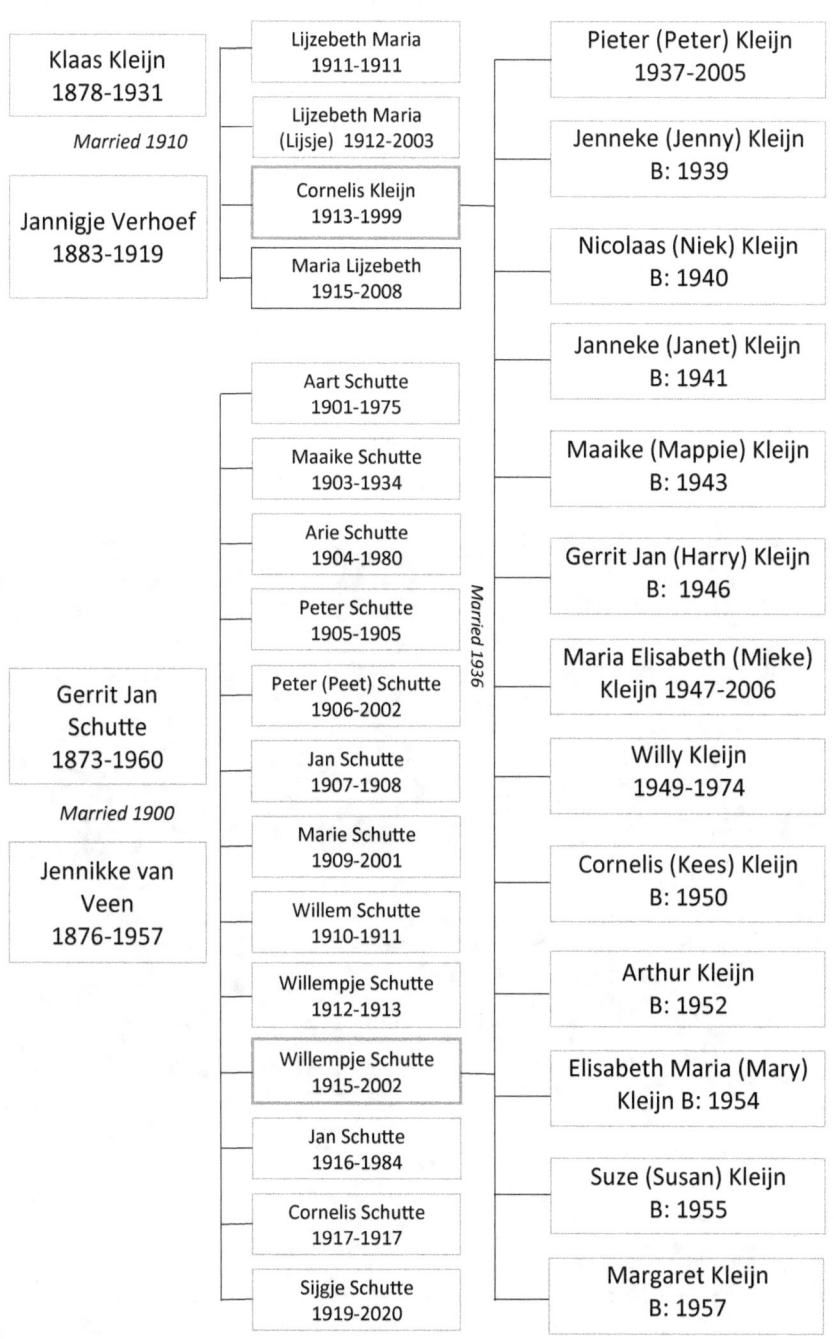

1. Hometown

"The Lord will record, when He registers the peoples: 'This one was born there.'"

~ *Psalm 87:6 (NKJV)*

My parents and grandparents and even my great-grandparents from both my Dad and Mum were all born and raised in that part of the Netherlands known as the *Alblasserwaard*. It is an area located in the southeast province of South Holland bordered by rivers on all sides; to the north is the Lek, on the west runs the Noord, to the south the river Merwede and on the east boundary is the Merwede-Kanaal, the Linge and the Oude Zederik which together form the boundary with the neighbouring province.

The *Alblasserwaard,* which covers about 25,000 hectares, is divided into seven local municipalities with 56 towns and villages that together, in 2020, house a population of about 170,000. Many of these small villages are only on average about 4 kilometres apart and, while the overall population has grown considerably from the time my parents were born in the early 1900s, a lot of the buildings in each village, including shops, churches, farmhouses and windmills from that era, still form a iconic part of the landscape.

Travelling through various villages in this district gives you a real sense of what it is like to step back in time. There are narrow dyke roads that are more suitable for the pre-car era and everywhere you look there's a proliferation of old farm houses and structures, some of which were built as long as 500 years ago. Demolition is a rare thing in this part of the world and buildings are well preserved and maintained, often kept updated to suit changing lifestyles. Heritage laws in the Netherlands are also stringently enacted to ensure the protection and preservation of historic buildings.

In 2017, my wife Rita and I stayed three months in the Netherlands and, as part of our research for this book, spent a number of days in a bed and breakfast farmhouse situated in Brandwijk, a small village where my mother was born. This farmhouse, known as 't Hoge Huis, was built in the early 1600s and besides the plumbing, electrical and kitchen having been updated, the core building is still exactly as it was when built.

The key element in the design of all farmhouses in the district, including this one, was providing safe refuge for livestock and people in case of flooding. This primarily involved sufficient height so that the second floor would be well clear of the highest possible flood level. Furthermore, there needed to be provision for ramps to be put in place in case of flood so the cows and other farm animals could be herded to the top floor where they would then stay for the duration of the flood. The house also had pulleys in place to hoist what was necessary to the top floor.

As floods in the region generally involved fast-moving waters that could threaten to wash away the whole building, the structure had to be built with solid foundations and walls to withstand these possible threats. Our time spent in the 't Hoge Huis farmhouse allowed us to witness the formidable strength and perpetuity of these buildings. We stayed on the top floor, which now serves as a bed and breakfast facility, and the enormous size of the exposed structural timber beams was impressive. 't Hoge Huis still stands firm today after more than 400 years despite having experienced countless floods during its time.

Since human settlement commenced in the *Albasserwaard* during the fourteenth century, fighting back water has been a defining factor in the planning and occupation of the district. During the course of the first 200 years of settlement there was a constant preoccupation with building dykes, waterways, dams and canals to allow the water to be drained from the land so it could become productive farmland. An extensive windmill network was developed to pump the water from the lowlands into the rivers that then flowed into the sea. The well-known and UNESCO heritage listed Kinderdijk group of 19 windmills all built in the early 1700s present a good illustration of the important role windmills played in protecting the Dutch countryside from flooding. After all, the *Albasserwaard* was predominantly below sea level, and before human intervention from the early 13th Century onwards, the area consisted of muddy floodplains and inaccessible wastelands.

Many of the waterways and dykes constructed two to three centuries ago have remained intact as have the townships and roads.

However, after the major flood of 1953 in South-West Holland and Zeeland (including the *Alblasserwaard*) in which 1,836 people lost their lives, the Dutch Government decided to develop a more comprehensive defensive mechanism to guard against future floods. Known as the Delta project, it involved building dams and storm surge barriers along the coast of South-West Holland and Zeeland. Thereafter, in the case of severe storms and flooding these barriers could be activated to protect the land. Despite being a very ambitious and costly project, it has nevertheless allowed the Netherlands to be predominantly flood-free for nearly 70 years.

The fact that the people of the *Albasserwaard* are surrounded by water - and have for centuries needed to fight its power - has had a distinct impact on the character and resilience of the people in the district. Before the development of the Delta works, a major flood occurred on average every 20 to 30 years and with those floods everybody's life and welfare was at risk. Flood waters didn't discriminate and affected both the poor and rich alike, with so many farmers over the years suffering severe financial hardship as a result of floods.

Historically, these small villages were places where everyone knew each other well and when storms threatened to break the dyke all hands were on deck to fill and build up sandbags to try and save the dyke. When the dyke did burst everyone needed to work together to save lives and stock. Then, after the flood, there was often a long period of isolation and hardship as the flood waters slowly receded over many months. The impact was acutely felt and experienced by all.

According to one of my Dad's half-cousins, who was 90 at the time I met him in 2017, this need to work together threw away any pretentions of class or status. As a consequence of these life-and-death situations, the district had a far better relationship between the farmers and the farm workers than in areas like the north of the Netherlands, where farmers were extremely class conscious and refused to even have a farm worker enter his house or eat with them. They also did little to improve or care for the worker's situation. The constant threats and need to work together caused the *Albasserwaard* people to become a far more egalitarian society than was the case in the rest of the country where those threats did not occur. Nevertheless, while the extreme elements of class and discrimination may have been absent in the *Alblasserwaard*, it was still an accepted tradition of general society during my parents' youth.

One of the benefits of the area's constant struggle with water was that many in the district developed experience and proficiency in the art of building dams, dredging, and pumping water. With the developing nations in the world needing to build harbours and dams during the 18th and 19th Centuries, entrepreneurs in the district were well placed to form companies and develop worldwide reputations for expertise in this area. Still today, the water industry is a major contributor to the economy of the district with many of these dredging and civil construction companies which have their origin during this period, still active worldwide and headquartered in the *Albasserwaard* town of Sliedrecht.

While my grandparents were all born in the *Albasserwaard* district, they came from different towns. My Dad's father Klaas Kleijn, was born in Streefkerk in 1878, while his wife, Jannigje Verhoef, was born in Brandwijk in 1883.

From my mother's side, there was Gerrit Jan Schutte born in Goudriaan in 1873 and his wife, Jannigje van Veen, born in Bleskensgraaf in 1876. At the time these towns were small villages with populations of about 400 each, surrounded by rivers and waterways. Between the villages were farmhouses, with the average farm plot not being much more than about 10 acres. All plots and farms were naturally divided by water ways and dykes with no fencing required. Farmers in the district concentrated on animal husbandry like milking cows, making cheese and keeping pigs. The land was unsuitable for grain-harvesting.

Up until the mid-20th Century the *Albasserwaard* was an agrarian society with the main economy revolving around the produce of farmers. Most careers outside farming were focused on servicing the needs of farmers and their families.

As with my grandparents, my parents were also born in two different towns although again in close proximity. Dad, Cornelis Kleijn, was born in 1913 in Streefkerk and Mum, Willempje Schutte, was born in 1915 in Brandwijk. Mum told me later that it was common to seek a marriage partner from a surrounding town rather than in one's own town. In fact, the small towns had so many family interrelations that it was often necessary to go to another village for a marriage partner to avoid family intermarriages.

People did not move around nor travel much at that time, so the tendency was for families to stay in their town of birth for life. The roots of many families living in the *Albasserwaard* can be traced back many generations. A member from my grandmother's Verhoef family traced the family back and found them living 400 years in the *Albasserwaard*. He published his findings in a book titled *Four Centuries Verhoef 1588-1988*. These long-term family roots in the district would be quite a common feature throughout the *Albasserwaard*, particularly amongst the farmers who had a tradition of passing on the farm from father to son. As a consequence, many people who grew up in those small towns and farms would have family connections with a large percentage of others in the community.

These family connections struck me when I visited the local museum in Brandwijk in 2017. My immediate family had left the district to migrate to Australia in 1952, then 65 years earlier. The lady at the counter gave her name as Alie Verhoef and after introductions and explaining my own family background it became obvious that we were distant relatives. She sent me to the local historian, Bep Tukker, who had the genealogical records of most of the families in the district. Upon visiting her, she also claimed to be some distant relation as the Tukker name appeared in the Verhoef genealogy. The family names of both my grandparents were well known in the district and understandably so as they had lived there for generations. My parents broke that cycle when they migrated to Australia in 1952. Having lived in Australia for 65 years, growing up without the extended family of grandparents, uncles, aunties and cousins, I found it an emotional experience to get that sense of roots and belonging, something that I did not experience in the adopted country. I felt as if this was "home."

2. Dad's parents

"The joys of parents are secret, and so are their grieves and fears."
~ Francis Bacon (1561- 1626)

Dad's father, Klaas Kleijn, was born on the 11th February 1878 on the Streefkerk family farm. He was the fourth child in a family of 13, of which nine survived to adulthood. No doubt, as was tradition in those days, he would have helped on the farm from his early years and would have had very little education. Eventually, he became a general builder's labourer. While some of his brothers became successful farmers and businessmen, Klaas didn't seem to have the mental capacity, nor the self-confidence to be self-employed or to make long term commitments. While he had a reputation of being a willing and hard worker, he didn't seem able to hold jobs down for long and so was often stretched financially. He was a member of the Dutch Reformed Church but there is no evidence that he was ever active in church life. As a youth he did attend catechism classes and had done his profession of faith in the church. When he married Jannigje Verhoef on the 1st September 1910 he was 32 years of age. His mother, Lijzabeth Kleijn-Verhoef, had passed away less than a year before he married, on 4th October 1909.

Dad's mother, Jannigje Verhoef, was born on the 25th July 1883 in Brandwijk. She was most likely born on the family farm as the Verhoefs had been farming in the district for many generations. Her mother, Maria Verhoef-Speksnijder, died when Jannigje was only 15 months old on 13th September 1884. Jannigje was the youngest of six children but two of her siblings died as infants and a brother, born just a year before her, died at the age of 11 in 1893. When she was five years old her father remarried to Dingena Maat who then became her stepmother.

Jannigje appeared to have difficulty learning and was considered to be a child who could not really take responsibility for herself. Some correspondence that she wrote as an adult has been preserved, and it shows a very slim and basic knowledge of language and spelling to the extent that her writing is a challenge to decipher. All indications are that, because of her difficulty in learning, she spent little time at school and so was given little opportunity to develop herself. She was simply classed as a 'slow learner' and with no proper diagnosis the cause of her mental disability is unknown.

She was, however, at the age of 21, entitled to a substantial inheritance from her mum, Maria Speksnijder. She was a farmer's daughter and had considerable wealth for those days. Jannigje only had to share the inheritance with her two siblings as the other siblings born from her stepmother were not entitled to any of her mother's wealth. This caused considerable stress amongst the siblings which wouldn't have made Jannigje's life any easier. Jannigje's father also had concerns regarding her ability to manage, in a responsible way, the amount of money that was due to her when she turned 21. With this in mind, through the courts, he arranged to become her legal guardian with power of attorney. He put this in place prior to the settlement of the inheritance to Jannigje. This gave him total control of the funds on her behalf. On the 19th September, 1906, the published report of the court case held in Dordrecht stated that, *"Jannigje Verhoef, of no profession, of adult age, unmarried, living in Gijbeland, province Brandwijk on personal request, due to her weakness of mind, has appointed a guardian."*

The settlement of her mother's will was executed on the 1st November 1906, only a few months after Jannigje 'voluntarily' gave to her father all power of attorney. She turned 21 in 1904 which would have been the legal date she was entitled to her inheritance. We can only assume that her father was able to have that delayed for two years to make sure that the 'legal protection' for her was in place. We can only surmise that she indeed was intimidated with the responsibility of that money and rather wished her father to take that on. Also, with her being single there was justifiably real concern that she might attract the wrong type of husband with that wealth.

Indeed, this was to be the assessment by the Verhoef family when Klaas started courting Jannigje. Here was an unreliable person, often without work and as a consequence often short of money, seeking the hand of their now-wealthy daughter. They could only assume he was after her money as she, being of slow mind, was not exactly an ideal catch for a young man. Their concern was heightened when it was announced that she was expecting a baby from him.

Jannigje's pregnancy posed a real dilemma for the family. They did not want the scandal of a baby born out of wedlock but neither did they consider them a suitable couple to take on the responsibility of marriage and raising a family. Furthermore, the Verhoef family really considered that the motive of Klaas was less about affection and more about the money. Jannigje's stepmother, Dingena, later revealed to the authorities that Jannigje really didn't want to marry Klaas and had preferred to be institutionalised, a sentiment she had supported. There was also the issue that the couple were second cousins. Whether this played a role in the discussion is not known but it reinforces how closely related and connected everyone was. Ultimately, the pressure of scandal and reputation in such a small town proved too much because, despite the many reservations and concerns, eventually both parents relented and gave the couple their permission to marry. On the first of September 1910, they were married with Cornelis, as Jannigje's legal guardian, signing a declaration agreeing to the marriage. By then Jannigje was five months pregnant.

I only have one photo from that day – a group shot of some 35 people: Klaas and Jannigje sitting at the front surrounded by their parents and grandparents and other family members and friends. Jannigje is dressed in black with a full-length dress and top that includes a collar covering her neck. She wears a wide-brimmed hat with a large decorative ribbon on the top. Her face is the only visible part of her body. Even her hands are inside a pair of black gloves. Klaas, next to her, is in a black suit sitting very upright with his head covered by a high-top hat. Their faces are expressionless.

The rest of the group wear an array of fancy dress and fashion typical for the day. Everyone wears hats. Some of the men have simple caps while others more formal black top hats. But none quite as high as what Klaas has atop his stony face. The women's hats reflect a remarkable range of styles and designs that reminds one of the hats worn at the Melbourne Cup. The diversity of dress standard would suggest that the family and guests were from a wide range of socio-economic backgrounds with differing levels of prosperity and status. Interestingly, only the stepmother of Jannigje, Dingena Maat, wore the traditional Dutch costume cap and dress.

Four months after this wedding, on the 25th January 1911, the couple had a daughter Lijzebeth Maria, who they named after both their mothers. Tragically the baby died five months later on the 30th June 1911 from, as recorded on the death notice, - "a serious but short illness."

Jannigje's father was still her legal guardian which meant that she could not make any independent decisions nor make financial transactions without his express permission. It is unknown what pressures were brought to bear and what made him come to this decision, but three months after the Kleijn couple married, Cornelis engaged a solicitor to officially resign as Jannigje's legal guardian. It is likely Klaas, and even his family, would have insisted on this. Klaas was after all, as husband of Jannigje, head of the household and would be expected to take responsibility for the financial affairs of his family. Klaas would have assumed that, with the resignation of his father-in-law as legal guardian, he would be given access to his wife's inherited wealth. While this may have been true for the ready cash that was available, most of the estate was tied up in property and, as later correspondence showed, any property sale had to be approved by Cornelis. This inability to have total control over his and his wife's affairs became a point of increasing frustration and conflict as the years went by and as Klaas' financial pressures increased.

3. Dad's Arrival

"Your eyes saw my substance, being yet unformed.
And in Your book they all were written,
The day fashioned for me,
When as yet there were none of them.

~ *Psalm 139:16 (NKJV)*

Dad, named Cornelis after his Grandfather, was born on the 5th November 1913. It took 18 months before he was baptised on the 4th July 1915 in the Streefkerk Dutch Reformed Church, the same day his younger sister Maria Lijzebeth was baptised. This delay beyond the customary baptism within a few weeks of birth might be a reflection on an unhappy relationship the couple had with the local church, which may have been restored after the birth of their third child.

As was the case with nearly all births in those days, he would have been born at home. When he was born Dad already had a 16-month-old sister, Lijzebeth Maria. She was given the same name as her sister who died at five months in 1911. After Dad, the family expanded with another girl, Maria Lijzebeth, born 18 months later. Naming children after close relations was then a long-held tradition. The second daughter was typically named after both the grandmothers, but in reverse order so that both were equally recognised.

Klaas and Jannigje had bought and moved into a small corner house right in the centre of Streefkerk. Klaas' parents lived in the same district a few kilometres away on a farm. The brick and tile house was typical for those days with a very small back yard and a steep gable roof with an upper story living space underneath it. Located a few blocks from the local church it was easy walking distance to the town's facilities and shops. Living in the centre of the village, not much could happen without the whole town knowing it. At that time there were few cars around, so people simply walked, biked or took a boat on the numerous waterways, to get around. To travel to some of the nearby cities, like Rotterdam or Dordrecht, boats were preferred as the most convenient transport. The *Alblasserwaard* area was, after all, surrounded by rivers and the towns and villages had historically all been developed along the riverbanks.

The population of Streefkerk in the early 1900s was about 800 people, with many living on the estimated 90 independent farms surrounding the township. The town itself would possibly have had a population of between 300-400, many of whom would have been employed on one of the surrounding farms. Others would have been engaged in farm services such as the provision of food, clothing, repairs, maintenance and building. The maintenance and expansion of dams and dykes was also a constant source of employment in the district. Electricity was not connected till 1928 and water in 1937. As new inventions and services were introduced the range of careers and occupations also expanded in the towns.

On the 28th July 1914, eight months after Dad was born, the First World War broke out. While the Dutch remained neutral in the conflict, they were nevertheless surrounded by the fighting enemies and were in constant danger of being dragged into the conflict. Because of this danger the Dutch declared a general mobilisation and had more than 200,000 soldiers on standby ready for battle. Many men were called up and spent the years in boredom at barracks being battle-ready in case the war broke out. Also, in the *Alblasserwaard*, many men were called up. My Dad's half-cousin, Arie Jan Verhoef's dad, for example, was called up in 1914 and, as a consequence, had to sell all his cows and leave his kids with other family members to comply with the call-up. Klaas Kleijn received an official exemption – the reason may have been his mental state but there is no indication of this on the exemption notice.

It appeared that both sides of the warring nations saw the neutrality of the Dutch as advantageous for themselves. So, despite some real threats of invasion by the Germans if they were refused access or cooperation during certain phases of the war, the threats were never carried out and each crisis passed without mishap.

This did not mean that the Dutch weren't severely affected by the international conflict. When Germany invaded Belgium and captured the city of Antwerp in mid-1914, over a million Belgians fled into Holland, clogging roads and pathways. South Holland was the gateway for these desperate people.[1] The Dutch reached out to them with generosity, opening houses and stores to feed and clothe them. Despite the extraordinary number of refugees and the challenges those numbers entailed, it was reported that the Dutch population as well as its civic leaders spared no effort to lighten the load of these destitute and homeless people.[2] While most stayed in towns in Zeeland which borders Belgium, Streefkerk, only 90 kilometres from Antwerp, was also affected by incoming refugees. Family photos taken during the time in the Streefkerk area show the presence of Belgian refugees. All available accommodation and resources located in the south of Holland were harnessed to cope with the massive refugee influx.

The war also severely affected the shipping capacity of the Dutch both for trade as well as fishing. Besides German boats torpedoing Dutch ships, there was also the danger of hitting strategically placed sea mines laid by the Germans. While their war was with the English and their allies, they could not tolerate Dutch ships plying the oceans and possibly assisting the enemy. By the end of the war the Dutch were left with less than 10 per cent of their fleet and consequently exports, imports and fishing had virtually ground to a halt. To add to this injury, towards the end of the war, Dutch boats in American or English harbours were confiscated by them to be used for the final war effort. The British and Americans were desperately short of ships and needed them to transport troops and supplies for the final offensive against the Germans. They took this action under an international law known as 'Angarie', which gave a country at war the right to seize and use the property of neutrals for the purpose of warfare provided compensation was later paid.[3]

The result was that the Dutch, while avoiding massive loss of life, by 1918 had its cupboards bare and its economy in crisis. Food became scarce and unemployment was rampant. This deteriorating situation severely affected Klaas and Jannigje Kleijn with their three young children. Klaas had a reputation as a hard and dedicated worker but also as someone who was difficult and argumentative. So it was hard for him to keep a job down. With the deteriorating economy he became particularly disadvantaged as work was scarce and employers had plenty of keen workmen to choose from.

Their marriage was, from the beginning, a very unhappy one. The few letters that have survived from them portray in stark detail how desperate the situation between them was. Possibly within the first 12 months of marriage, Klaas sent an undated letter to his sister, Niesje, requesting her help to wash his clothes claiming his wife was neglecting her duties. In the letter he relates that he has a job in town and is willing to pay his sister for the washing. He claims that his wife treats him with disdain, does not want to do anything for him and constantly scolds him whenever he is home. He regrets not having kicked her out of the house and feels tremendously unhappy and sad. The only mitigating factor is, he wrote, that he is still in charge of the purse so he can go and do what he pleases. Obviously, the withdrawal of guardianship by his wife's father shortly after their marriage had given him a measure of financial independence. From this letter it appears to have been an important issue for him so it can be assumed he was instrumental in pushing for control of his wife's finances.

The pressure in the marriage increased when he lost his job and spent more time at home. Cash became scarce and he started talking about the need to sell some of the properties that his wife had inherited. Early 1918 he sent a letter to an agent instructing him to sell two properties valued at a total of 5,600 guilders. He asked the agent to move quickly and, if the price appeared too high, to come back with a revised price. The agent approached his wife, Jannigje, saying he would not sell the land unless the family agreed and a solicitor was engaged. He made the point that the property was from Jannigje's side of the family and she and her family needed to agree to the sale.

In desperation, Jannigje wrote to her parents for advice. Her husband was becoming increasingly irrational and demanding and she feared for her safety. She closed the letter by saying the kids are all well and healthy.

There is evidence that the mental health of Klaas was deteriorating during this time. He was feeling persecuted, was hearing voices inside his head and began imagining that his wife was unfaithful to him and was attempting to poison him. This was further aggravated when his local friends stirred him up with claims of infidelity on the part of his wife with another man and that he should keep a check on her. And since it was well known in the town that she was the one with the money, when he appeared to be short, villagers would again play on his insecurities by suggesting he go and see his wife and ask for some money.

The unemployment, the relentless pestering of his friends, the financial pressures and his inability to access what he considered his own, as well as suffering in a loveless marriage was, in the end, more than he could handle. He couldn't sleep, thought that people were out to murder him and became more and more paranoid and unstable. During 1918 he wrote a number of letters to the town mayor naming people who he thought were sleeping with his wife and asking the mayor to warn them to stay away from his house or he would take matters into his own hands. In the meantime, due to his fear of being murdered, he bought a large knife for protection which he carried with him at all times, even taking it to bed. Fear kept him indoors after dark.

Jannigje had her hands full with her three young children and a struggling husband. By the end of 1918 the eldest, Lijzebeth, was six, my Dad, Cornelis, was five while the youngest, Maria, was three. By Dutch law, introduced in 1901, all children from the age of six had to attend six years of school. It can be assumed that Lijzebeth was by this time attending the local school. According to the undated letter written by Jannigje to her parents, possibly some time during 1918, the children all enjoyed good health. Later reports reveal she was a faithful, loving and caring mother and her supposed unfaithfulness was simply a figment of Klaas' imagination, instigated and fed by the shenanigans of his friends. With her limited mental capacity, Jannigje would have struggled with what to do regarding Klaas' financial demands and efforts to sell properties that she had inherited. Before marriage, with her dad as guardian, she had never been confronted with the need to make any financial decisions. It would have been challenging, in the circumstances, for her to provide some sense of stability in the household for the sake of her children, while at the same time coping with her husband's deteriorating mental health.

4. That Fateful Day

"Yet man is born to trouble, as the sparks fly upward."

~ *Job 5:7 (NKJV)*

It was a Thursday, the 20th of February 1919, the day that my Dad and his two sisters would never forget. On that day, about 8.00 o'clock in the morning, their dad snapped. Klaas attacked his wife Jannigje, first with an axe and then with his knife to her throat. He then walked from the scene, first to notify the local doctor and then, to report the incident to the police where he gave himself up.

With life-threatening injuries, Jannigje needed urgent medical attention. Her head had been seriously injured by the blows of the axe, so arrangements were made by the doctor to have her taken to the Diaconessenhuis in Rotterdam. This hospital, established in 1892 by the Dutch Reformed Church of which Jannigje was a member, was considered one of the most advanced hospitals in the country. However, to get there Jannigje had to be taken to the boat harbour by horse carriage, then by boat for a 20-kilometre trip to Rotterdam harbour and then again by horse carriage to the hospital. This whole trip would have taken between four to six hours. Most likely the doctor would have been by her side for the journey. She arrived critically ill with serious concerns for her chance of survival.

Urgent efforts were made to contact Klaas's family a few kilometres away on the farm where Klaas was born. On arriving at the scene of the attack the family would have reached out to the distraught and traumatised children. The Kleijn family then notified Jannigje's family, the Verhoefs, who lived on a farm in Brandwijk, about 13 kilometres away, sending a telegram with the simple words, *"Daughter seriously injured. Tragic event."* Three days later, on the 23rd February, both the family Kleijn and family Verhoef received a telegram from the hospital 'Diaconessenhuis' with the words – *"Mrs. Kleijn has died."*

The three young children's world was now thrown upside down. They had lost both parents - their mum dead and their father taken away by the police. Furthermore, the scandal of it and inevitable gossip that would have been rife in that small village where everyone knew each other was something they would have to cope with and grow up with. Humanly speaking, the odds were against them to be able to grow up as normal, balanced adults.

There have been some different versions of the circumstances that led to the event. My Auntie Lijsje, as the oldest Lijzebeth became known, would later recall that that morning her dad was outside on the dyke with a few friends who had goaded him to check out what his wife was doing, suggesting she was with another man. He then supposedly rushed home, grabbed the axe and attacked her. Various versions of this story seemed to have been accepted by family members as somewhere near what happened. Family members also claimed that one of the friends responsible for telling him these untruths felt so awful after the attack, blaming himself for the tragedy, that he committed suicide.

Auntie Lijsje, who was six at the time, still had, in her 80s, graphic memories of that day and the trauma it caused. The children were in bed when the incident occurred, and she was the first one to awaken. One of her most vivid memories was seeing a lot of blood. Dad, who was five at the time, never spoke about the occasion to his children and seemed to have blocked the event out of his mind.

Klaas himself told the interviewing judge that he was up early that morning, chopped some wood and got the fire going. He left the axe next to the fire. His wife got up at 8 a.m. and started making him a coffee. He had visions of her trying to poison him and thought he witnessed her putting something in his coffee. Reason left him. He grabbed the axe next to the fire place and attacked her.

Meanwhile, in the town and the surrounding villages everyone soon heard about the fatal assault which served as fodder for gossip for many years. Remarkably, the media was low key about the event. Newspapers were virtually the only means of gaining information in those days and there were many publications in circulation to fill that need. Yet, in contrast to what we experience in the media today, this act of domestic violence only featured in a few lines buried in the papers under the local news section. Before Jannigje died, the wording, which appeared similarly in a number of newspapers, read:

> *Yesterday morning, a certain K., in Streefkerk committed a murderous assault on his wife by swinging an axe at her head and causing serious brain injury. The lady is in a serious condition. The attacker, who cannot be held accountable, has been taken into safe custody.*

A few days after her death it again was mentioned in a few newspapers with the wording then being:

> *A 35-year-old lady, who was, by her husband, a certain K. in Streefkerk, wilfully attacked on the head with an axe, has now died as a result of the injuries inflicted.*

There are no wasted words, no background or details, just factual information with persons not named or identified. The notice also makes the point that the offender was considered not responsible for his actions. Was this an intentional protection of people's privacy by the media?

Jannigje's body was taken back to her birthplace, the family farm in Brandwijk from where the funeral procession took place. Her three young children were considered too young to attend the funeral. Then six-and-a-half years old, Auntie Lijsje, later recalled peeping through the front door keyhole to observe the procession. It hurt her deeply that she was not able to attend her mother's funeral.

Rev. H.J.L. Poort, pastor since 1896 of the Dutch Reformed Church in Streefkerk where the Kleijns were members, had a close knowledge of the family and, particularly of Klaas Kleijn, who grew up in the town. Shortly after Jannigje's death he sent a letter of comfort and support to the family:

> *Dear family,*
> *I wish to express to you with a few words my sincere condolences with the tragic and sad event that has unfolded. It fills also me with great sadness and distress. I have known Kleijn since he was a young boy attending my catechism classes, and while he had a mental weakness, never could I have imagined that he*

would be responsible for the death of his wife and in such a horrible and shocking way. And, although I have known Jannigje for a shorter period, and was aware of her particular peculiarities, nevertheless I found her a quiet, soft and caring person who was a loving mother for her children.

Only just recently they both promised me that they would again read God's Word daily together with the children and that they would faithfully use the new Bible that they had. And now everything has turned out so differently. But also this has not happened outside God's providence and will. One day it will be revealed that God's ways are wonderful even if they are for us now painful. His wisdom is deep and his mercy everlasting. May God give you the grace and comfort so that despite this period of suffering your hearts may be lifted up to him. Despite this heavy trial he continues to be faithful providing we bow our knees to Him, our loving God.

May the Lord, who has burdened you with such a heavy cross, comfort you and give you His mercy and peace.

Yours in Christ.

Rev. H.J. Poort

5. The Aftermath

"The Lord is near to those who have a broken heart."

~ Psalm 34:18A (NKJV)

Immediately after the incident, Klaas Kleijn was taken into safe custody to Dordrecht, a city about 20 kilometres south of Streefkerk. This city was the main servicing centre for the *Alblasserwaard* district in terms of law and order, so the courts, judiciary and police were all headquartered there. The judge, under the direction of the town mayor, ordered an investigation into the mental state of Klaas Kleijn and whether he could be held responsible for his actions. A Dordrecht doctor, D. Stolp, was appointed for this task. He interviewed Klaas a number of times and others in the course of his investigation, including his doctor and pastor. On the 26th of February he made the following recommendations after giving a summary background of the event:

> *On the grounds of the reported events outlined and the responses received from Klaas Kleijn, we consider him to be suffering insanity which he experiences in the form of extreme <u>paranoia</u>. We regard him not being accountable for what he has done and recommend that it is necessary to have him admitted to a mental*

> *institution for his own welfare, for his family and for public safety.*

There was to be no formal court case with hearings, presentations and defence. The judge used the advice of one physician, presented in a three-page report, to declare Klaas Kleijn insane and to have him admitted to a mental institution for one year. Under an 1884 law governing the State supervision of insane people, a judge was empowered to rule, that if someone has committed a punishable offence but, due to their mental weakness could not be held accountable, that person could then be ordered to a mental asylum for a period of twelve months. During those twelve months regular records were to be kept of the patient's condition and then two weeks before the expiry of the twelve months his condition was to be again assessed by a judge to determine whether ongoing residency in the insane asylum is required.

So it was that on the 1st March 1919 Klaas was admitted to the government-run insane asylum in Medemblik, North Holland. About 170 kilometres from Streefkerk, it was a challenging distance to travel at that time, so family members were not in a position to make regular contact except via letters.

Meanwhile, discussions were taking place between the Kleijn and Verhoef families as to what to do with the three young children. Ideally, they should stay together as siblings but this was not to eventuate. The final decision was that the eldest, Lijzebeth Maria (Auntie Lijsje), was to be cared for by Klaas' younger sister, Niesje Kleijn, who was 30, unmarried and probably still living at home. Two years later Niesje married Huig de Haan so Auntie Lijsje moved in with them in Streefkerk. They never had children of their own.

From all accounts and Auntie Lijsje's own reports she endured a terrible time. Niesje treated her with contempt, not extending any love and compassion. Despite getting excellent grades at school, at age 12 she had to leave school to seek work. Her schoolteacher even offered to foster her - which Auntie Lijsje would have loved - but Niesje would not agree to this.

It appears she treated Auntie Lijsje as a useful means of acquiring monetary gain. Under her foster agreement she was entitled to claim all expenses incurred to care for Auntie Lijsje. She meticulously recorded every expense and made sure she didn't miss out on any entitlements. It has been said that by the time Auntie Lijsje turned 21, at which time she could claim her inheritance, Niesje's reimbursement claims had virtually exhausted the entire amount.

Some family members have suggested that Niesje was very upset that her brother had brought the Kleijn family name into disrepute, and with Auntie Lijsje being his eldest daughter, she took her anger and frustration out on her. The Netherlands was in the midst of a depression so it has also been suggested that her need for money at the time played some role in her outlook and actions. Whatever the reason, my Auntie Lijsje was brought up in an abusive, unloving environment. She finally escaped this situation when she married Dirk de Haan in 1933 at the age of 21.

Despite experiencing such severe trauma and growing up in an unloving household, Auntie Lijsje developed a tremendously warm and affectionate personality, reaching out to help others at every opportunity. Even her foster mother, Niesje, despite treating her so badly, received loving care and attention during her old age when she moved close by Auntie Lijsje so she could care for her. Auntie Lijsje had seven children and died in 2003 at the age of 91.

My Dad, Cornelis, was taken up by his grandfather, Cornelis Verhoef, after whom he was named. Dad's grandmother, Maria Speksnijder, had died 35 years earlier in 1884 but his grandfather had married again with Dingena Maat in 1888. They lived and worked on a farm in Brandwijk and had a further ten children, seven of whom reached adulthood. When my Dad was taken in by the family in February 1919 there were four unmarried children still in the family home: Maria Jantje aged 25, Marinus Jan (21), Janna Cornelia (19) and Jan Cornelis (14). His grandfather was 69 and his stepmother 57.

Marinus Jan married Maria Pietertje Jannigje Bongers a year later on the 1st April 1920 and remained on the farm with his new wife, in time taking over the farm from his father. Grandfather Verhoef died in 1931 when Dad was 18. A year after his death, in February 1932, Dad moved from the farm to join his youngest sister who stayed with Pieter and Miek Verhoef. They lived in a house near the Brandwijk town centre and Dad stayed there four years until his marriage in October 1936.

The youngest of the three children, Maria Lijzebeth (Auntie Marie), at just 3 years and 8 months at the death of her mother, was taken up by the oldest brother of her mother, Pieter Verhoef, who in 1900 had married Maria (Miek) Elizabeth Tukker. A childless couple, by all accounts they welcomed the opportunity to foster Auntie Marie. They doted on her, treating her like she was their own. She was encouraged to study and take a career of her choosing.

The trauma of losing her mother and seeing her mentally ill father haunted her. With that experience she developed an interest in studying mental health and psychology. However, that option was not available to her when she needed to make the choices, so she went for nursing and later specialised in midwifery. After the Second World War, she worked in that capacity for an extended period in what was then Dutch Indonesia. Returning back to the Netherlands, she set up her own midwifery practice in Amsterdam. She became a very independent, driven, and strong-willed individual who did not take kindly to injustices. In areas neglected by the general society, like the slums of Amsterdam, she was always available to deliver babies regardless of the mothers ability to pay. She never married and died in November 2008, aged 93.

Most challenging for the three young children in the early years after their mother's death, besides coping with the traumatic and violent way of losing her, was that they were separated from each other. They all ended up in quite different households and had little opportunity to actually get together. As soon as they could they started writing letters to each other. Sometimes, in school holidays, they were invited to come together for a period, usually at Pieter and Miek Verhoef's place. The Verhoef's were generous and empathetic hosts, excellent foster parents for Auntie Marie, and where possible reached out to both my Dad and Auntie Lijsje. Dad used to recall how, as young children, they so looked forward to those times together.

No doubt, the special circumstance and trauma they experienced as youngsters had a profound effect on their relationship as siblings. They had a unique understanding of each other that kept their relationship strong and supportive throughout their lives. When one looks at such a traumatic experience by such young children in light of today's knowledge of mental health and childcare it is remarkable how they all seemed to manage to grow into adulthood as seemingly well-balanced and stable individuals. That certainly didn't come about because of any special psychological attention they might have received because of their circumstances.

According to the Child Mind Institute of Western Australia, children between the ages of 3-6 who experience such a traumatic event would develop some or all of the following symptoms: intense and ongoing emotional upset, depression, anxiety, behavioural changes, difficulty eating and sleeping, withdrawal and difficulties at school. Their tips for dealing with children after such a situation is making the child feel safe, acting calm, maintaining routines, sharing information about what happened, listening well, helping them relax and enjoy themselves. One hundred years earlier none of these tips would have been implemented. Instead, the siblings were separated, my Dad was put in a household where the event was never mentioned or discussed, and he was put to work on the farm at a very early age. On top of that, he would have been acutely aware of his situation and the disgrace that his father had brought on the family name. Everyone in the district was aware of what had happened, including all his classmates. Did he experience bullying and discrimination as a result? How did he manage to cope and stay positive about his own future?

6. Klaas Kleijn: Ward of the State

"If only I could have restrained myself at that instant."

~ *Klaas Kleijn*

Under the 1884 Dutch National Law for the Insane, the mayor in a local town had the authority to have someone detained without trial if that person was deemed a risk to society. And so it was that the Mayor of Streefkerk authorised the detainment of Klaas Kleijn after he attacked his wife. This became a bone of contention for Klaas, who considered himself innocent of murder and who relentlessly campaigned over the next few years to have his case considered by a trial and judge. He was not told of his wife's death till many months after the event and when told he considered it a lie and fabrication. With his paranoia he didn't trust anyone, treating any information with suspicion, always thinking someone was out to get him. If his wife was dead, he reasoned it was not a result of what he had done. It must be the neighbour, who had previously threatened him, who was to be blamed.

In the limited number of letters that have been preserved he pleads his innocence and appeals to his family to write to the chief judge in Dordrecht to request a trial. He does not want to be locked away indefinitely in a mental institution and is confident that if a trial was held and witnesses were called, he would be freed with a fine.

Desperate, and not accepting that she is dead, Klaas pens a letter to his wife, undated but written possibly a few months after his incarceration, in which he pleads with her to write to the chief Judge to urge him to allow him to go to trial. To help his case he even suggests that she should admit some fault to the judge because her constant nagging had driven him to that point. In it he also writes how he is missing the children and she must write to him to tell him how they all are. He also asks her to send some regular money so he can supplement his food. While he claims the food is okay the portions are far too small, and he has already lost 18 pounds (or 8 kilos) in weight.

If he wasn't already, during his incarceration Klaas became a prolific letter writer. Three letters addressed to the Court in Dordrecht appealing for a trial have survived. The first one dated 16th March 1919 was written only two weeks after he became a resident in the asylum. The next one was written a year later in March 1920 and the final one in June 1920. They are all lengthy double-sided letters of about 400 to 500 words each. His growing frustration at the thought of being locked up in a mental institution for the rest of his life comes through very strongly. He wants to get back into society to work and to be with his children. He considers his incarceration a gross miscarriage of justice. In September 1919 he even appealed to the Queen of the Netherlands, Queen Wilhelmina, with a lengthy letter to consider his case.

It is doubtful that any of these letters were actually sent. Being a mental institution, everything that the patients did would have been closely monitored and their letters censored. However, the reports from the staff at Medemblik do record his constant writing and note taking and the letters written to his family would, in all probability, at least all have been posted. The family do report corresponding with him.

He seemed to write regularly to the grandmother of his wife, Marrigje Bons-Speksnijder. Despite her apparent difficulty forgiving him he encouraged her with the words, *"Grandmother, being angry is human but staying angry is from the devil. Please grandmother, read the Bible, Matthew chapters six and seven, read it carefully."*

Often he was quite spiritual in his letters and encouraged his family to be faithful to God. Writing for the birthday of his wife's grandmother, Marrigje, who turned 87 on the 12 May 1919, he wrote, *"God is good and faithful in that he spared you for so many years and I hope that God may give you still more but, when you die, may you then inherit eternal life with God."*

He continued in the letter reflecting on the terrible sorrow he had caused earlier in the year and how the reality of it was now starting to sink in. *"If only I could have restrained myself at that instant,"* he wrote, *"and then I would still be with my wife and children. For, grandmother, my sorrow is heavy but my regret comes too late."* He wrote further, *"We had talked about living separately but she insisted on keeping everything, including the children, but that was not easy for me to accept. Now I wish I had accepted it as I would now still be a free man, but it is now too late."*

With every letter to family members he appealed for gifts of money, cheese, meats and tobacco. It is quite apparent that the provisions given to the residents were quite meagre and did not seem to satisfy Klaas' appetite.

Klaas' sister Niesje Kleijn, wrote to the Medemblik

Institution management on at least two occasions, first in April 1919 and then again in July 1919, to enquire how her brother was going and whether he would likely be given his freedom soon. In the July letter she particularly mentioned the need to know so she could give the solicitor handling her brother's affairs advice as to what to do with their home.

The reply she received was:

> *The condition of your brother has not changed much. He has got more used to the surroundings and enjoys his household activities. Nothing much however has changed in regard to his mental condition. It is impossible to predict beforehand how long he would require care, however at this stage there is no indication of any improvement or healing.*

Klaas' brother Fop, two years his elder, was appointed as his guardian. He was a successful businessman operating from the town of Stolwijk about 40 kilometres north of Streefkerk. He had developed a business producing a brand of cigars and selling them through retail cigar shops right across the country. To manufacture the cigars, he employed about eight specialist cigar makers. He was given the responsibility of looking after Klaas' affairs and his actions would have a big influence on the life of his institutionalised brother. He became the contact for the Medemblik Institution, arranging payment for his brother's care and attended to any legal documents or decisions that needed to be made in respect to Klaas.

As was normally the case for poor residents, the institution had approached the Streefkerk Council for payment, but they initially refused, saying Klaas and his family had their own means to pay. Fop arranged to make the payment but concluded that Klaas' money would run out within a year. He put pressure back on the Streefkerk council who eventually relented and agreed to commence paying from December 1919. Legally the local council was ultimately responsible for their own citizens if they happened to end up in a mental institution. The Dutch Central Government made no contribution to this cost.

Under the 1884 Law for the Insane, records had to be kept and made available for inspection of everyone who was institutionalised. During the first fortnight of a person's stay the notes on their condition had to be completed daily, then weekly for the next six months and after that, monthly. These notes would form part of the annual appraisal. Based on these notes a judge then had to rule whether the person would be institutionalised for another 12 months.

The same applied to Klaas whose notes were taken and filed. His notes show that initially he suffered from a lot of sleeplessness and stomach pains but after a month no mention is made of that again. The notes show that Klaas seemed delusional. He did not understand the seriousness of his situation, and as time went by, became more and more convinced his neighbour killed his wife. His wish to go to trial was often noted. There were occasional references to him suffering from hallucinations and hearing voices. In April 1919 he was tested using the then accepted Binet-Simon method developed in 1911. This test for less gifted people would then determine at what age level their mental capacity had developed. This test gave Klaas' mental state as equivalent to a 10-year-old. He was described as a patient who was easy to deal with and who could readily be distracted away from his hallucinations and peculiarities. He had a good relationship with other patients as well as personnel and doctors.

After the first twelve months the assessment, as submitted to the judge and signed by the director of the Rijks Krankzinnigengesticht in Medemblik, read:

> *This patient (Klaas Kleijn) is suffering from insanity in the form of imbecillitas, accompanied by hallucinations, illusions, memory distortion and changing and coherent delusions. Continuing nursing in an asylum institution is essential.*

The Institute in Medemblik, being a government organisation, was designed for individuals that needed to be urgently placed but after a first-year trial that person would be relocated to another institution, preferably one that was located in the province of the patient's home town. For Klaas that would mean the province of South Holland.

His guardian brother, Fop Kleijn, made enquiries and eventually settled on St. Joris Gasthuis in Delft, South Holland, about 50 kilometres from Streefkerk. So, on the 10th April 1920, after a 13 month stay in Medemblik, Klaas was transferred to the St. Joris Gasthuis. Concerned about the ongoing cost and being aware that the Streefkerk Council was a very reluctant payer, Fop had looked for the cheapest option. This Gasthuis had three class structures, third class being the most economical. So Fop arranged for Klaas to be registered as a third-class patient.

7. Life at the St. Joris Gasthuis

"Compassion asks us to go where it hurts, to enter into the places of pain, to share in brokenness, fear, confusion, and anguish. Compassion challenges us to cry out with those in misery, to mourn with those who are lonely, to weep with those in tears. Compassion requires us to be weak with the weak, vulnerable with the vulnerable, and powerless with the powerless. Compassion means full immersion in the condition of being human."

~ *Henri J.M. Nouwen*

Klaas was now in an institution that had for centuries accommodated and cared for the mentally ill. Initially, in the late 14th Century, the St. Joris Gasthuis had been established as a drop-in centre for the town's destitute. However, since the destitute were often also suffering from mental illnesses, the institution grew to become the place where the insane were kept. With the city of Delft growing and prospering during the 16th and 17th Centuries the services offered by St. Joris Gasthuis were in constant demand. There were no laws or rules governing care, and it was still generally believed that insanity was the work of the devil, so treatment often had spiritual connotations. It was not until national laws for the insane were introduced - first in 1841 and then further expanded in 1884 - that organisations like St. Joris Gasthuis had to really review their methods of operation to ensure compliance with the new regulations which were also being policed by random government inspections.

There had even been some talk of closing the St. Joris Gasthuis down. It seemed so difficult and expensive to make the required changes and the institution seriously questioned how the extra income required for these adjustments would be generated. However, there remained quite some pressure on Delft to increase the number of places for the insane living in the district, which was one of the main objectives of the 1884 law. Each district was required to ensure it had sufficient accommodation to house the mentally disturbed in their area.[4] So eventually, after more than ten years of discussion and debate by the Gasthuis board and the Delft City Council, plans were adopted and approved for a major building development on an area of land just outside Delft. The old inner-city address would be updated and renovated but the main expansion and construction would be on a larger rural block just outside the city.[5]

The new buildings were designed to cope with three classes: upper, middle and lower or 1st, 2nd and 3rd. In the 3rd class the sleeping quarters catered for 25 residents per room. They were designed as two-storey wings, the upper floor being the sleeping area and the lower for living and kitchen. Each set of 25 residents had their own outdoor garden. A central building, which formed the main entrance, housed the administration area, the doctors and visitors' rooms, as well as a church building used by both Catholic and Protestant residents. The facilities catered for males and females, but the buildings and entry points were kept separate.[6]

These newly built facilities were officially opened in 1893 with 370 resident patients. By the time Klaas arrived in 1920 the number of residents had grown to nearly 1000. There was a big turnover with a new person arriving nearly every day.

The class system played a prominent role in the way the organisation was run and managed. Third class was simply the bottom of the rung and entitlements were very limited. Food was basic with virtually no variety, potatoes with beans being the standard dish. A small piece of meat was available just for the Sunday. Sugar for coffee and tea or butter for bread were not afforded those in 3rd class. So, while 1st class could be enjoying a three-course meal, together with wine and cigars, the 3rd class languished, often near starvation being given just the bare necessities to keep them alive.[7]

This must have been particularly grating for Klaas, whose parents were farmers and whose wife had been given a substantial inheritance. And the class system didn't just stop at food, it also affected clothing, access, privacy and, in 3rd class, it came with the demand to do daily physical labour to supposedly pay for their care. First class residents had their own bedroom and enjoyed privacy. One can imagine the challenge for Klaas of sleeping in a common room with 24 other mentally disturbed patients.

The cost of care for Klaas, despite being placed in 3rd class to keep the expenses as low as possible, nevertheless seemed to be an ongoing issue of concern for the Town of Streefkerk. After the family claimed it had exhausted Klaas' own funds, the local town was then legally responsible for ongoing costs. Streefkerk Town Council had already made a number of enquiries regarding the possible term of Klaas' stay and whether he might soon be released. As his stay was reconsidered by the court on an annual basis there was always the possibility that a judge might rule that at a certain point he was well enough to be released. After all, the institution aimed to provide care with the objective of the patient experiencing demonstrable improvement and sufficient healing of their condition. However, each year seemed to go by without any word of progress about Klaas' condition.

In April 1924, after four years of covering costs, it was evident that the town tried to find ways to either expunge the costs or at least minimise them. *"This cost,"* the Mayor wrote to the management of St. Joris Gasthuis, *"is a burden for a small town like Streefkerk":*

> *I consider it my duty, with an eye on the financial affairs of the community, to ask you if it is possible to further drive down the costs of caring for Klaas Kleijn. This is important for us as we get no support from our Federal Government for these costs.*
> *It would be a great financial advantage if Klaas Kleijn could be transferred to the Belgische Kolonie Geel. I have sought permission from the Federal Minister of Internal Affairs and am now seeking your cooperation with this.*

There is no record of how the St. Joris Gasthuis responded. What is known is that Klaas was not transferred. Were they able to reduce the cost of caring for Klaas as the Mayor of Streefkerk suggested and thus avoid the complexities of following through on the transfer? Had they found some other ways to cut expenses even further by reducing Klaas' access to food and resources? We do not know but from evidence it can be assumed that Klaas' situation did not improve and possibly worsened following this Mayoral request to introduce further cost cutting measures.

The Mayor's request for a transfer to a Belgian institution, Belgische Kolonie Geel, is an interesting one. At the time, that institution was a world leader in integrating mental patients into families. When the Mayor wrote the letter in 1924 there were a total of 550 Dutch mental patients at that institution. The system of integration was ground-breaking and very effective. The transfer would probably have served Klaas well. It can be assumed that the costs there were covered by another institution or charitable organisation so the Town of Streefkerk would have been released from any further financial liability. The Mayor had done his homework and even got the approval of the Federal Minister. Why it was never acted upon is a mystery.

It is known, however, that Klaas continued to hope for an early release. His frustration is evident in the letters that have been preserved. He drafted more letters to the Queen of the Netherlands, one in April 1920 and two in August 1920. His letters are showing more confusion than his earlier ones and much of the wording just doesn't make sense. However, it is clear that he wants the Queen to intervene in his case so he can become a productive person in society.

In November 1920 he addressed a letter to his father-in-law Cornelis Verhoef and his wife, Dingena. He appealed to them to write back and to visit him with the children. "Oh Father, Oh Mother," he wrote:

> *I have not seen my children now for 21 months. Please come quickly. I would so much like to see my lovely children. Yes last Saturday I was full of hope that I*

*might see my son on his birthday (*Dad's birthday the 5th November – he would have turned seven*). I went to God in prayer for him "O God may your blessings rest on him so he may grow up as a God-fearing person and that soon he may be with his Dad again and that I may be back in society."*

He further appealed to his parents-in-law to go to the judge to request a trial for him. He had expectations that following a fair trial he would be released. As with each letter, even those addressed to the Queen, he asked for food, fruit, cheese and tobacco.

There are no records of Klaas ever having written to his Dad, Bastiaan Kleijn. His mother had died a year before he got married and it is quite possible that he had no relationship at all with his own dad after his assault on his wife. His Dad died in 1924, five years after the attack.

As required by law, St. Joris Gasthuis, each month, took a note of Klaas' condition. This report was put forward each year to the judge to determine whether he should stay another year. While at the end of the first year a detailed summary was submitted, there is no evidence of any detailed assessment for the following years. It seemed simply a procedural requirement and presumed that Klaas would stay as a patient. There was never any indication that his condition might be improving or that he might eventually be released.

For the total period of just over 11 years that Klaas was in the Gasthuis, there are six handwritten pages summarising his condition every month from the period he was admitted on the 20th April 1920. The notes indicate a steady deterioration of both his mental and physical state. He remained very suspicious of staff, thought they were withholding incoming letters and parcels sent to him and constantly championed his innocence and continued his unrelenting quest for freedom.

There were increased references to him hallucinating. By 1926, he reportedly was self-harming by bashing his head. By 1927 he was often screaming and hitting himself. As a result, in February 1928 the notes refer to him as having an extremely large swollen forehead.

He continued to hear voices, was agitated, hallucinating, delusional and inflicting self-harm. While often screaming and extremely unsettled, he was not aggressive.

In March 1931 he was in bed with pneumonia. By May he had a sarcoma growth on his leg and in August his condition was described as deteriorating fast.

The last entry by staff was September 1931. Klaas, they wrote, was dead. He died September 8, two months before Dad's 18th birthday. He was 53. Eleven and a half years of suffering at the Gasthuis had come to an end.

All the wing accommodation buildings of St. Joris Gasthuis, where Klaas and the majority of the residents stayed, were demolished in 1990. However, the main entrance and the church, with some halls, have been kept. One hall has been turned into a museum.

The equipment on display gives an indication of some of the severe methods that were used to control patients during Klaas' time. Calming medication was not introduced until the 1950s so other methods were used to control difficult patients. Physical restraints, straitjackets, electric shock treatments, solitary confinement, water treatment and submersion for long periods as well as dark room isolation were meted out when deemed necessary.

Some restraints and treatments were given under the guise of helping the patient but, in other instances, punishments were dished out to those that 'misbehaved' or had the temerity to try and escape. Escapes were routinely attempted and resulted in being locked up in isolation for six weeks.[8] A 1950s staff member admitted in an interview that electric shock treatment was often used as a punishment, twice a week. A number of staff members interviewed for the book, *Van Koningsplein naar Lazarusklap*, about St. Joris Gasthuis (first published in 1994), recall how the constant threat of attack and assault by disturbed patients would inevitably lead to the use of physical constraints for the safety of the staff. They speak of their initial horror and reluctance at using some of the methods but, as the practices were commonplace and as they were not the management, they had to accept the situation.

There is no doubt that Klaas, with his constant screaming, agitation and tendency to self-harm, would have been subjected to a range of different restraining treatments. Many of those treatments are now known to be harmful to mental health, and, often, to the physical health of a person. It is worth considering if the self-harm came about as a result of these 'treatments' or were the treatments used as a response to self-harm?

In 2017 I spoke to a volunteer who was helping to set up the museum and cataloguing the material.

He was an elderly retired man who had started work at St. Joris Gasthuis as a 17-year-old lad and was employed there for the rest of his working life. As a youngster he'd been aghast at the treatment given but when querying it he was told that was how things had to be done. He was given no professional training and just had to follow orders. He now finds it difficult to explain the reasons for some of the treatments given, like the bathing of patients where they were placed under water and forcefully kept that way by a restraining blanket that just kept their head above the water. The patient used to be kept there all day and at the end of that time their body was totally weakened and needed treatment. This often led to other diseases and infections.

From all accounts, Klaas entered the institution a healthy person. Eleven years later, at the age of just 53, he died, a sick and broken man. There is no reference in his notes to any treatment he might have received. There seemed to be no legal requirement to record and submit this information when the annual review was due. Nor are there any records of the visits he might have received from family members or members from his church. Did he get any pastoral support from a minister?

Mum told me later that the three children would together visit their dad once a year. However, Auntie Lijsje told one of her children that apparently she only went once and was so shocked with what she saw that she was unable to ever go again. Auntie Marie told family members that she used to go more often, independently.

Speaking to the archivist of the Dutch Reformed Church in Streefkerk where Klaas was a member, he was unable to find any references to spiritual support for Klaas after the tragic event in 1919. There seemed to be no references to any visits made in consistory minutes or reports.

Klaas himself appeared to become very spiritual, judging from the content of the few letters that still exist. Unfortunately, the church at the institution was only accessible to 1st class patients so Klaas, in all likelihood, would not have attended there. The church was built to accommodate about 50 worshippers so never in the planners' or church leaders' mind would it have been considered a place of worship for all 1000 residents of St. Joris Gasthuis. It remains a mystery what the church leaders of that time saw as their calling with respect to members who happened to be third-class residents in the institution.

A day before Klaas died, on the 7th September 1931, St. Joris Gasthuis sent a telegram to Fop Kleijn, Klaas' brother and guardian, to say that his condition was serious.

Fop then sent a telegram to the families where Klaas' three children were staying: Niesje Kleijn, Cornelis Verhoef and Pieter and Miek Verhoef. Pieter and Miek Verhoef went immediately to see him on the 8th but, by the time they got there, he had already died. It was reported to them that Klaas had passed away peacefully.

The funeral was held three days later on the 11th September 1931. The procession went from the St. Joris Gasthuis to the Jaffa cemetery in Delft, a distance of about two kilometres, where he was buried. All three children, Auntie Lijsje, who was then 19; Dad, 17; and Auntie Marie, 16, were in attendance.

In the arrangements made after Klaas' death, all attempts were made to minimise the expense. As grave sites were divided into four classes, with fourth being the cheapest, Klaas was buried fourth-class. Legally the fourth-class graves could be cleared out after only 10 years. All other classes were generally family graves with a minimum 20 years rental life. From information received from the administrators of the Jaffa Cemetery, a 10-year site was usually provided when no rental money had been paid. Klaas' grave was cleared for reuse on the 14th April 1947, nearly 16 years after he was buried. His bones were placed in a common grave with others. No markings or name plaques were made, and the area used by the cemetery to dispose of the bones when clearing graves is not accessible to the public. In all likelihood that area now forms part of a modern housing estate that was developed on part of the original cemetery grounds.

8. Dad's Formative Years

"There are only two lasting bequests we can give our children - one is roots, and the other, wings."

~ *Hodding S. Carter (1907-1972)*

As has been related earlier, after his mother's violent attack and death in February 1919, and the institutionalisation of his dad, Klaas, Dad was taken up and cared for by his grandfather from his mother's side, Cornelis Verhoef along with his wife, Dingena Maat. His grandfather had remarried after the death of his first wife in 1884, Maria Speksnijder, who was Dad's grandmother. From that first marriage there were now two surviving sons, Pieter and Cornelis, both of whom were married and moved out of the family home by 1919. Pieter and his wife, Maria (Miek) Elizabeth Tukker, accepted my dad's youngest sister, Auntie Marie, as their fostered daughter.

Dad, at five years of age, was cast into a family of adults. His grandfather was 69 and the four children still at home from his grandfather's second marriage were aged between 14 to 25. Having such a young addition to the family would have been a challenge especially for grandfather Verhoef who was very conscious of increasing limitations due to age. Since his first marriage in 1874 he had fathered 16 children, nine of whom were still alive. The farm work commitments were relentless and that, combined with a busy household, would have taken its toll on his health. In 1919 he writes to the family, *"Considering the attachment I have with C. Kleijn, I wish it to be considered for the boy to stay with me for as long as my health and strength allow. But at 69 years of age I am not in a position to care for his clothing or washing."*

He then goes on to outline the cost: 80 cents per day and 20 cents per night. Because Dad was entitled to an inheritance at age 21 those caring for him were able to charge all expenses and have them paid for by the executor of the will of his late mother, Jannigje. The days he stayed on his grandfather's farm were always carefully recorded and accounted for.

In 1932, a year after his grandfather died, a calculation was made of the total indebtedness accumulated during the preceding 13 years of enjoying his grandfather's hospitality. A final settlement was agreed to and a formal legal document drafted to declare that neither my Dad, C. Kleyn nor his grandfather, represented by his surviving wife Dingena Maat, had any further liability or claim against the other. The document also stated that they had sighted all the accounts, calculations and payments made and declared that everything was found to be correct and in good order. The document was signed by my Dad's two guardians, uncles from each side of the family, Fop Kleijn and Pieter Verhoef. At 19 he was considered underage, so all Dad's finances were still the responsibility of his two appointed guardians.

Growing up with uncles and aunties, all a lot older than him, would have initially been a lonely experience for Dad. There was also the legacy of what his mother experienced when she was still at home before her marriage. His mother had experienced rivalry within the family due to her inherited wealth from her mother, which her half brothers and sisters were not entitled to. Dad was now in a similar position, a young boy who had an inheritance which none of them could benefit from. This inevitably must have led to some jealousy and underlying friction.

This tension over inheritances was highlighted to me in a discussion with one of Dad's half-cousins in 2020. He related how their grandfather, Cornelis Verhoef, was unceremoniously kicked off his farm by his own two sons when they came of age at 21 inheriting the farm through the death of their mother, Maria Speksnijder. Maria came from a wealthy farming family owning a number of farms and properties, including the one she was living on with her husband. When she died in 1884 her inheritance bypassed her husband and went straight to her three children, one being Dad's mother.

The two sons insisted they take over the ownership of the farm. Their Dad, despite farming it for more than 25 years, had to move out to make way for his sons. Dad's grandfather was then forced to buy another farm, and this is the farm where my Dad came to live after the death of his mother.

Dad's uncles, with whom he now found himself growing up with, were children of Cornelis' second wife, so half-brothers to Dad's mother and the two uncles who had been responsible for removing their father from his beloved farm. And Dad was, of course, the son of one of those three children who came to inherit all that wealth from their dad's first wife. Speaking to my Dad's half-cousin it was obvious that there was still an element of bitterness left by the event that had affected his father and grandfather nearly 140 years earlier.

Dad missed his sisters terribly. They even went to another school, he in Brandwijk, his two sisters in Streefkerk. Only his eldest sister, Lijsje, who had already been to school for a year, could write letters at this stage. In December 1919 she wrote a letter to both my Dad and her sister Marie, to wish them a happy new year. Her foster mother, Niesje, wrote that Lijsje was so happy at the opportunity of being allowed to write to her siblings. It appeared to have been a special favour given to her by her foster mother. From reports, my Auntie Lijsje's life was very strictly controlled by her foster mother. With Dad also now going to school it wouldn't be long before, he too, would be starting to write letters to his sisters. It was for them a lifeline of support and care for each other.

School was compulsory for a minimum of six years, starting at age six. This meant that many already left school at twelve years of age. Dad had eight years of schooling and left at the age of 14. He later would recall his time at school with a certain fondness. The school he attended was a Christian school and from Grade One he had to learn a Psalm every week. This was the only homework given. From Grade Four onwards he also had to learn a Lords Day from the Heidelberg Catechism, which was one of the Reformed doctrinal documents. The main focus of learning was on Maths, Writing and Reading with a bit of History and Geography thrown in. There were no sporting activities.

The desks were all lined up in rows with the boys on one side of the room and the girls on the other. Each desk was equipped with an ink well for dipping their pens in when writing. Some amazing penmanship skills were developed from those early years of concentrating on the style and ink flow.

Wooden clogs were the standard wear for the school children. At school was a special clog room where a spare pair was kept to be worn just inside the classrooms. They changed the clogs as they arrived in the morning and left in the afternoon. Shoes were only worn on Sundays or special occasions.

Growing up on a farm, Dad was introduced very early to farm work. Children in the family were considered a natural resource to help, where possible, with farm duties. Schools were tolerant and understanding of the fact that children as young as ten often had to work on the family farm. During summer months, farm children were given special leave for up to six weeks to assist with the hay harvesting.

Farm children who had to milk cows were given extra time off from school. From the age of 13 Dad had to join the milking team to milk about 20 cows by hand. This meant getting up at four every morning and in the afternoon leaving school half an hour early to participate in the afternoon milking session. So, while the official annual school holidays were only for two weeks, farm children were given special dispensation so they could help at home for an extended period of time. With so many people in the district relying on farm income, no bureaucratic roadblocks were put in the way for them. Also, a career in farming was the natural choice for farmers' sons, so being absent from school to work on the farm was considered a natural evolution to becoming farmers themselves. I'm not sure how well those farm boys could concentrate at school getting up at 4 a.m. in the morning. Dad did acknowledge that he often used to fall asleep at the desk in school.

For leisure and games, farm boys invented their own recreation and entertainment. Rarely were there readymade toys bought for children. Balls were made from discarded bike tubes, hoops from old bike rims and discarded wood turned into carts, aeroplanes, windmills and trains. Fishing, skating, exploring and jumping ditches were other favourite pastimes. The area was, after all, surrounded by rivers and canals.

Building rafts to float across the water was also a popular undertaking.

As there were no other young children in the home, Dad sought the company of children his age elsewhere. His Uncle, Arie Verhoef, a farmer living nearby, had children just a few years older than Dad, so he often played with them.

One day while jumping creeks, a common way to challenge each other's jumping agility, Dad misjudged and, missing the bank, ended up in the water. His arm slammed into the bank, resulting in a broken arm. This was early 1925 when he was 11 years old.

His Auntie Keet, who at 25 was still single and living at home and was probably Dad's main carer, wrote a lengthy report of the episode to Dad's sister, Lijsje, to explain why Dad had not been responding to her letters.

The doctor came for a house visit around 10 p.m. that night to inspect Dad's broken arm and, after a cursory inspection, declared it was a bad break in two places and needed to be set. Held down by his uncle, auntie and granddad the doctor went to task setting the arm in plaster. Dad yelled out in pain throughout this whole process. There was no access to general anaesthesia in those days.

However, there was worse to come.

To be certain everything was okay, the arm was x-rayed.

It was not okay.

Auntie Keet wrote what happened next, a few days later, when the doctor made another home visit:

> *"The arm had to be broken again. The doctor pulled his arm one way and Uncle Piet pulled Kees' shoulder the other way to try and straighten the arm. Kees was yelling out in pain, it was just unbearable to witness*

and listen to. Then you heard his arm snap like a piece of wood. The doctor then kept his arm straight by tying it to a plank. He now is on the mend but has to be helped with everything."

Auntie Keet's four-page detailed letter, one of the few preserved from that period, revealed a deep compassion and love for Dad and his siblings. She appeared to have great empathy for Dad and his circumstance and acknowledged the importance of Dad writing to his siblings. It appears the letter is fundamentally written to assure Dad's sister that, while he would love to write, she should not take that wrongly as he cannot write letters due to his broken right arm. She provided further reassurance, writing that he looked forward to continuing to receive his sisters' letters: *"He was very happy receiving your last letter,"* she wrote, *"and has now requested me to write to you."*

Also evident from the letter is the number of uncles and aunties that he was surrounded with and who got involved with his welfare when necessary. When Keet signs off the letter she passes the greetings on to Dads' sister from Opa and Oma and no less than three Aunties and four Uncles! – all family that Dad was surrounded with.

The letter also refered to Dad's state of mind. Keet wrote that within a few days he is no longer in pain and is happy and singing again. Also, because Dad is severely restricted and house bound, his cousin Kees, the son of Uncle Arie, often dropped by to play. She also reported that Dad had received notice that he had been promoted to Grade Six. Each year children would anxiously await news on whether they would be moved to the next grade. Many did not, so when they were promoted that was a joy they shared.

The letter gave a very positive reflection of Dad's progress from a very troubled start at age five to developing into a normal well-adjusted eleven-year-old boy who has a generally happy and positive disposition.

Later that year, on the 19th October 1925, Dad and his two sisters joined in the 25th wedding anniversary celebrations of their beloved Uncle Piet and Auntie Miek. They were at all times a loving and caring couple for the three siblings. Dad and his eldest sister Lijsje wrote a poem for the celebrating couple. Neatly written, probably by the 13-year-old Lijsje, it gives an indication of the depth of love they had for the couple and the extent of their own maturity at such a young age. Following is an English summary of the words:

> *Where so many are gathered,*
> *On your silver wedding feast,*
> *Where so many faces reflect,*
> *Joy and happiness.*
> *We come as well,*
> *Your niece and nephew,*
> *Hoping that this anniversary poem,*
> *May express joyful tones,*
> *In tune with the festivities of the day.*
> *May blessing come down on your home.*
> *May God be with you always,*
> *And may He crown you with a Golden wedding feast.*
>
> *From Lijsje Kleijn and Cornelis Kleijn*

Original Dutch wording:

> *Waar zovelen samenkomen,*
> *Op Uw zilveren Bruiloftsfeest,*

Waar men uit zoveler blikken,
Ongeveinsde Blijdschap leest,
Komen we ook, Uw Neef en nichtje,
Hopende, dat ons bruilofts dichtje,
Blijde tonen geven mag,
In het feestlied van deze dag.

Zegen daalde er op Uw woning,
Onverbreekbaar was Uw Echt;
Van Uw Liefde is rijke loning,
U deze feestdag weggelegd,
God zij met U al Uw dagen,
Tot Uw huis eens moog gewagen,
Van Feestzang, dubbel schoon,
Op Uw gouden bruilofts kroon.

Van Lijsje Kleijn en Cornelis Kleijn

Their sister Marie, who was 10 at the time, also put together a moving poem in honour of her adopted parents:

How quickly did I see my mother,
And my father disappear.
Lonely, lonely and lost,
I stood with bitter tears.

Then you took me with you,
And gave me protection and love in your house;
I found in you my parents back,
Found with you a welcoming home.

Thankful for your generous love,
I beg on this, your anniversary.

"*Dear Father in Heaven
Reward them for the love they have shown me.*"

From Maria Kleijn

Original Dutch wording

*Ach hoe gauwe zag ik mijn Moeder,
En mijn Vader henengaan.
Eenzaam, eenzaam en verlaten
Stond ik hier met bittren traan.*

*Toen hebt Gij mij meegenomen
En gekoesterd in Uw huis;
'k Vond in U mijn Ouders weder,
'k Vond bij U een vriendelijk thuis.*

*Dankbaar voor Uw grote goedheid,
Smeek ik op Uw feestgetij.
"Lieve Vader in den Hemel
Kroon hun liefde werk aan mij."*

Van Maria Kleijn

9. In the Work Force

*"Let the beauty of the Lord our God be upon us,
and establish the work of our hands for us;
yes, establish the work of our hands!"*
~ *Psalm 90:17 (NKJV)*

When Dad had his 14th birthday, on the 5th of November 1927, he left school to join the workforce. His grandfather told him he could choose a career between being a butcher, milkman, or baker. He never enjoyed killing animals so butchering was not for him; being a milkman involved a lot of work out in the cold at night which he also didn't like, so he settled for baker. No doubt through family connections, he secured a job with baker Huib Vlot who operated from Dad's birthplace in Streefkerk.

While the Global Depression years did not officially start till 1929, the Dutch economy was already struggling, with many unemployed. Dad related later how wealthy people were even resorting to paying businesses to employ their sons so they could learn a trade and be productively employed, so at the time he considered himself fortunate to be able to get a job straightway. He started work as a trainee baker on the 7th December 1927 on wages of 50 cents per week, plus board.

By the time Dad started working in the bakery, he had

already worked long hours for two years, getting up 4.00 a.m. each morning to help milk the cows. This introduction to long working hours served him well when he started in the bakery, where the hours were just relentless. He worked six long days a week starting at 5.00 a.m. and finishing at 7.00 p.m at night. The Friday shift was longest, finishing at midnight and then starting at 3 o'clock Saturday morning again. There were no holidays or additional time off. The only day free was Sunday which was then culturally seen as a rest day for catching up on sleep and attending church. It's not surprising that employers had to offer accommodation as part of the salary package as workers could just roll into bed when they finished, which is what they did.

As the trainee baker, Dad was the general assistant to do all the menial tasks, including helping others. There was little structured training and a boy was expected to do what he was told. Any arrogance or unwillingness would lead to instant dismissal. Most young trainees had no other expectations; they had grown up in a disciplined environment where they learnt early on where their place was in life. Their boss and parents were the ultimate authority figures and, generally, young lads would work hard and try to please.

Dad did say later that the lack of sleep during those years was a constant challenge. As soon as he relaxed, he would fall asleep and he even had, on occasions, fallen asleep while riding his bike. Dad said it was just as well there were no cars around in those days because he would have been at high risk of being run over. Staying awake in church on Sundays was also difficult, not only for Dad but also for the many farmers who were up at 4.00 a.m. Sunday morning to milk the cows.

When Dad first started working, electricity had not yet been introduced to the bakery. This meant that the ovens had to be stoked with wood and a lot of the mixing was done by hand. The Dutch enjoyed and continue to enjoy a wide range of pastries, cookies, breads and cakes, so being a small village bakery, they had a full range. During festivities, like Sinterklaas, the demand for particular delicacies would increase and the bakery employees were expected to work right through the night in order to fill all their orders.

Late each Saturday night Dad biked the 10 kilometres home to spend Sunday with his grandparents and family on the farm in Brandwijk.

In July 1929, after 20 months, Dad left, moving to a bakery in Schoonhoven, a larger town on the other side of The Lek River. It is unknown why he left his first job. His reference from his boss, H. Vlot, makes no mention of it and simply says that Cornelis Kleijn was there for one year and eight months and as a trainee baker fulfilled his duties honestly and faithfully.

Maybe it was the attraction of working in a newly equipped modern bakery. The Kok family had bought new premises in 1929, strategically located on Harbour Street, and set it up with the latest equipment and facilities together with an attractive shop front. Dad's conditions and wages were likely also better, although the financial crisis was about to get serious in the Netherlands.

The bakery, Bakkerij Kok, is in 2019, still run successfully by the same family. On its website it reflects on those early difficult years after its 1929 establishment:

> *The Crisis years had started and there was a need for hard work. Many labour-intensive hours were worked for little pay. The family in the meantime had grown to ten children and as soon as the child's legs and arms*

were strong enough, they were roped into helping in the business.

The situation in the bakery was no different to that on the farms. Children were a ready resource to help in the family enterprise, particularly in those difficult economic times. So, while Dad's renumeration might have been a bit better than the 50 cents a week he earned at the previous place, any increase would have likely been very modest. There also were still no holidays. That simply was not part of the culture or mindset in those days. Dad said that the only time he got time off was between jobs. Maybe that was another motivation to move from time to time, provided you had the next job lined up.

Dad stayed at his second bakery job even shorter than the first, a total of 15 months. From the historic report of the bakery as given on their website, it would appear that he might have been competing with the growing family involvement by the Kok family. After all, they admit in their historic reflection that the ten children were all put to work as soon as possible so they could save outside wages. It is possible Dad felt increasingly insecure. Mr. Kok gave him a glowing reference so there seemed to be no bad feelings with Dad leaving. "*I declare,*" he wrote, '*that C. Kleijn has worked diligently, faithfully and honestly and I highly recommend him."*

His next job was with a bakery run by the Brokking family situated in Jaarsveld. This was more than 20 kilometres from Streefkerk and even further from Brandwijk. H.A. Brokking was an old established business that had, until 1913, also owned a windmill for grain production. When Dad joined, the grain production side of things had been integrated into another corporation and the bakery was kept as a separate business. The Brokking name is still prominent in the Netherlands within the baking fraternity. Dad worked there till the end of March 1933 when he had to leave after being called to serve in the Army for six months. Brokking gave him a complimentary reference in a similar vein to his previous ones. He wrote, *"Cornelis Kleijn proved to be an honest, diligent and reliable worker and that's why I would recommend him to his employer in the future."*

The year Dad started working for the Brokking family, 1931, was a difficult and emotional year for him. In January of that year his grandfather, Cornelis Verhoef, under whose care he had been since he was five years old, died. Just eight months later, on the 11th September his dad, Klaas died at the age of just 53. While no reference is made to his passing in any of Dad's correspondence of the time, there is evidence that he did attend the funeral with his siblings. The occasion would have brought back into focus all the awful events they had experienced as young children. Just two months later, in November 1931, his Auntie Keet married and left the family home. She had for many years been a great support for Dad as is evidenced by some of the correspondence she wrote on his behalf. Her leaving the home left a big gap for Dad with now only his elderly Step-Grandmother still in the family home. He writes about this to his sister Lijsje, *"With her (Keet) marrying it will be very quiet here on Sundays with only Opoe [Grandmother] here. I think I better also get married soon."* He was eighteen at the time and decided to leave the farm and move in with his Uncle Piet and Auntie Miek in their Brandwijk home. One of his grandfather's sons, Marinus Jan Verhoef, had taken over the running of the farm.

10. Army Life

"In fact, the highest obligation and privilege of citizenship is that of bearing arms for one's country."

~George S. Patton Jr. (US General, World War II)

Under the Dutch military law of 1922, 19,500 men annually were mandated to be conscripted to join the army. Each year about 63,000 nineteen-year-old males were available for the draft. 23,000 of them were selected and, after health and other checks, the final figure would need to come in at the required 19,500. The initial term of service was five and a half months for infantry and artillery conscripts, and fifteen months for cavalrymen. Dad was conscripted for the infantry and artillery service so he served for a relatively short period – from the 20th March to the 2nd September 1933.

1933 was also when Hitler came to power. The Dutch had, since the end of World War One, progressively downscaled its defence expenditure. While they had maintained neutrality in the First World War, the Dutch nevertheless had been on full alert during those four years with over two hundred thousand soldiers on standby. After the war they no longer saw any threat and, by 1933, were spending only 20% of their 1918 military budget. However, with Hitler coming to power in January 1933, that situation would change dramatically over the next few years. Dad was fortunate that he was conscripted before the changes were made because the conscription periods were over the next few years progressively lengthened to two years. Dad was able to get back home and in the workforce in under six months.

Dad seemed to be pretty relaxed about spending six months in the service. There was no threat of war and it seemed like a bit of an adventure. He wrote to his sister, Lijsje, on receiving the news of his conscription that, *"I think you can learn a lot and you also experience a few new things."* Dad was stationed at the Army training barrack in the township of Bergen op Zoom, which was about 65 kilometres south west of his home. The barracks had been a strategic defence location for centuries, being near the southern border of Holland.

Letters sent to his sisters during his army service reflect a very positive experience and attitude. In a letter written within a few weeks of starting he wrote how he is enjoying it and is particularly pleased with his role, for he has been allocated to a specialist team that is trained in signalling. This role needed constant focus and attention as he learnt and studied the complicated codes of light signalling. *"I have got such a relaxing, easy life,"* he writes. *"We sit around for days just learning the signals. It beats marching all day."* He also appreciated the pay he received, one guilder and eleven cents per week.

He did acknowledge that the domestic work they had to do took some getting used to, like making your own sandwiches, doing the dishes, making the beds, sweeping the floors and polishing your shoes. He even had to learn sewing and knitting.

He wrote that he spent a whole two days learning knitting. His fingers were sore after the experience! The standards were exacting and they were strictly supervised. Likewise, the food was good, the camaraderie amongst his team excellent and, in the evenings, they had a special common room for playing all sorts of games together. For Dad, who was used to such long hours of work under pressure, the army service must have seemed like an idyllic lifestyle. At Easter he was able to enjoy a 4-day break. Usually over Easter he was working in the bakery right through the night to meet the demand of customers for special Easter breads and treats.

Dad was in a group of 30. He was really impressed with the training and the insistence on best practice and standards. He enjoyed the periods when they would spend days in the forest practicing the art of war and learning to live in tents and be self-sufficient. It appears like his group was very supportive of each other and, in the six months, developed a strong sense of comradeship. When not on a joint exercise there was a roster for different activities like guard and sentry duties. In each letter to his sisters or family he reinforced just how much he was enjoying the life and experience.

During the period there, Dad was also in a position to attend regular church services, attend catechism classes and Bible study evenings, as well as socialise on the weekends with fellow Christians. After church on Sundays he nearly always ended up at someone's place for lunch. According to him it beat sitting in the dormitory on your own. On free Saturdays he would also go out with friends and even enjoyed occasional swimming at the beach. He wrote of spending days relaxing at friends' places on the sofa with a cigar and tea and radio. That, according to him, was the life!

Because of the high concentration of so many young men in

the area, the churches made sure they had a presence in the district to give spiritual support and extend hospitality to those in the armed services. My Dad really benefitted from the presence of the church and its focus on reaching out to the Christian servicemen and welcoming their participation. In that short six-month period he became totally immersed in church and community life. It was probably also the first time he had been in a position to be able to devote quality time and attention to his church life without suffering from sleep deprivation.

In Dad's last letter from the army barracks dated the 29th August 1933 to his sister, Lijsje, he expands on the farewell program for his last week in the military. Every day during the last week there was some event, either with the Bible study club, the catechism students, the army group or church people. Evening festivities with chocolate milk and cigars, a day out at the beach, another afternoon in the nearby forest and then the last day rounding it off with official military parades and a ceremony. Interestingly, Dad received a formal diploma certificate in recognition of his completion of the required six months of military service.

11. Back in the Work Force

*And whatever you do, do it heartily, as to the Lord
and not to men, knowing that from the Lord you
will receive the reward of the inheritance; for you
serve the Lord Christ.*

~Colossians 3:23-24 (NKJV)

While he was in the army his Uncle Pieter had already made enquiries regarding a baking opportunity for Dad in Oud Alblas, which was only 8 kilometres from Brandwijk. His wife, Miek, went and visited the owner, Mr. Rees, at his bakery to make further enquiries on behalf of my Dad. Mr. Rees was looking for a baker who had experience and could work independently. While Dad felt he still had certain aspects of the bakery trade to learn he was confident of being able to satisfy the requirements of the job.

So, within a week of leaving the army Dad was in a new position closer to home and now employed as an experienced baker. He enrolled at the bakery training school in Dordt and attended classes there every Monday night to expand his knowledge. His boss coached him and supported him in his studies. He wanted my Dad to upskill as soon as possible, so the weight of the baking was not all on him. It appears that he was close to retirement and most likely wanted to slow down.

While Dad enjoyed the work, coming straight from the army, where there was so much social interaction, he initially found it very quiet. As was common for the time, his sleeping quarters were on the premises and, with just the elderly couple around, it was a challenging time of acclimatisation for him socially. Nevertheless, he persevered and, as a result, became an experienced and professional baker. He admitted to his sister that, with his increased status and responsibility, he gave new attention to his dress standard and behaviour. He was no longer the boy who was there to help everyone, but he was now a young mature gentleman who learnt how to converse with clients, suppliers and workers.

On weekends he stayed at the home of his Uncle Pieter and Auntie Miek in Brandwijk. With his Opa Verhoef having passed away in 1931, and his uncles and aunties now married and out of the family home, he felt more at home with Pieter and Miek. They were always most welcoming and helpful. They lived in a spacious and stately family home of 11 rooms and two bathrooms so there was always room for guests. Meanwhile, Dad's sister, Marie, who they had adopted as their daughter, had been living in Amsterdam for some years already, first to study, but later to work at an aged care centre.

Dad's financial welfare, as well as his access to some free time seems to have improved substantially with his new job. He often had Saturdays free and was able to attend weekly catechism classes and youth Bible study evenings every Wednesday and Thursday. This meant that he not only stayed with Pieter and Miek on the weekends, but also on the two nights he had the Bible study and catechism commitments. He enjoyed the community life and his involvement with church activities. He attended the Reformed church in Brandwijk where his uncle and auntie were members. Brandwijk was his hometown, and became the focal point for all his social and church activities.

He joined the local shooters club and became one of its best marksmen. Every Saturday evening, he was there with the members practising and holding competitions. According to his Auntie Miek, he was one of their best shooters and often came home with first prize, which might be a box of cigars or a tin of coffee. His army life must have given him a taste for shooting, something he never followed up on in later life. Maybe, after the horrors of the war, his attitude to guns changed because, to my knowledge, he never again owned a gun and certainly never spoke of his talents as a sharpshooter.

On one of the first Saturdays he had free in October 1933, he hired, for the sum of two guilders and forty cents, a car for the day to drive to Dordtrecht to attend to some shopping. This was an incredible expense equivalent to two week's wages when he was in the Army. He seemed determined to improve his dress standard and presentation and came home kitted out with a complete new outfit, including shirt and tie, overcoat, raincoat and a top hat.

Excitedly he wrote to his sister about the thrill of driving a car that could with ease cruise along between 20 and 25 kilometres an hour. His Auntie Miek wrote to Dad's sister, Lijsje, that Dad is now a real gentleman and all the components of the outfit he bought suited and fitted him perfectly. Maybe at the age of twenty, with his eldest sister Lijsje getting married in November, he was also thinking of a future wife and the need to look the part.

In 1933 the Netherlands was in the depths of the Depression. Forty percent of the workforce was unemployed, and the country was facing a growing debt crisis. Many faced poverty and hardship. It appears that Dad was largely unaffected by this huge crisis in his country. Family connections, inherited wealth and also the ability to work hard and be flexible all gave him some shelter and security. He was never unemployed and, with both his parents passed away, he was, on November 1934, at age twenty one, entitled to a substantial inheritance. No doubt, this gave him the confidence to spend when he had cash and to maintain a certain standard that was, to him, quite normal.

He continued to enjoy his work and growing experience at the Rees Bakery in Oud Alblas. The location, the working conditions as well as the opportunity for learning all suited him. He stayed there until the time came when, in September 1936, he was in a position to start his own business. Mr. Rees gave him a positive parting reference with the words, *"He did his work and trade with exceptional commitment, loyalty and honesty and therefore I can, without reservation, recommend him to any future employer."*

12. Dad Finds his Future Wife

*"How do I love thee? Let me count the ways.
I love thee to the depth and breadth and height
My soul can reach…"*

~Elizabeth Barrett Browning
(1806-1861)

In October 1933 Dad started attending the pre-confession classes under the leadership of Reverend C.P. Boodt, who had been a pastor of the Reformed Church at Molenaarsgraaf-Brandwijk since 1928. He was a very influential leader who was a powerful preacher and who also felt called to awaken his congregation to the danger of the rising Nazism. He was fondly remembered by both my parents for his wise, scriptural counsel and his genuine love for his congregation.

During his time there, he identified some members of the congregation as being overzealous, judgemental and lacking in humbleness. After a minor incident involving an elder who was outrightly and immediately condemned and judged, Rev. Boodt preached on Ecclesiastes 7:16 which reads, *"Be not overly righteous, nor be overly wise: Why should you destroy yourself?"* It was reported that this sermon made a big impact as did many of his other sermons. In 1936 he left

Molenaarsgraaf-Brandwijk to take on a ministry position in the Reformed Church of Leerdam.[9]

My parents often spoke with respect and awe of this wonderful, wise and faithful pastor who never compromised on principle. They both felt privileged to have been taught by him in those early, formative years of their life. My mother, Willempje Schutte, two years younger than Dad, also attended the same pre-confession classes under the leadership of Rev. Boodt. Both Dad and Mum, with a number of others, made their public profession of faith at the church service held on the 1st April 1934. It was a joyful occasion. Mum writes in her diary on that day: *"God is Great and his Greatness unfathomable. That also I may belong to His chosen congregation, that also I may confess His name. That Christ also died for my sins. Thank God that it is not only the significant people in this world but also poor servant maids that God accepts."*

The text for the sermon on the day of their profession of faith was from Matthew 28 verse five: 'But the angel answered and said to the women. *"Do not be afraid, for I know that you seek Jesus who was crucified."* My Mum's mother had this text engraved on a piece of wood as a gift for Mum to remember the occasion by. This engraved text had a prominent place on the walls of my parents' various homes for many years.

During the months of attending the pre-confession classes, Dad got to know Mum and was determined to get to know her better. She only lived a few houses from where Dad stayed on the weekends at his Uncle and Auntie's place. On the 3rd June 1934, just two months after their public profession of faith, Mum was invited with a few others to the Verhoef's house and it appears that either that evening or within a few days he asked her to be his girlfriend which she then accepted. There seemed to be no hesitation – she was madly in love with him, as she indicated in her diary notes. *"Isn't love wonderful. You can't understand or grasp what love is. He (Dad) has got a great need for love as he has no father or mother. I am sometimes concerned that I am unable to satisfactorily fulfil that need. But God will be with me. It is so beautiful to know that someone loves you and you can reciprocate that and so make each other so wonderfully happy. I hope that, with God's help, we can achieve that."*

Only just over a week later, Pieter and Miek got a taste of what it was like having someone courting in the house. Miek wrote to Marie, Dad's sister, on the 11th June about how the night before Dad came home late from visiting his new girlfriend. Pieter and Miek were both in bed, but still awake. Dad, not wishing to disturb them and thinking they were asleep, very quietly undressed himself downstairs. Taking his shoes off he carefully crept upstairs trying not to make any noise. However, because he had taken his shoes off, he slipped and crashed with a loud bang on the floor. Miek explained in the letter how they just couldn't contain themselves and burst out laughing.

It appears as if the courtship was approved by Mum's parents, Gerrit Jan Schutte and Jennikke Schutte-van Veen, as well. In a letter dated the 17th June and addressed to her son, Peet, Jennikke wrote: *"We have got a new friend in the house. Wimp is courting Cornelis Kleijn, the brother of Marie. He is a fine lad, very quiet at home. Rev. Boodt said he is a nice serious young man, and that is something for the minister to say."*

13. The Schutte Family

*"He causes the grass to grow for the cattle,
And vegetation for the service of man,
That he may bring forth food from the earth."*

~Psalm 104:14 (NKJV)

The Schutte family can be traced back in the Alblasserwaard district to 1770. My grandfather, Gerrit Jan Schutte, was born on the 30th November 1873 in Goudriaan, a small village just eight kilometres west of Brandwijk. My grandmother, Jennikke van Veen, was born on 3rd December 1876 in Bleskensgraaf, another small village in the Alblasserwaard about four kilometres east of Brandwijk. The Schuttes were predominantly farm labourers and shop keepers. My grandfather left home at age ten to take employment on a farm. It is not known what education, if any, he might have had, and, as compulsory six year schooling was not introduced till 1901, it can be assumed that, being from a working-class family, his education would have been minimal. His dad was a farm labourer so they would have had limited means.

The reality for many families was that the money was so tight it was a relief when one of the children, even at a young age, could find work that could at least provide for food and accommodation. For the parents, it was one less mouth to feed. Gerrit Jan was the sixth child, born from a family of eleven. Of those eleven children, five passed away within two years of birth and another four died at the young ages of 13, 21, 30 and 32. My grandfather had only one sister who lived to a mature age of 58. He himself outlived all his siblings by over thirty years when he died in 1960 at age 87.

My grandmother, Jennikke van Veen, also came from a working-class family with very little means. According to my Mum, she had no formal schooling but was taught basic writing and reading skills at home. She kept a writing pad and even late in life was still often seen practising her writing. With no phones and little opportunity and money to travel, the only method of communication with friends and family was through letter writing, even when someone lived only a few kilometres away. Thus, writing was a very necessary skill to accomplish. Her letters and parts of her writing books that have been preserved show a simple yet neat style of writing that lacks the decorative and flowing style of those taught the craft at school. Her vocabulary is simple, and her spelling largely based on phonetics rather than the correct spelling.

The other feature of her writing is her expression of her committed Christian faith. Her letters demonstrate a strong faith and hope, and often provided encouragement to the recipient to trust in God's providence in their lives. Her writing pads contain sections from books or publications to practise her writing with the common theme of serious theological and Biblical material. There seemed to be no room for lightheaded or jocular verses.

With her serious intent to follow Scriptures she would join the 'Doleantie' movement when it came to her village, Bleskensgraaf, and the neighbouring Brandwijk and

Molenaarsgraaf in 1897. This led to the institution of the Reformed Church in the area. Its members chose to separate themselves from the state sponsored Dutch Reformed Church, which to their mind had become decadent and self-serving, as well as unfaithful to Scriptures in many areas. They considered that its leaders were caught in the grip of the age of Enlightenment, leading them to question many of the fundamental truths that were summarised in the Church's confessions. The newly instituted Reformed Church wished to go back to the foundations fought for in the 16th century Reformation by John Calvin and others who lived by the mantra 'Sola Scriptura', by Scripture alone.[10] Members of the Reformed Church considered John Calvin as their spiritual father and so are often referred to as Calvinists.

Nationally, the 'Doleantie' or the 'aggrieved' movement, started in 1886. This was 52 years after the Secession in 1834, when, under the leadership of Hendrik de Cock and others, some 120 congregations separated themselves from the Dutch Reformed Church for much the same reasons as those that separated in 1886. These two independent and separated groups, the Doleantie and Secession, then merged in 1892 to become known officially as the Reformed Churches of the Netherlands. In total they represented 8 per cent of the Dutch population with a membership of 370,000.[11]

The established state sponsored church did not take kindly to its members leaving and starting another denomination doing everything in its power to make life difficult for the breakaway groups. Their influence was substantial: their official head was the Queen of the Netherlands and its members were representative of most leaders and influential decision makers in the district. However, this did not deter believers like my grandmother who felt principally committed to be part of this movement. Faith and trust in God had always played a big part in people's lives in an area where there was a constant threat to life and property from floods. And so, the movement to a strong faith-based church found fertile ground with many people in the Alblasserwaard district.

Despite initially not having Government support nor support from the elite, this new denomination, with incredibly driven and committed members, soon were to have significant influence. The leader of the movement, Abraham Kuyper, even became the country's Prime Minister in 1901. His motto was that the Lordship of Jesus Christ covered all spheres of life including state, schools, church and society. His passionate leadership resulted in the institution of Christian schools, Christian universities, a Christian political party, Christian newspapers, and Christian unions. His vision was that Christians needed to be active and involved in all areas of society and so influence, through Scriptural norms, the direction that society takes. With all these institutions being established during this period under the banner of the Reformed Church in conjunction with the committed Calvinist work ethic of its members, it became for this Church denomination the golden age of influence and prosperity. The Reformed Churches experienced a major rejuvenation and revival.[12]

The initial worship services of the newly instituted Reformed Church where Grandmother attended was held in the barn of farmer A. Brouwer in Brandwijk, which was situated in the back section of the farmhouse.[13] This farmhouse was already then famous for its 'three stones' embedded into its front wall that depict the height of the flood waters. The highest was in the year 1740, then 1819 and the lowest stone represented the flood level in 1809. It is also the farm where my grandfather, Gerrit Jan Schutte, the future husband of Jennikke van Veen, worked for all his adult life.

As a teen, Grandmother was introduced to the art of sewing and knitting. She became very proficient in this and worked in this field until she got married. Her older brother, Cees, was a professional tailor, so Grandmother would most likely have learnt from him and assisted him.

There are no records of how my grandfather and grandmother met. They did not attend the same church as my grandfather was still a member of the State-sponsored Dutch Reformed Church. Possibly they met at the Brouwer farm where Grandfather worked and Grandmother attended the Sunday church services of the breakaway group.

At this time, she would have been 21 years of age. Brandwijk was an easy four-kilometre bike ride from her hometown of Bleskensgraaf and would have been a place for grandmother to visit and possibly shop. Not every village carried all the necessary goods that people required so it was not unusual to visit villages to seek out individual items.

Whatever the circumstances, Gerrit Jan Schutte and Jennike van Veen, my grandfather and grandmother, met and committed themselves to each other in marriage. The ceremony took place in Brandwijk on the 14th November 1900. Grandfather was 27 years of age and Grandmother 24. Grandmother, having been through the church struggle and with a passion to be a member of what she saw as the true church, the Reformed Church, persuaded Grandfather to agree to leave the Dutch Reformed Church and join her as member of the Reformed Church of the Netherlands.

My grandparents bought a house, together with my grandmother's brother Cees and sister Maai, located right next door to the newly completed Reformed Church Building in

Brandwijk. The house was divided into two separate living areas with Cees and his sister taking over the front half of the house so he, being a tailor, could use the front room for his work. He set up tables and equipment under the front windows to make use of the light and to display and promote his business.

My grandparents lived in the rear section of the house which consisted of a combined living kitchen area, a small adjoining bedroom and an upstairs attic. In the lounge there were two curtained off cupboards built in the walls which were referred to as 'Bedsteden' – a boxed bed in the wall. There was no bathroom or laundry but outside there was a small work shed, next to which was a toilet of sorts – a hole in the ground under a seat. A number of times during the year the wastage from the toilet was dug up and recycled for use in the vegetable garden.

Water in the house came from just one single pump in the kitchen area. For personal washing they used a portable basin and jug that was often kept beside the bed for easy access in the morning. The pump in the kitchen took a lot of effort to just get a single bucket of water from it so it was often easier to simply scoop a bucket of water from the canal running across the road from the house. The canal was also used for washing clothes and any other domestic utensils or cloths that needed cleaning and washing. On the canal bank was a small step and platform which was used for this purpose. This house was about as basic as any available, with minimal space and no facilities to speak off.

When travelling from Australia in 1975 and visiting the house, Mum could not believe how small the space was and how it had been the home for such a large family. Her parents had even taken in their grandmother and cared for her at a time when most of the children were still at home. The house contrasts sharply with the 11 room two-bathroom home where the Verhoefs lived and where Dad had often stayed. The Verhoefs were located only 200 metres away in the same street.

Shortly after my grandparents got married, they moved into this home. It was to remain their home for the rest of their married life. It was only after my grandmother died in 1957 that my Grandfather eventually moved out to live the final years of his life with his daughter, Sijgje, and her family.

Living next to the church proved to be an advantage for my grandmother as she was able to take on the role of sexton and cleaner of the church. Besides that, she kept herself busy doing the traditional household chores of those days like cooking, sewing, cleaning as well as maintaining a substantial vegetable garden. As their children grew up, she was the main influence and educator of them. Her husband was always working or resting and left the bringing up of the children mainly to her.

Those that remember her say she was a stern, but friendly and caring, mother who worried a lot about her children and impressed on them the need to live by the Bible. While she was not a reader and had limited reading ability, she did read the Bible regularly. The Bible was always located in a prominent place in the lounge and, as one of her grandchildren later said, for her the Bible was an open book. Church was important to her as was the contact she had with the minister, who was for her a mentor and pastor. Sometimes she would have difficulty following all the different dogmatic debates about the church and so became confused. Rev. Boodt would then talk to her and in simple terms assure her of God's grace and covenant promises.

Some of the senior people in the district who knew her claimed many sought her advice and she would also reach out to those that needed help. While uneducated, her wisdom and insights were appreciated. Even the pastor's wife, Mrs. Boodt, as a young mother living next door in the manse, sought her advice and support. She later told Mum how she acutely missed that support when the pastor's family moved away in 1936 to Leerdam, admitting to weeping on occasions when she no longer had that ready access to my grandmother. Grandmother somehow did this all under the radar and never spoke about any of it. No doubt people could trust her to keep things confidential. Years later, in 1975, when Mum spoke to Mrs. Boodt, she was surprised to hear from her how much her mum had meant to her at that time when they were in their first congregation as a young ministerial couple.

My grandmother was typical of a generation of people who were committed to serve the Lord in all aspects of their life but who, through limited education, could not always grasp the theological debates that raged amongst the more learned people. Abraham Kuyper was particularly conscious of the need to communicate and support the 'kleine luyden', people of limited influence and education and who had, in the main been neglected by the elite. He formed Christian Unions and counselled that all people had God-given talents that they could develop and use in His service. While previously the Christian message to the lower classes had been one of needing to simply accept their station in life, Kuyper gave them vision and hope.

My grandmother encouraged her sons to learn a trade and to develop their talents. While there was not much opportunity for education due to financial limitations, a trade could be sought early in life. With the girls in the family it was different. Except for the more progressive people like the Verhoefs, who encouraged Auntie Marie to get an education, in the Schutte family the girls were simply introduced into domestic service or dressmaking types of activities in preparation for future marriage and motherhood.

My grandfather was, and remained, a farmer's labourer all his life. Since the early 1900s he worked on the Brouwer farm which was an easy walking distance from his home. It was one of the larger farms in the area with 25 hectares of land and milked between 20 and 30 cows each day. Each worker would milk by hand between five to seven cows. This would take about two hours morning and night seven days a week. After morning milking, Grandfather went home for a quick breakfast, then worked on other aspects of the farm that included caring for the pigs, cheese making and the seasonal cutting of the hay. He would be able to go home for lunch and siesta for two hours, returning at 2.00 p.m. and then be allowed to go home again at about 5.30 p.m. for dinner. During the summer months they might still do another few hours of work on the farm till about 7.30-8.00 p.m.

On Sunday there was no extra work undertaken outside milking and Saturday evening was also always free. This all equated to about 75 hours of work per week during the summer months, and about 60 hours during the winter months. Without a break! Year in, year out! There were no provisions for holidays and even when he had to attend funerals, he needed to make sure that the cows would still be milked. As there was also no provision for retirement, he worked well past his retirement age. He went on to work more than 50 years at the Brouwer farm.

The grandson of the Brouwer that employed grandfather in the early 1900s, Piet Brouwer, recalled in 2017 how grandfather was part of the furniture there and had a reputation of being a very reliable and trustworthy worker. He was particularly good with sharpening scythes and cutting grass so in retirement he often used to come to sharpen the cutting tools and cut some grass. Piet's father told him that he had to give free milk to my grandfather every day for as long as he lived after retirement. Piet remembers him coming in at 4.30 p.m. each day to collect the milk, but while he was there, he would inevitably also do a few odd jobs. Piet had very positive memories of my grandfather and knew he was appreciated by his father.

Despite these relentless hours on the farm, during the winter months when there was no evening work, Grandfather developed a hobby repairing clocks and watches. When at home and not resting he was always in the corner of the lounge attending to his clocks and watches. Self-taught, he became very proficient in this and was even given the honour, of which he was quite proud, of repairing the clock in the town tower. While he never charged cash for his work, he was given things in kind like cheese, fruit and other consumable items that went towards sustaining his family.

While working on his clocks and watches he always sat in the corner, behind his desk, and rarely participated in any conversation. He was known as a very quiet man who kept to himself. One of my cousins, who would often visit as a youngster, was always amazed at the skill he had in dealing with the delicate pieces of a watch with his large farming hands. According to him the only time he would speak was when some delicate piece dropped on the ground and he would get everyone looking for it. The room always had lots of clocks that would, at the turning of the hour make a range of chiming sounds. So, while Grandfather was sitting in the corner behind his desk busy with his watches and clocks, Grandmother would be sitting near the fireplace knitting and sewing and keeping a conversation going with whoever was there.

Another peculiar feature that some recall about my grandfather was that he wore a gold lobe in his left ear. Apparently, this was a tradition from where he grew up. It was an insurance to pay for his funeral in case there was no money.

He was not a heavy smoker but occasionally lit up his pipe. He was, however, constantly chewing tobacco which he would then from time to time spit out in a bowl before then taking in a fresh batch. Mum never got used to that and referred to it as a disgustingly filthy habit. Smoking was not frowned upon and in fact encouraged. One of my oldest cousins, Jan Smit, remembers that there was a sign in the lounge that read "Contented Smokers do not Cause Unrest." When he was about 12 and visiting, Grandmother gave him some money to buy some cigarettes for himself at the local store. It was the first time he bought cigarettes, and he recalls it being a packet of Blue Ribbon. This then led him to becoming a smoker for the next fifty odd years!

Grandfather never got involved much in church life. With no education, with restricted reading ability, and with the unrelenting demands of farm work he really had little time or energy to do much else. He was never appointed to consistory or to any other role within the church community. He was known to often sleep in church – after all he had to get up at 4.00 a.m. every Sunday morning to milk the cows before church. One of the family members, a half-cousin of my Dad, recalled in 2017 how, as a youngster, he used to sit behind my grandfather in church and he and other farm workers simply could not keep their eyes open. As he was always sitting behind my grandfather the pastor asked my Dad's half-cousin specifically to give my grandfather a prod if he fell asleep. However, my Dad's half-cousin felt empathy for those farmers and the hours they worked and was reluctant to disturb my grandfather during the church service.

My grandparents experienced extreme poverty for most of their early married years when they had a young growing family. While Grandfather always had a job, the pay was so little that there was often not even enough to feed the family. Only the most essential things were bought, and the vegetable garden became an essential source for the daily needs of the family. When I spoke in 2017 to some of the Verhoef farmers in the district, they recalled that the Schuttes were so poor during the depression and war years that they often had to organise the children to eat somewhere else. Farmers, who had more access to food, would try to accommodate and help out where possible.

My grandparents welcomed their first son, Aart, on the 30th December 1901. A total of thirteen children were born during the next eighteen years with the last one, Sijgje, born on the 14th October 1919. My mum, Willempje, was number ten and born on the 10th March 1915. Of the thirteen, four only lived for about three months and one lived for about six months. Eight reached adulthood but then another daughter died in 1934 at age 31.

My grandmother was unable to produce breastmilk and that seemed to be one of the main issues in trying to keep a baby alive. Medical advancement had still to arrive especially for the poor. The wealthy did have better access to doctors and could afford it. My grandparents had no money to pay for anything that was above and beyond the normal necessities of life. My mother once related a story of how one of her brothers was near death at three months. The doctor came, gave the child a cursory inspection, declared that his feet were already cold so there was no hope for him and then abruptly left. The family was left to deal with the dying child whom the doctor had effectively declared as dead. The pastor, arriving a short time later, advised my grandmother to try and feed the child some egg yolk. This they did and the child survived and lived a long healthy life into his eighties.

This instance does reflect the disadvantage people with no money or influence had. Many in the community, including the wealthy, were aware of this latent discrimination by doctors. A half-cousin of my father, Kees Verhoef, who is now into his 90s and spent his life as a practising doctor, related in 2017 how his father had warned him about this attitude when he commenced his studies. His father told him that he would support him to become a doctor providing he treated everyone equally regardless of class or influence or the ability to pay. His father threatened to disown him if he ever heard that his son did otherwise. This was a powerful message to a son starting his doctor's career and one that he carried with him all his life.

With the relentless poverty, the death of so many children and the heavy demands of work and a growing family, my grandparents would not have had an easy life. Yet there is no evidence of complaining. They had a strong faith that sustained them and gave them comfort in times of grief. They were able to give their children a safe and stable Christian environment that equipped them for their future lives.

14. Mum's Early Years

*The rich and the poor have this in common,
The Lord is the maker of them all.*

~Proverbs 22:2 (NKJV)

While Mum was the tenth child, when she was born on the 10th March 1915 there were only three surviving brothers and two sisters. The oldest, Aart, was then 14, Maaike 12, Arie 11, Peter (Peet) 9 and Marie 5. The family also cared for and had in the house Grandmother's mother who was in her 80s. The boys all slept in the attic, the girls in the small bedroom adjoining the lounge with the youngest sleeping in the bed cupboard in the lounge. My grandparents also slept in the bed cupboard built into the lounge wall.

After my Mum, Grandmother had three more children, two sons and a daughter. One son died within 5 weeks of birth. Then there was Jan and finally the youngest, daughter Sijgje, born 14th October 1919, who died on the 7th June 2020 aged 100.

My mother, Willempje, was named after Grandmother's brother Willem. She had named one of the boys Willem, but he had died within three months from birth. The next baby born, a girl, was then named Willempje, but she also died within seven months. My mother was the next baby born so she received the same name. She became generally known as Wim although her mother referred to her as Wimp and her first employer, Mrs. Donner, called her Wimpje.

She was fortunate in having some older sisters who spoilt her and gave her attention. When birthdays came along it was her older sisters who showered her with love and presents.

At six years of age she attended the local school, together with her sister Marie who was eleven by that time. School was about a half hour walk so she was usually accompanied by her sister and others that lived in the area. She did not enjoy school. They were surrounded by wealthy people; next door lived the minister's family, across the canal lived the mayor and his family and in the same street were a number of well-to-do, established farmers. The Brouwer farm, where her dad worked, was also just across the canal.

All these children from these diverse backgrounds and means were all thrown together in the classroom. No doubt their clothing, mannerisms and personal hygiene were all quite contrasting, so it was fertile ground for bullying and pestering. Mum certainly felt inferior and considered that the teachers also treated the poor different to the others. She was able to keep up with the learning, but seemed to get no recognition for it, compared to others. The fathers of the farmers' daughters were in the consistory, school board and in other community activities but her dad was not involved in anything and so had no influence. Somehow, she felt this and wrote about it in her diary. She was also the victim of bullying by some of the girls and consequently kept more and more to herself. By the time she was eleven, she was looking forward to turning twelve, the legal age for her to be able to leave school.

It was a Christian school, so they had to learn a Psalm from the Bible each week. In her final years there was also a Lord's

Day from the Heidelberg Catechism to memorise each week. Her mum also talked to her a lot about faith and Scriptures. While her mum had little education and read with difficulty, she was nevertheless able to follow the Sunday sermons and discuss them with her children. She instilled in her children very early in their lives a love for the Lord and a love for Sunday worship. At an early age, Mum already started her spiritual journey, as is revealed in her writings. At age ten her Dad slipped on the wharf while loading a boat and fell in the river. Not being able to swim he could have easily drowned as was so common in the district, with its extensive canals and waterways. However, he was saved, and she writes, "I could see God's hand in helping my dad, so he did not drown."

The dilemma of what to do when she left school weighed heavily on her. Her sister Maria had a job with a dressmaker. Maybe she could do with extra help. Her eldest sister, Maaike, had already moved out of the house with her eldest brother, Aart, to work at a milk business in Zwijndrecht, a town about 26 kilometres away. In January 1927, just two months before she was due to leave school, Maaike came home for a weekend to celebrate her 24th birthday with her family. The minister's wife, Mrs. Donner, also came to visit from next door to congratulate Maaike on her birthday. As the minister's wife she was very active in the congregation and wished to be more so but with two young children at home she was a bit restricted. What she wanted was someone in the house who could keep the children occupied. She had decided that my Mum would be just the right girl, so she mentioned that to Maaike.

It was settled and a week after leaving school, Mum joined the Donner family to take care of their two young children, a girl, two and half years old, and a boy, one and a half years old. Mrs. Donner was very good for Mum and made a commitment to teach her a lot of domestic skills like washing, cleaning, cooking and sewing. Her initial duties were just caring for the two children and keeping them entertained, but, in time, Mrs. Donner wanted to train Mum to take on the responsibilities of a house maid.

Mum loved the work and the environment. Mrs. Donner took her under her wing like her own daughter, read stories to her and gave her a taste of another type of life. However, within six months, in August 1927, Rev. Donner received and accepted a call to Broek op Langedijk, a town in the North of Holland about 125 kilometres from Brandwijk. This caused a bit of a dilemma. Grandmother was not too happy for Mum to go with them there, but the Donners were keen to keep Mum with them. Mum was also enthusiastic to stay with the Donner family and go with them. Mrs. Donner was a very committed, humble lady and she cared for Mum, which eventually swayed my grandmother to let Mum go with them. The agreement was that she could come home for a break every four months, and, if she ever got homesick and wanted to leave, they would raise no objections.

So, after the goodbyes and packing her things, Mum left home at the age of twelve and a half to live in with the Donner family in their new town. Initially, she loved it. The children enjoyed her company, she was supported and encouraged by the pastor and his wife and she also found friends in the church community. She no longer felt the stigma of being different and poor as she was now dressed and acting like she belonged to the Donner family. Mrs. Donner taught her all she could and grew to love her as her own more and more. Mrs. Donner also became increasingly more active in helping out with disadvantaged and needy community members. She took in children from time to time and gave Mum an example of what the community of saints should look like. She instilled in her a drive to help others.

However, the natural gravitational pull of home started to slowly grow in Mum. It probably began when she was home for a break in June 1928 during which period her Oma died. Her Oma had lived with the family for many years and Mum had developed a bond with her, often spending time talking with her and in later years, when her eyesight had started to fail, even spent time reading to her. Mum was there for the funeral and found it difficult to leave her grieving family to return to the Donner family. She felt herself distancing from her family and felt particularly sad for her mother. On reflection she started to regret the way she had, initially, so joyfully left the family home and considered what her mother must have felt. She even sent a letter asking her mum for forgiveness. This was, of course, the last thing that her mum expected. Her mum had not taken any offence and there was nothing to forgive.

Despite this, Mum persevered, but continued to look forward more and more to her breaks when she could return home, which was happening about every six months. Meanwhile, she was increasing her skill set under the coaching and direction of Mrs. Donner. As the children grew and needed less attention, Mum took over more of the domestic roles of cleaning, washing and cooking.

After a lot of hesitation Mum eventually did speak with Mrs. Donner about her homesickness and desire to go back to her family home. Mrs. Donner just couldn't understand it. How could she be unhappy? They had treated her like their own child and the privileges she enjoyed was something she would never have been able to enjoy at home. Mrs. Donner was also concerned that my Mum would find it difficult to fit back in with her own family after such a long period away. After all, the lifestyle in the pastor's house was so different. How could Mum possibly get used to the frugal and basic lifestyle that would be experienced in the Schutte household? Mrs. Donner had developed a close relationship with Mum, trusted her implicitly and had invested enormous time and energy in her personal development. Mum had been trained and taught by her to the point where she was capable of taking on more responsibilities. How could she possibly think of leaving now? Mum felt awful about having raised the matter with Mrs. Donner and decided to soldier on.

However, things came to a head and one time while at home, the issue was so pressing her that she confided all of this to her sister Marie. Marie realised the seriousness of the situation and immediately told her mum, who then undertook to speak to Mrs. Donner. Shortly after, in October 1930, Rev. Donner came to visit and Grandmother told him that Mum was suffering homesickness and wanted to come home. He relayed this to his wife, and reluctantly she agreed for Mum to leave them and return home in six months' time. This would give her time to find a replacement and also give my Mum more time to learn some more skills.

She had just been enrolled into sewing classes. Mrs. Donner seemed to genuinely love Mum and while sad to see her go, still wished the best for her and so continued to support her training. On her last birthday with the family on the 10th March, just a few weeks before she was due to leave, they organised a memorable party for her and showered her with presents. In her diary, she lists the many presents she received from them, but then also mentions the 12 letters and five cards she got from family and friends. Then, a few weeks later, after emotional farewells Mum left to start a new stage in her life back with her own family. It was the 30th March 1931, and she had just turned sixteen and had been with the Donner family for four years.

During those four years, Mum had maintained good contact with her family and friends via letters and cards. Hundreds of letters were received and sent. Over 100 cards sent to Mum in that time have been preserved. Some came from friends, but most came from her siblings, particularly from her sisters Marie and Sijgje. The Donner family also sent her regular cards while she was holidaying at home with her parents. They addressed her by her full name, Willempje, while her siblings and friends simply called her Wim. The Donner's cards to Mum have warm messages of greeting and at times include unique scribbles and 'hello' messages from the two young children. They no doubt missed her when she was away.

Coming home, Mum had presents with her for all her siblings and parents. Mrs. Donner had taught her to buy some small presents for her parents each time she came home but seeing she was now coming home permanently, she made a special effort to spoil them all. It appears that the allowance she received while with the Donners gave her a bit of flexibility to be able to spend money on a few luxuries. The Donners had also bought her clothes so she was always suitably dressed. Mum bought her dad a wallet and it seems he was just so happy with it. "A real leather wallet," he exclaimed. Mum wrote in her diary that he had never been spoilt with fineries and barely had enough money to buy the essentials.

During those last six months while Mum was still with the Donners, Grandmother had successfully lined up another job for Mum with the local town mayor who lived just across the canal. By now Mum had developed very useful, practical skills as a domestic worker in the homes of the upper class, so it appears the local mayor had no hesitation in employing her. No doubt Rev. Donner, who would have known the Mayor from his time as his pastor, would have given a glowing reference.

It was quite a different experience for Mum, for here she was not part of the family, but a work maid, who was expected to do her work without complaint. The hours were long, from 7.30 in the morning until 7.30 in the evening. Nevertheless, she enjoyed her work and was able to do what was required without complaint. And she enjoyed the fact she could be home every evening.

Grandmother was beginning to struggle with her health and needed one of her daughters at home to help with the daily chores. At this time Marie, five years older than Mum, was remaining at home helping her mum. However, she had marriage plans, and when she left, the responsibility of staying at home and helping Grandmother would fall on Mum. And so, it was arranged with Grandmother that, after eighteen months working for the local mayor, Mum left to take the place of Marie, who got married on the 25th August 1932.

Interestingly, Mum's brother Peet got married on the same day to save costs. All the festivities were held together. As an interesting aside there was debate about what colour the wedding dress of the brides should be. Marie, being a country girl from poor parents would wear black, as it would seem presumptuous if she wore white. However, a city girl, Peet's wife Jo, insisted on wearing white. So, there were two siblings married together with the one bride in black and the other in white.

After six months, grandmother began to regain her strength and health again, so Mum was able to take on a few other jobs. The minister next door, Rev. Boodt, who had taken over as minister of the church after Rev. Donner had left, asked for some help as did another church family where the mother was sick. It so happened that over the next three years until Mum got married, she juggled a number of jobs while working at home to help her mum. She wanted to be busy and so enjoyed the opportunity of helping out in a number of families.

The family was then struck with tragedy. Mum's eldest sister, Maaike, had just delivered her second baby, a boy. Within a few days, however, complications arose and she became seriously ill. She died in hospital on the 2nd January 1934, within two weeks of the birth of her son. Mum, then 19 years, wrote in her diary: "*Maaike died peacefully with a smile on her face. Here it was manifested: the believers can face death joyfully, without any fear. Death is then an entrance into eternal life.*"

It was, nevertheless, a terrible time of grieving for the family. Maaike was the happy, joyful person in the family who would liven things up, just by her presence, and she was now gone. It was a very difficult time for grandmother and mum's presence was now certainly needed in the family home.

Three months later on 1st April 1934, Mum did her public profession of faith, together with Dad and some others in the church, under the leadership of Rev. Boodt. Two months later Dad asked Mum to become his girlfriend. Mum was 19 and Dad 21.

15. The Happy Couple

"Rejoice, O young man, in your youth, and let your heart cheer you in the days of your youth."

~Ecclesiastes 11:9a (NKJV)

Grandmother, it seems, harboured real concerns about the class difference between the Schuttes and the Kleijns. People in the district just did not marry anyone outside their class and the worlds of the Kleijns and Schuttes were poles apart. She told her daughter that Kees Kleijn had grown up and lived with farmers and his mother was a farmer's daughter, while her dad was a simple farmers labourer. There were colossal differences involving all aspects of life for those of differing social classes, including access to services, money, and influence. Mum had experienced that contrast in her school years and been the victim of a lot of bullying, as a result. Now here she was thinking of marrying someone from that class which had given her so much grief during her formative years.

The Schuttes lived in a small house with no luxuries or conveniences. Grandfather Schutte's pay never allowed the family to buy anything but the bare essentials and for many years, they could not even feed their children properly. Contrast that to Kees Kleijn's environment, where he grew up in spacious homes   He had never suffered want and always had access to anything he needed. In recent years, he had spent most of his time with his Auntie Miek and Uncle Pieter who lived in a luxury 11 room 2-bathroom house just down the road from the Schutte's humble abode. Grandmother Schutte was acutely aware of her humble status in life and how differently the privileged in society lived. Could this cause problems for her daughter in her relationship with Kees Kleijn?

Mum, on the other hand, did not see this as an issue at all. She was in love and cared deeply for Kees Kleijn, who demonstrated a sense of humbleness and empathy when integrating with the Schutte family. There was no indication that he ever had anything but the deepest respect for the Schutte family, despite their impoverished lifestyle. He developed warm relationships with Mum's brothers and some of them remained firm friends for the rest of their lives. He soon became totally accepted by the family and was treated like one of their own.

Going to the same church and both having a strong commitment to their faith certainly helped seal the bond of trust and respect. Grandmother Schutte was a deeply religious person whose faith meant so much more than temporary riches and this would have had an impact on her attitude towards Kees Kleijn. Then she also received a glowing endorsement from her minister Rev. Boodt who was very supportive of the courting couple.

For Mum, life now revolved around the weekends when she could spend time with Dad. She wrote in her diary: "The week days take so long but the weekends seem to fly past." Dad regularly hired cars over the weekend, so they could drive and visit family members spread out in the villages across the Alblasserwaard district. He enjoyed driving and the freedom the vehicle gave them to go where they wished, without the often lengthy times needed to wait for connecting buses and transport. Cars in 1934 were still very basic and travelling at 40 kilometres an hour was about the maximum the cars could take. Dad commented once that if he went any faster the car would start swaying across the road. He once had an incident, when driving along with Mum, that a wheel came loose and catapulted past them into the canal. It was just a matter of retrieving the wheel, bolting it back on and continuing the journey. Most things in the car could be fixed with a few simple tools.

On Sinterklaas Day, the 5th December 1934, Dad spoiled Mum with the gift of a fancy handbag and ladies gloves. For Christmas they stayed together at Mum's sister, Marie, and her husband, Henk, who lived in Klundert, a town about 40 kilometres south of Brandwijk. They had been married just over two years ago and had one son Jan, now 12 months old. Mum and Dad really enjoyed the company of this couple and they always remained close.

In the nine months since Mum and Dad had been courting, they had introduced each other to all of their extended families through personal weekend visits. They seemed to enjoy the social interaction and fellowship that family life offered. Mum wrote in her diary, *"Through going out visiting with Kees I have come to love him more and more."* These were happy times for the young courting couple, and they were seemingly accepted and embraced by members of both sides of the family. They were also both positively engaged in church life, enjoyed Bible study fellowship and Rev. Boodt's sermons. Often, when writing in her diary on a Sunday evening, Mum would summarise the day's sermons and engage with the key points raised. They both made a conscious effort to not only listen to the sermons but to also see where practical applications could be applied in their own lives.

16. Sickness Strikes

"God employs several translators: some pieces are translated by age, some by sickness, some by war, some by justice."

~John Donne (1572-1631)

Travelling home from their 1934 Christmas visit with Mum's sister, Marie, and husband Henk, Dad was suddenly overcome with severe abdominal pains. He had to rest for a while before the pain subsided sufficiently to allow him to continue the journey home. During the next few weeks, he had the occasional painful burst but, as was generally the case in those days, he just stoically soldiered on. However, by the end of January it became too much for him to bear. After relentless pain for two days, he visited the local doctor who had him immediately admitted to the hospital in Dordrecht.

He was diagnosed as having a severely inflamed appendix, but due to the infection they could not operate. This was now a serious and life-threatening situation. There was no penicillin to treat the infection – that was not introduced till 1943 – so every care had to be taken to build the immune system and not introduce foods that might aggravate the situation. For Dad this meant a strict diet of 15 grams of water and 15 grams of milk every hour. The whole focus was on fighting the infection and getting his condition stable enough so an operation could be performed to drain the accumulated abscess from the area surrounding his appendix. By day five he was finally allowed a cup of Bouillon in addition to his strict water and milk diet. The pain was subsiding slowly and by day seven he was allowed three cups of Bouillon as well as a cup of tea. Those visiting him could see the weight just falling off him. By day eight his temperature was going down so everyone saw that as a sign that the immediate threat to his life might have passed.

Every day he had a steady flow of visitors. Mum used the bike to visit, taking about an hour to cover the 18 kilometres from Brandwijk. Nevertheless, she was determined to see him every day. Dad's Auntie Miek was also a regular visitor and would keep Dad's sister Marie updated on Dad's condition by a regular stream of letters, most of which have been preserved. Often, there were so many visitors that they would need to enter the ward in turns, so it would not be too busy for Dad. There was no shortage of support or concern for his welfare from family, community and friends. Considering that at that time thousands of people died in the Netherlands each year from such a simple ailment as an inflamed appendix, the concern and worry was very real and valid. Whether he would survive this crisis or not had been the question in everyone's mind.

On the thirteenth day the doctors considered the time right to operate just to clean out the infected area and drain all the accumulated pus. This was considered a very dangerous, but necessary, first step in the intervention. Further delay could result in poisoning and death. Removal of the actual appendix would have to wait for another time, after Dad had regained his health. The intervening operation to clean the area of infected material was considered a success, but the recuperation was a very slow process. He maintained a limited diet, but now with a little more variety to build his strength. It was three weeks before he was allowed out of bed for some first steps.

After just over five weeks in hospital, Dad was finally discharged for further healing at home before needing to return to have the appendix removed. At home with his Uncle Pieter and Auntie Miek, he continued his convalescence under the supervision of the doctor who came to visit every two days. At each visit, the doctor prescribed the amount of walking he was allowed to do, the exercises needed and the food he could eat. He even advised Dad to stop courting Mum for a period, as his health was so precarious. According to his Auntie Miek, he had no intention of having anything interfere with their ongoing courtship and commitment to each other.

His convalescence was very slow. For four months he was restricted to the home, not allowed to work and was required to follow a prescribed regime of exercise, walking and diet. It was a hard road for him, especially as, in time, he felt more able to take on things. He did spend a lot of time reading and, according to his Auntie, had just about read every book in the library. On the 27th June he was finally considered well enough to be admitted back into the Dordrecht hospital to have his appendix removed.

This time everything went well, there were no complications, and he was discharged from the hospital within ten days. After a further five weeks of healing at home, he was finally cleared to go back to work on the 5th August 1935, more than six months from when he was first admitted to hospital.

It was a remarkable and intense journey for my Dad and the attention that he received from doctors, hospital staff and others was just amazing. For the whole period of the six month recovery his condition, what he ate and drank, his movements and exercise were all closely controlled and monitored by his medical team, with the whole focus on getting him back to good health. While some of the treatment meted out might be ill-advised from today's 'enlightened' medical perspectives, the commitment and dedication demonstrated by the medical staff was certainly outstanding. Did he get that sort of treatment and care because of his family connections and their ability to pay for them? Would a Schutte, with no money, influence or connections have received the same consistent treatment for the whole six months?

The Dutch were to introduce compulsory health insurance in 1941. The central Government of the Netherlands had never accepted responsibility for the health care of its citizens. So when Dad was in hospital, it was up to the local government to provide for the medical care of the poor in their locality. The upper class paid their own way. [14]

If a Schutte ended up in hospital they would be reliant on their local authority to cover the costs. We have earlier seen the impact that relying on the support of the local authority had on the treatment and care that Klaas Kleijn received while institutionalised in the St. Joris Gasthuis. The Streefkerk Council, where Klaas Kleijn had lived, did everything in its power to ensure that the least possible money was spent on Klaas Kleijn. While some authorities had better reputations than others, the general principle certainly applied that if you had no personal funds to pay for your medical treatment and needed to stay in a hospital in the 1930s in the Netherlands, you were at the mercy of the generosity - or otherwise! - of your own local authority. It is hard to imagine that a local authority, during the difficult Depression years, would have endorsed and supported the six months of care that Dad was privileged to enjoy.

During the period of Dad's sickness, Mum also became ill. Her face, hands and body were covered in blisters while the inside of her mouth was so swollen she could hardly speak or eat. Doctors were baffled by her condition and were unable to come up with an explanation or diagnosis. After two weeks of bed rest her condition slowly improved, but it still took at least another month before she regained her strength. While the doctors could not come up with a diagnosis, Mum thought it was the result of stress dealing with Dad's prolonged illness. Especially when, in the early period, there were real fears for his life. This had all taken a toll on her. Besides visiting Dad every day, she was required to attend to her work commitments, both at home with her Mum and with two other families she regularly worked for. She believed it had been this particularly busy and stressful time for her, that had been the cause of her illness.

Grandmother Schutte encouraged her daughter, saying that the hardships they experienced as a couple was a blessing before marriage because, through it, their love and commitment for each other was really put to the test. Mum agreed and could write in her diary that their love for each other had become stronger as a result, and that they now always wished to be together.

By August 1935 both were back in good health and at work and could start planning for a long term future with each other. They announced their engagement. It was a bit unexpected, but Mum's sister, Marie, and her husband, Henk, were over on holidays and they suggested that if they were going to get engaged, they should do it while they were there so they could celebrate with them. This little bit of encouragement was all they needed, so, without much fanfare or planning, they got engaged, exchanged the appropriate rings and vows and celebrated with the family and some close friends.

A week later Mum heard that Rev. Boodt and some consistory members were travelling to a deacons' conference in Broek op Langedijk where she had lived with the Donner family for four years. It was now over four years since she had left them. How she would love to visit them again. 'Could she have a ride?' she asked. There was one seat vacant so, in the company of four men, she was able to drive to Broek op Langedijk and spend the day with the Donner family. The bonds were still strong, and she thoroughly enjoyed her time with them.

17. Charting a Life's Path

"I find that the great thing in this world is not so much where we stand as in what direction we are moving: To reach the port of heaven, we must sail – sometimes with the wind and sometimes against it – but we must sail, and not drift, nor lie at anchor."
~Oliver Wendell Holmes, Sr.
"The Autocrat of the Breakfast-Table." 1858

Now that his health challenges were behind him, Dad didn't waste any time in planning for his future. He did not want to remain working for a baker but was keen to become self-employed. While he enjoyed his work with baker Rees in Oud Alblas and could possibly have taken over the business due to Mr. Rees' impending retirement, Dad was concerned about being able to keep his clients. Most of the clients were members of the state-sponsored Dutch Reformed Church while Dad was a member of the breakaway group, The Reformed Church. Many of the Dutch were upset with those leaving the established mother church and had no compunction in showing this displeasure by avoiding, if possible, doing business with them. Because Mr. Rees was still a member of the Dutch Reformed Church, Dad felt that many of Mr. Rees' customers would buy their bread elsewhere if Dad took over the business.

He placed a 'Wanted to Buy' advertisement for an established bakery in the local paper. Seven different bakeries and business were offered to him and in the first week of August 1935 he went to inspect one of them in Dordrecht. His Uncle Pieter and Mr. Rees were both happy to assist and advise. The business in Dordrecht involved a bakery and shop that sold, besides bread products, a range of goods like cheeses, eggs and other dairy products. The total investment for the freehold shop and business, including stock, was just over 20,000 guilders. Dad seemed confident that he was able to purchase something at that price. While no official records survive as to the size of the inheritance he collected a year earlier when he turned twenty one, it can be assumed that he would buy something that he could afford rather than starting a business with loans.

After some months searching, in February 1936 he eventually settled on a bakery in Oud Beijerland, a small town 40 kilometres west of Brandwijk. The buildings were comprised of a bakery, house and shop, and after inspecting all this with a few of his uncles and Mr. Rees, he decided the business was solid with a good track record that he could build on. Handover of ownership would be in September. The settlement date of the business helped determine the marriage date of Mum and Dad. They decided to marry in September just before moving into the baker's house. Things were starting to fall into place for this young couple. Mum became excited about setting up the house and helping in the shop. During the next months they made a few visits to the place to orientate themselves and plan for their future.

In March 1936 their beloved pastor, Rev. Boodt, received and accepted a call to go to the Reformed Church of Leerdam. Before he went, they arranged with him to officiate at their wedding. His willingness and commitment to do this meant a lot to my parents, particularly my mum.

On the 10th March Mum celebrated her twenty first birthday. From Dad she received a Singer sewing machine, one that she was to use for the whole of her married life. It is now in the possession of one of her Australian grandchildren, our daughter Susan Dykstra. A few months earlier on Dad's twenty second birthday on the 5th November 1935, Mum gave him a fancy round glass-top smoke table that had all the different attachments required for serious smokers, a cigar holder, match holder and ashtray. Dad also kept that for the whole of his married life and it eventually ended up in my own lounge as a memento of the heyday of smoking days in the past.

By mid-June 1936 Dad and Mum both resigned from and left their respective jobs. Dad wanted to spend time working in the bakery he was buying in Oud Beijerland so that when he did finally take possession in September he would be fully conversant with all aspects of the business. Dad had, by that time, been working for Mr. Rees in Oud Alblas for nearly three years and had developed a very trusting and warm relationship with him. Mr. Rees had spent a lot of time with Dad, inspecting and advising on the various bakeries and businesses he had been looking at. It seemed like, despite knowing he was going to lose Dad as a valuable employee once he bought his own bakery, he was nevertheless happy to support him and see him succeed. He had been a valuable teacher and coach for Dad.

But first Dad and Mum had a few weeks of holidays, knowing that once they started their own business, they would have little opportunity to take breaks. They spent some time travelling around, sightseeing and visiting friends and family. They loved travelling together and enjoying the cafés in the small villages. They even spent time swimming at a beach.

They stayed a few days in Amsterdam with Dad's sister, Marie, and while there also visited the Rijksmuseum, which they thoroughly enjoyed. They spent three days with the Donner family in Broek op Langedijk. Mum had been there less than a year earlier, just after her engagement to Dad. She obviously was very fond of the family, for her and Dad to spend three precious days of their holidays with them. They had a marvellous time there and Mum also enjoyed catching up with their two, now grown up, children.

The holidays came to an end and Dad then took up working in the bakery he was about to buy. However, about a month after starting there, a crisis developed. A new bakery had started in town and a price war was going on. Bread from all the outlets in the town was heavily discounted in the hope of growing or at least maintaining market share. Profits in the meantime were plummeting and Dad was starting to get worried. Would this price war continue, or would it be over by the time he took the business over in September? There was no way he wanted to get into a business that had no prospects of making a profit.

On the 6th August 1936, Dad made the decision to withdraw from the purchase. He must have had a contract that allowed him to pull out within a certain time frame. As a couple it must have been a difficult decision, particularly for Mum. She had been there many times and had the setting up of the house all planned. How she had looked forward to starting their married life there. Now, only about six weeks before the planned wedding date they had no business, were unemployed and would possibly have to delay the marriage. It was a challenging situation for them. Mum wrote in her diary, "Man can decide but it is God who determines."

However, Dad seemed to remain positive. A week later he

visited his Auntie Niesje, who then wrote to Dad's sister Marie, about the visit. She wrote that Dad told her about not going ahead with the purchase, but that he was already looking at other opportunities. Auntie Niesje was happy that he did not go headlong into a potential disaster and had the courage to walk away from it.

Less than a month after walking away from the deal, Dad had found something in Sliedrecht, a town only 10 kilometres south of Brandwijk. He had come across a milk round that was available for purchase. In the same town was a row of double storey units under construction that were being offered for sale. The units were due to be completed by the 1st of October so there was an opportunity, for little extra cost, for a purchaser to make changes to the building to suit their personal needs. Dad had an idea of converting the ground floor into a shop with the living area upstairs. He thought a milk round could be nicely complemented by a retail dairy and milk products business. After consulting with Mum and other members of the family he went ahead and bought both the milk round and a double storey unit on Kleindiepstraat 9, Sliedrecht.

Mum was ecstatic. Their wedding date could now be confirmed, and they could plan for their future. "I can't thank and praise God enough for this wonderful blessing," she wrote in her diary.

Nevertheless, Dad still had some military obligations and was due to spend another 17 days in military service. This was part of the initial conscription requirement. It was nearly three years since he spent six months in the military, and he was required to keep up the training by spending another 17 days at the same camp in Bergen op Zoom. He was keen to get this commitment over with before he was married and starting the business. He had previously enjoyed army life but with new purpose and commitments it was now just an annoying interruption. However, he was pleased that the army agreed for him to complete his obligations then and not later.

Two and a half weeks before the proposed wedding day, tragedy struck. On Saturday the 19th of September, Dad's sister Marie, moved back from Amsterdam to live with her adopted parents, Auntie Miek and Uncle Pieter. On Monday they all decided to visit Lijsje, Dad's other sister, in Streefkerk, about 10 kilometres away. The three took their bikes for a lovely visit with Lijsje for about one-and-a-half hours. Then it was back on the bike to pedal home. On the way they stopped for a brief rest on a dike along a canal. Suddenly, without warning, Pieter collapsed and died from a massive heart attack. He was fifty-nine years.

He was so loved by Dad and his two sisters. His home had always been welcoming for them, a haven, and he always had their welfare at heart. Pieter, as a brother of Dad's mum Jannigje, had real empathy and understanding of his sister's children and had felt blessed to be able to care for them. He understood their lows and the burden of the trauma they carried and had always been there to encourage and counsel them. In a letter written by Miek to Marie a year earlier, in response to Marie's wish to buy them a substantial gift in appreciation of their care she wrote:

> *What we did for you both (Dad and Marie) was done with sincere love and we consider the greatest gift to see how well you both are doing. That gives us the pleasure. We can say that the Lord has richly blessed us through you and we hope and pray that in your continuing life's journey, with God's blessing and to his honour it may continue to go well with both of you.*

They had given them a godly upbringing and guided them as best they could to live a life of thankfulness and service to God. If Dad or his sister Marie were struggling, they encouraged them by directing them to their Creator, who always had the best things in mind for His children, even if that was sometimes difficult to understand. Just three months before he died, Pieter wrote a letter of encouragement to Marie, at a time when she must have been struggling with some disappointments in her life. This letter, one of the few surviving from Pieter, gives a good picture of the depth of feeling and concern he had for his adopted daughter and how strongly his counsel was motivated and underpinned by his faith. He wrote:

> *Now don't take offence to what I write because you know we always have the best intentions and wishes for you. But Marie, where do you think our setbacks come from? You do know that, don't you? Might it not be possible that God's hand is in this, that He is moulding you through this disappointment. I know we so easily think we don't need that, but God is doing things for our benefit even when we don't see it or want to see it especially when we are in the middle of the situation. However, we have to accept bad times just as we do the good times. Oh, Marie, I can sympathise with your difficulties, but you cannot let your spirit become despondent. Why do we have faith? Surely also to be able to be patient in times of hardship and setbacks and not let grief and sadness overtake us? On top of that, you and I have nothing to complain about as far as having access to material things, we can get everything that we need. Besides that, you also have a loving*

family. Consider how many have nothing, no loving family, home or material goods. Please do look at the positive sides of your life and you will realise there is so much you can be thankful for.

For five years since he left the farm after his grandfather died in January 1931 Dad had made his home with Pieter and Miek, his adopted parents. It had been a critical time for Dad as he had begun to develop his career, been seriously ill and spent months at home in convalescence. He had started courting his future wife while in more recent times, he had been searching for a business to buy. Pieter accompanied him on all the business inspections, and, while admitting he wasn't a businessman, nevertheless, gave sage advice that Dad respected. And now, just two and a half weeks before Dad's big day, the marriage to his beloved, Pieter was gone. How Dad would have loved for him to be a witness of that day and how happy Pieter would have been to see his adopted son, who had such a traumatic start to his life, now happily entering into marriage with a committed Christian girl.

Yet it was not to be. Should they still go ahead with the wedding? They decided that yes, indeed, the wedding would go ahead, but the festivities would be low-key. So it was that first they attended to the funeral of Pieter, and then, only a week later on the 8th October 1936, they got married.

As was the custom in the Netherlands, the official wedding ceremony was carried out by the Mayor of the town. On the morning of their marriage the couple first walked to the Town Hall to have the marriage officially carried out and recorded by the Mayor. After this they walked to the church for a special wedding service to encourage them and to seek God's blessing for their marriage. It also involved them giving vows to each other based on a set of questions developed by the church and on the biblical principles of marriage. As arranged previously, Rev. Boodt came from Leerdam to lead the service and officiate at the wedding. The chosen text was from Psalm 23 on the words – "The Lord is my Shepherd."

There were very few people in the church, and at night, in the home of Mum's parents, only close friends came as well as the girls from the Bible study club to pass on congratulations. It was a low-key event, as was appropriate in the circumstances when many in the family were still overcome by grief. As was traditional for someone from Mum's background, she wore a plain, long black dress, while Dad wore a black suit with a top hat.

At the end of the evening, Mum's brother Aart drove the couple to their just completed house in Sliedrecht. There was no time for a honeymoon. Dad had to start at 4.00 a.m. the next morning to do the milk round with the current owner, so that he could show Dad the ropes. Mum recalled later how Dad was an hour late and how angry the man was at having to wait.

18. The First Years of Marriage

*"Jerusalem the golden,
With milk and honey blest..."*

*~" Jerusalem the Golden"(Ewing)
Text by: Bernard of Cluny
Trans. by: John Mason Neale 1818-1866*

The house my parents moved into was a modern, spacious just-completed two-storey building. They had the ground floor changed so it included an open room with a large display window facing the street that could be set up as a retail shop. Besides the shop area, the ground floor also had a dedicated kitchen, toilet, a living room and storage room as backup for the shop. Upstairs were four bedrooms. Then there was also the attic, which many in the Netherlands used as both storage space and sleeping quarters, if necessary. For a just-married couple, Dad and Mum had plenty of space.

They moved in on their marriage day and immediately committed to working the milk round and setting up the shop, which was to be launched a week later on Saturday the 17th October 1936. Advertisements promoting the opening in the local papers had been placed so there was no turning back. So, in their first week of marriage, Dad was learning the ropes in relation to the milk round and in his spare time was, with Mum, working setting up the shop in time for the grand opening. It was a busy week.

The day before the opening Mum had an outbreak of boils and blisters which covered her mouth and face. She did not think she should be speaking and dealing with clients in the circumstances. It was a similar condition - but not as severe – to what she had suffered a year earlier, when Dad had been seriously ill. This time it took her a fortnight to get her health back.

With Mum out of action, Dad made other arrangements, employing a part-time assistant. The opening was a great success. Over 70 guilders was collected that first day. It seemed like everyone in the town had come through the shop. The shop specialised in dairy products including a range of cheeses, yoghurts, custards, butter and milk.

The milk Dad sold was advertised as being 'TBC free' – this meant the milk would have been pasteurised by the farmer Dad bought it from. Milk had been identified as one of the causes of the spread of tuberculosis, which in those times, without penicillin, was often fatal. Getting milk that was 'TBC free' would have given Dad a competitive advantage as it was not yet a general standard within the industry.

More than ten years later, following the war, the Government finally introduced legislation making pasteurisation of milk compulsory. This revolutionised the industry with farmers now generally selling their milk to large milk distribution centres which had the expensive pasteurising equipment to treat the product to government standards. They would then sell to retail outlets like my Dad's.

In 1936 Dad could still do business direct with the dairy

farmer, negotiate his prices and conditions and then buy the milk in 10-gallon drums which he picked up himself twice a day after the morning milking and, again, after the afternoon milking session. This ensured the freshest milk possible. For home delivery, which he did with bike and cart, the clients provided the containers in which he would pour the ordered amount from the ten-gallon drums. Those coming to the shop would take their containers with them and again the required amount was poured into their own container.

The other selling feature Dad promoted was that he kept everything refrigerated in summer, so customers received their goods in a cool condition. The shop was new and, as a consequence, Dad incorporated the latest technology including electric refrigeration.

The business kept them both very busy, despite having a part time assistant. Dad was on the road most of the day, going house to house with his milk cart. Mum and the assistant worked in the shop from nine o'clock in the morning until nine in the evening, six days a week. While the shop income dropped after the initial opening day, it remained steady and they were both pleased with the consistent turnover. Three months after starting, Mum wrote in her diary, "*The business is going well. For this we can be thankful to the Lord.*"

Mum never really felt that she was cut out to be a shop keeper and was not so comfortable with chatting and making small talk with customers. She said later that, while Dad had never complained about her work, and she did it with total commitment because it was their business, she considered herself unsuitable and not a natural fit for the job. On the other hand, Dad was eminently popular with clients and could chat and engage with them in a natural way. He had the confidence and customer relations skills that she felt she lacked.

They had a busy social life with family and friends visiting regularly, many times not just for a day, but for a number of days. There was a real interest in what they were doing and how the business was going. The house was spacious enough to accommodate extra people when required, so guests staying overnight was not a problem. Their beloved Pastor, Rev. Boodt, also dropped by a few times when he was in the area. Both my parents enjoyed his company and counsel and missed his sermons. They often compared their current minister with Rev. Boodt but had to remind themselves that each minister had different gifts and talents and, as long as the sermon was true to Scripture, they should not complain.

Six months after they were married, Mum's older sister, Marie, fell ill so Mum took in her oldest three year old son for five weeks. Mum enjoyed having the young lad around and looked forward to starting a family of her own. After three weeks the boy's mother, Marie, also came to stay. Being away from home and able to relax and be cared for by my parents helped her in her recuperation process. After two weeks she was able to go home again and take her young son with her.

Thirteen months after they married, on the 28th November 1937, their first child, Pieter (Peter), was born. He was named after Dad's dear uncle, his adopted dad who had tragically died from a heart attack just before their wedding, and who was still sadly missed. The birth took place at home. Mum had been serving in the shop till 10.00 p.m. Saturday evening. By 5.30 a.m. Sunday morning, baby Peter arrived. There had been little notice and Dad only just managed - in the early hours of the morning - to round up the doctor and midwife, who both arrived just on time to attend to the birth.

What joy and happiness for my parents! Mum was overwhelmed with not just the joy and wonder of it all, but also with the responsibility. She wrote in her diary, *"It is a major concern and responsibility to raise and nurture him before the Lord as having received him from His hand."* Mum was instructed to stay in bed for ten days after the birth as was the norm in those days. So, Peter was presented for baptism the following Sunday in the presence of just Dad who made the baptismal vows also on behalf of his wife. This was a very common practice in the Reformed Church in those days, as they believed there should be no unnecessary delays for the child to have God's promises of the covenant confirmed and baptism administered.

Motherhood seemed to agree with Mum and she thoroughly enjoyed the time she could spend with her child. The working hours of the shop assistant were increased so Mum could spend more time in the house with young Peter. She must have quickly developed a reputation for being an effective parent because, twelve months after Peter was born, she was asked to care for a young two-year-old boy whose mother could not cope with him. The boy would not eat or sleep and was losing weight. The mother's doctor had suggested that if a home was not found soon where he could be induced to eat and sleep, he would need to be admitted into hospital. Mum had the same doctor and, after discussions with him and the parents, agreed to take care of the boy for six weeks. The parents were not allowed access to him during that period and the doctor would monitor his health.

The boy had been the master and his mum, while fussing over him all day, could not get him to obey. He was down to 24 pounds (10.8 kilos). The first few days with my parents were bedlam. Kicking and screaming he refused to eat. In the end, Dad and Mum together held him down and force fed him. When they put him to bed, he jumped out straight away. So they bound his legs and arms, tying him to the bed so he could not get out. They maintained this approach, never giving in. By day three, he gave up fighting, started eating independently and stayed in bed, getting a good night's sleep. By the end of the first week he was acting like a normal happy child, singing and playing. The doctor, on his first visit after a week, was delighted with the progress and commented that he had never seen the child so happy. After the six weeks he had put on six pounds and was reunited with his parents, a totally different boy.

Three months later, on the 25th February 1939, Mum had her second child, a girl she named Jenneke (Jenny) after her mother. All went well and even quicker than the last time. Again, it was on a Saturday afternoon - she was helping out in the shop when she gave a warning to Dad to get the doctor and someone to help in the shop. In under an hour she had the healthy baby girl. They were overjoyed at the blessing – first a boy and now a girl.

The tranquility of their lives was soon to be interrupted, however. The clouds of war were gathering pace and Hitler, who had now been in power in Germany since 1933, was becoming more and more threatening. The Dutch, while maintaining their insistence on being independent, nevertheless felt increasingly threatened by Hitler's aggressive and belligerent attitude. On the 28th August 1939 the Dutch declared a general mobilisation. All classes of conscripts since 1924 were called to active duty. Dad was conscripted in 1933 so was in the group called to serve. A new Commander in Chief of the Army and Navy, L.T.G. Reynders was appointed to oversee the situation and prepare the country for possible war. Some 300,000 men were called up and remained completely mobilised until the German invasion nearly nine months later on the 10th May 1940. [15]

While for Dad the call up was not unexpected, when it actually came it still sent enormous shockwaves through both my parents. They received little notice. Dad had to leave already on the 29th August, the day after he was called up. He was able to organise a reliable person, a Henk van der Haren, to take over his work. Henk also slept in the house to ensure Mum was not on her own. The uncertainty and real possibility of war played on their minds and they wondered whether they would see each other again. *"If we did not know there was a Father in heaven who is in control of all things we would despair,"* Mum wrote in her diary.

19. The Spectre of War

*"Each one hopes that if he feeds the crocodile
enough, the crocodile will eat him last. All of them
hope that the storm will pass before their turn
comes to be devoured. But I fear greatly that the
storm will not pass. It will rage and it will roar
ever more loudly, ever more widely."*
~ *Winston Churchill – 20th January 1940*
(Comment directed at the neutral nations.)

The Dutch had great difficulty coming to terms with the fact that they might have to participate in a war. All Dutch Governments, from 1880 onwards, had espoused neutrality as their foreign policy. Not since Napoleon had the Dutch been seriously engaged in war. Never in Dutch history had the Netherlands fought Germany. Their First World War experience, where through neutrality they had avoided bloodshed and involvement in war, had remained the foundation of their policy right until close to the breakout of the Second World War. Even as the evidence was mounting that there was a major build-up of German troops near the Dutch border in late 1939, many in government and in the armed forces still refused to accept the inevitable.[16]

However, what seems to have been forgotten by present day commentators was that, for the Netherlands to maintain neutrality in the First World War, it had boasted a strong defence force of two hundred thousand trained men, armed and ready for battle.[17] Anyone who wanted to ignore Dutch neutrality during the First World War was going to have to face a very formidable and battle-ready foe. After the First World War, with no foreseeable threats, the annual defence expenditure was slashed to the point where, by the 1930s, it was only 20% of what was spent in 1918. There was no political will or unity within the Dutch Government to change this situation.

With war possibly on the horizon, by May 1939, the Dutch Government was in crisis. The Finance Minister, J. de Wilde, refused to use deficit spending to finance the increased defence programs required, and subsequently resigned. This led to the downfall of the Government and, despite the Queen intervening and asking a number of prominent leaders to form Government, the political situation remained in paralysis for two and a half months. It was supremely unfortunate that this collapse came at such a critical time when strong and decisive leadership was needed. Finally, on the 10th August 1939, seventy-year-old Dirk de Geer was able to form a cabinet and took over as Prime Minister. Just two weeks later, on the 28th of August, he declared a general mobilisation of troops throughout the Netherlands.

However, the push for neutrality remained. When the Second World War broke out on the 1st September 1939 with the German invasion of Poland, the new foreign minister, E. van Kleffens, prepared a proclamation of neutrality which he publicly declared. As foreign minister, he still hung on to the hope that Germany would not attack the Dutch. Even as late as the eve of the invasion of the Netherlands on the 10th May 1940 he was reported as having said that he did not think the Dutch would have to fight.[18] Even as war raged around them, many leaders in the Netherlands still failed to grasp the true intent and danger of Hitler and his National Socialist agenda.

The policy of maintaining neutrality caused divisions and hampered serious preparations for war. Every effort was made to avoid offending the Germans or give them cause for invasion. These overt efforts at neutrality also meant that defence systems and intelligence could not just be aimed at Germany as the only possible enemy, but all borders had to be protected equitably – including those with the French, English and Belgians. The naivety of maintaining and defending this neutrality policy was just astonishing since the rest of the world was readily moving towards full-scale conflict. It also meant that the Dutch could not negotiate treaties in case of attack. Both France and England took exception to the Dutch and their neutrality. In a January 1940 speech, Churchill strongly criticised the Dutch policy and urged them to oppose Nazism. Displaying his unique and inimitable way with words he said, "Each one hopes that if he feeds the crocodile enough, the crocodile will eat him last."[19]

For Churchill and for many in the Netherlands (including the Dutch Queen), there was no uncertainty about the evil of Hitler and the need to oppose and defeat him at all costs. However, there were sufficient numbers in the Netherlands, particularly in areas of influence, that still clung to the belief that they could stay out of the conflict.

In her autobiography, the Dutch Queen Wilhelmina wrote that, for her, the war was not five years but ten years - as she had lived under the shadow of the imminent invasion for five years prior. She became acutely aware of Hitler's agenda for Europe already in 1933 and had no doubt that the Netherlands was part of his overall strategy. She reminded Dutch leaders to read his book, *Mein Kampf*, where Hitler had laid bare all his twisted views of Germany's place in the world and his attitude to the Jews. She wrote: "*Until late 1939, countless people slept peacefully on the comfortable cushion that was known as neutrality. It gave a false sense of security but, unfortunately, it had in its grip many people who carried major responsibilities for the nation.*"[20]

The result of this was disastrous for the defence of the country. There was dysfunction at government level but also within the armed forces. The Commander-in-Chief of the Army and Navy, L.T.G. Reynders, appointed in August 1939, resigned in February 1940, after only five months in the position. He was convinced that Germany would not attack. Intelligence coming in from Germany that gave valuable information about Germany's plans for the Netherlands was simply dismissed as unreliable. The Minister of Defence A.Q.H. Dijxhoorn, clashed with him on policy and in the end demanded his resignation. Retired Major General H.G. Winkelman was then appointed in his place. This was five months after the start of the Second World War and three months before Germany was to invade the Netherlands. Time was of the essence and still there was no responsible leadership to rally and unite the country on the difficult path forward. The Dutch did not get their 'Churchill' in their hour of need.

Another challenge for the leaders in the Netherlands was the strength and influence of the Dutch Nazi Party. (NSB: Nationaal-Socialistische Beweging.) In 1935, the party had gained 8% of the votes and two seats in the Dutch Senate. In 1937, as some of its more extreme elements were revealed, its vote dropped to 4%. Nevertheless, the party still gained four seats in the House of Representatives and five seats in the Senate. For a new party this was a substantial achievement. [21]

With some 50,000 members, its influence and presence were everywhere. Many would not necessarily declare their membership openly, but they would, if holding positions of influence, promote Germany and undermine any and all Dutch efforts to discredit Hitler and his movement.

To counteract the danger of this spying and sabotage, the Dutch Government outlawed Nazi organisations and the wearing of political uniforms. The distinct party uniforms of the NSBs now became illegal to wear. However, the spying and working for German interests by the NSBs continued unabated. Papers regularly reported on spy plots and instances of sabotage. Even international papers in New York gave extensive coverage to the rampant, unchecked espionage carried out by the NSBs in the Netherlands.

By the end of 1939, the Government security forces started becoming proactive in seeking out these spies and arresting them. On the 23rd of January 1940 they arrested 21 NSBs who were accused of collaborating with the Germans on the borders of the country. A week later, two men were arrested in Rotterdam for transmitting weather conditions to Germany. On the 21st of April, a Dutch Nazi editor was arrested. He had information on all the troop movements in the Netherlands and was relaying this to his German contacts. On 5th May, just five days before the invasion, 21 people were arrested who were considered dangerous to national security. Most were NSBs and included one member of parliament.[22]

British Prime Minister Neville Chamberlain, as well as Churchill, made more appeals to the Dutch to reconsider their neutral position. Democratic countries in the world needed to unite to fight against Germany, they said. Having another foothold in Europe would have served the Allies well at this stage. However, instead of agreeing, the Dutch military fired at

British aircraft crossing Dutch airspace on their way to attack the Germans. Allowing such a passage would be seen by the Germans as a breach of their neutrality.[23]

Dad and Mum, as well as their extended family, were never in any doubt about the evil nature of Nazism and the need to resist it. Nazism attacked the core values of Christianity, so committed Christians across the country saw the organisation for what it was - an ungodly movement that attacked freedom of religion and speech. The persecution of the Jews and treating them and other minority groups as subhuman was against God's ordinance of love and respect for every human being as being created and precious in God's sight.

Already for many years since the rise of Nazism in 1933 Reformed pastors, including my parents' previous pastor, Rev. Boodt, had warned against its evils and of the need for Christians to resist and to defend the norms of the Bible. As editor of the weekly church paper, *De Reformatie*, Professor K. Schilder became an influential leader in this regard. He was highly instrumental in the 1936 General Synod of the Reformed Churches of the Netherlands, where it was stated that it did not see membership of the NSB organisation as being compatible with Scripture and Confession. The Synod encouraged pastors and consistories to counsel and, if necessary, censure and discipline those that still sought to be members.[24]

However, there was a movement within the Reformed Churches that disagreed with this. This was led by the son of the well-known Abraham Kuyper, Professor H.H. Kuyper, and Professor Hepp, both very influential people within the leadership of the Reformed Church. Kuyper publicly declared his opposition to the Synod 1936 decision and stated that if the church started putting members under discipline because of

NSB membership it would be inviting big trouble. In return, Schilder continued to strongly challenge him on his stance towards Nazism.

These conflicting views held within the Reformed Church leadership led to more and more arguments and division between these two very different, but influential, leaders. They had no hesitation to use the power of media to espouse their opinions - Kuyper as editor of the weekly, *De Heraut,* and Schilder as editor of *De Reformatie.* However, within a few months of Germany invading the Netherlands, Schilder was captured and his paper forcibly closed. He was no longer able to publish his views.

Kuyper, on the other hand, was never interfered with by the Germans due to his neutral stance and so was able to publish his paper, *De Heraut,* without interruption throughout the war years. So while, on the one hand, there were many extremely brave and principled pastors who risked life and limb to maintain what they saw as faithfulness to Scripture, there was another group within the same church that tolerated NSBs and promoted the acceptance of German leadership. Many pastors and people hiding Jews were captured and murdered as a result of NSBs providing information to the Nazis. Some of those NSBs were sitting in the church benches and then informing the German authorities when they heard their pastor warn in his sermon against the evils of Nazism. Even mentioning the Dutch Royal family in public prayer from the pulpit was a reportable offence.

20. Called Up For Service

"We must be ready to allow ourselves to be interrupted by God."

~Dietrich Bonhoeffer

When Dad was called up for service on the 28th August 1939, he was 25 and had been married for less than three years. In those three years he had never been separated from his wife and now he had to leave without knowing how long he would be away or what the future might bring. His two sisters, Marie and Lijsje, had both come to Sliedrecht to wish him well and say their goodbyes. After leaving home, Dad went past the home of his adopted mother, Miek, in Brandwijk, as well as his in-laws, the Schuttes, who lived nearby, to say his farewells. The seriousness of the situation and the imminent threat of war and its possible consequences for those enlisted was in the forefront of everyone's mind. The power and ruthlessness of the German war machine was by then well-known, reinforced by incoming reports of violence in neighbouring countries.

Within a week of being in the army, Dad wrote to both of his sisters. He was in Zeeland, the southern part of the Netherlands, sleeping with ten others in a farmer's shed and got his meals from a travelling kitchen van. There was general chaos and a very subdued atmosphere with everyone expecting the worst very soon. On Sunday, he attended an outdoor field service run by an army chaplain and wrote that he enjoyed the sermon which gave comfort in the circumstances. Most of all, he wrote about missing his wife and children and the uncertainty about how they are going, not having yet heard from them.

In the meantime, Mum, at home with the two children, was taking the separation badly. Despite support from the neighbours and a reliable worker, as well as visits from her mother and her husband's sisters, she just could not cope with the situation. It started to affect her health and sense of wellbeing. While she had sent three letters within the first week, Dad wrote that he still had not heard from her. Postage to the many diverse locations of the soldiers would have been a challenge and there were delays in delivery. Because of her obvious distress, her brother, Peet, suggested to her one day, "Why don't you go and visit him?" She asked, "Would that be possible, and how would I get there?" Peet was a resourceful brother and organised a friend to drive Mum and the two children to see Dad at the Army camp in Zeeland. At the time it was about a three-hour drive by car.

And so, within two weeks of leaving home, Dad was suddenly surprised with a visit from his wife and two children. They had been unable to give him advance notice of them coming so his initial reaction was one of shock, thinking something was wrong. However, that soon passed. He managed to get a few hours' leave; the weather was perfect, and they could all spend about four hours together in an area of farmland, just besides the camp. Mum wrote in her diary, "After that visit everything seemed different. We had seen each other again and been able to encourage each other."

A week later, Dad got his first break since being enlisted:

two days' leave which he could spend at home. There had been high tension when the Second World War started after the German invasion of Poland on the 1st September 1939, but, after a few weeks, the Dutch relaxed again and allowed their soldiers leave. After that, Dad had leave virtually every week, except when there were group exercises or when the threat of war seemed to rise. This would happen whenever there was another insurrection somewhere in Europe or when Germany or Italy were taking over more territory or when reports came through that an invasion of the Netherlands was imminent.

Whenever there was a crisis, there would be a flurry of activity, but if, after a few weeks, nothing eventuated, everything seemed to revert back to a more relaxed routine. In the interim, the soldiers, while obviously massively inconvenienced by having been taken away from their homes, were certainly not under the same pressure as those fighting on the war fronts. The whole approach on the field reflected what was going on at policy level. The fact was that many leaders *still* entertained the fanciful idea that the Netherlands could stay out of the war.

The newly appointed Commander-in-Chief, H.G. Winkelman, was well aware of the army's limitations and had no illusions about the Netherlands' ability to defeat an attack by Germany. His forces, while totalling 280,000 men, had minimal training and were ill-equipped with no tanks and limited artillery and anti-aircraft guns, most of which dated from the First World War. His strategy was to try and delay an invading enemy long enough until aid might arrive from Allies. However, the problem was this: There had been no negotiations or treaties drawn up with the Allies, for that would interfere with the neutrality policy of the Dutch Government.

Winkelman concentrated his forces mainly in the southern

provinces, along the main access roads and bridges and along what had become known as the Grebbe Line – a line of 85 kilometres that ran north to south and had rivers and lakes as part of its natural defence. It was a line of defence that had been developed since the war with the French in the late 17th Century. So, with men of limited training and aged equipment the Dutch forces intended to use old embattlements and the country's extensive waterways and dikes to its best advantage in case of attack.

On the 10th May 1940, at 3.55 a.m. German forces invaded the Netherlands. The country that had prided itself on being a trading nation that wished to stay clear of conflicts was now being overrun by the well-trained and determined military force of Germany. The Germans had planned the invasion for months and, with their network of spies in the Netherlands, were up-to-date with knowledge of troop movements and defence tactics. Their explanation of the invasion was that they had to take over the Netherlands as they had information that the English were going to use the Dutch territory to invade Germany.

The Germans came in their thousands. They were transported in trucks, tanks and armoured vehicles from the German borders where they had been gathering for weeks. Others parachuted from planes while others, once a few airports had been captured, landed in troop carrier planes. Aircraft were used to bomb strategic positions and army locations. Many Dutch soldiers died in the early morning while they were still in their bunkers. Everything was quickly and efficiently executed. It was from this lightning style of war that the term *Blitzkrieg* found its way into our vocabulary.

It took just five days before the Dutch had to surrender and accept German occupation. While that might appear a very short time, Hitler became impatient when he did not have the Dutch surrender immediately within the first day. The Germans considered the Dutch their natural allies and had hoped there would be little resistance. Part of its first-day strategy was to take over the airports around The Hague, where the Queen and seat of Government were and capture the Queen and Cabinet. However, to their surprise, they were met there with fierce resistance and, so, after initially taking the airports they had to surrender them again, thus denying them the possibility of more German troops landing into this area.[25]

By day three, the Commander and Chief, H.G. Winkelman, had to tell the Queen that he could no longer guarantee her safety and recommended her leaving. Already on the day before, the Queen herself had made arrangements for her daughter, Juliana, and husband Bernhard to travel to England. The Queen and the Cabinet left and were able to safely make it to England. Winkelman was handed total authority and became the head of State for the Netherlands.[26]

By day four the Germans were losing patience and decided to force the Dutch into submission by bombing the cities, starting with Rotterdam. On the 14th May, at 1.30 in the afternoon, they mercilessly started bombing the residential district of the city causing massive damage, loss of life and raging fires. Some 40,000 people lost their homes and 900 civilians died. If the Dutch did not surrender, they were told Utrecht would suffer the same fate the next day. Winkelman felt he had no choice but to lay down arms and surrender. He signed the appropriate capitulation documents at 10.00 a.m. on the 15th May 1940. It was to be the beginning of five years of brutal German occupation of the Netherlands. Winkelman was offered a position working with the Germans, but he refused to cooperate and spent the full five years of war in internment.

After the war he was decorated and considered a hero by the Dutch citizens.

In those five days of fighting 2,200 Dutch soldiers and over 2,000 civilians lost their lives. Thousands more were wounded. It had been a bloody and fierce battle and later analysis of the fight indicated that in the circumstances, with the odds stacked against them, the soldiers had fought bravely and with fierce determination. It had not been the walkover that had been anticipated by the German leadership.

21. Fears for Dad's Safety

*"The truth is, of course, that what one regards as
interruptions are precisely one's life"*
~ Collected Works of C.S. Lewis
(1994)

Dutch citizens everywhere were confronted with the breakout of war. Mum was woken up early on Friday the 10th of May by the deafening din of planes overhead. She went outside and saw the sky dark from the many planes. In the distance, she observed paratroopers filling the sky as they were dropped from military planes. It was full-on war. Everyone was on the street, observing and discussing. No one worked that day or slept that night. Sirens were constantly blaring. The family had to seek shelter in a neighbour's cellar nearby.

The following day, as people were starting their weekend, a bomb dropped so close by that it shattered the windows of my parents' house and shop. From this point they lived in constant fear for their lives. How would it end?

But Mum's biggest concern was for Dad. Where was he and was he safe? Five months pregnant, she was already entertaining the possibility of having a child that would not know its father. Death and destruction seemed everywhere. Just hours after the bomb dropped close to the family home, her brother Peet, with wife Jo and four young children, arrived. They were forced to flee their home because of the intense fighting and had walked with their four young children from their home in Dordrecht to my parents' home in Sliedrecht - a distance of about ten kilometres. They were seeking shelter with plans to go to his parents, Grandfather and Grandmother Schutte in Brandwijk, where they thought it might be safer. Their presence and their tales of what they had seen and experienced further reinforced to Mum the desperate situation for the army and for Dad.

Peet, with two of his boys, went by bike to Schutte's place the next day to ascertain whether they could stay there for a period. He thought the small villages in the *Alblasserwaard* would be a safe haven, away from all the violence that he had encountered in the city of Dordrecht. However, while travelling through the area he was shocked by the destruction. Bleskensgraaf, a small town only four kilometres from his parents' home in Brandwijk, had been totally destroyed by German bombing the previous day. Only the church was still standing but was so badly damaged that it would need to be rebuilt. Apparently, there had been some army trucks parked in town which the German fighter pilots had seen as a reason to bomb the area. Buildings that stood for hundreds of years were now just piles of rubble. The Schuttes, as well as Dad's auntie and foster mother Miek, who lived in the same Brandwijk street, had packed their essentials and were ready to flee at a moment's notice. No one felt safe in the current turmoil and situation.

Notwithstanding, the Schuttes were obviously not going to refuse hospitality to one of their own children despite their own difficult situation. Peet, on returning to Mum, related what he had seen and how much destruction there was. Hearing this,

Mum became increasingly aware that she might never see Dad again. Thinking him gone, she even wrote a final farewell card addressed to him, writing that God had given her the strength to accept the worst if that was His will.

Unbeknown to her, during the five days at war Dad had been in places where there had been no direct engagement with the enemy. Nevertheless, he was transferred three times in five days spending the last two days in the region of Leerdam, which formed part of the Grebbe Line of Defence. However, according to a letter Dad wrote to his sister, they had no enemy contact and so he was not involved in any action. This was in contrast to many other spots along the defence lines where the Germans had set their priorities. During those five days there were reports of heavy fighting on many fronts, but Dad was spared that plight.

For six days Mum lived in uncertainty, expecting the worst for Dad. The Dutch capitulated on the fifth day, the 15th May. What would then happen to those 280,000 soldiers that had taken up arms? Dad was evidently aware of his wife's deep concern as he made a special effort to get a message to her that he was alive and well. He had a contact in the area where he was stationed, a Mr. Korevaar, whom he visited and to whom he appealed to get a message to his family. Mr. Korevaar travelled the 20 kilometres to Brandwijk to bring the message to the Schuttes. Mum's brother Peet was there, so he, in turn, travelled the ten kilometres to Sliedrecht to pass the message on to Mum. What joy! Mum was overwhelmed and according to Dad's foster mother Miek, who was there, Mum wept uncontrollably with happiness. "Thanks be to the Lord," Mum wrote in her diary.

Three days later, on the 19th of May, Dad suddenly appeared at his family's front door. Borrowing a suit from Reverend

Boodt, his previous pastor, who now lived close to where he was stationed, he found his way home to reunite with his family. His visit was not sanctioned and came with considerable danger. As he had no official leave he could only stay for about an hour before he had to get back to the Boodt residence, replace the suit for the army uniform and get back to his camp unnoticed. Mum wrote that it was a wonderful and emotional reunion. However, uncertainty regarding their future remained. Would all the soldiers become prisoners of war and be transported to Germany? Dad had to go back and wait for the outcome and then decide how he would respond. He certainly had no wish to go to Germany and to possibly be put into German factories to work on the war effort. He was determined to resist if that did eventuate.

A week later, on Saturday the 25th of May, Dad again arrived home. He and most of the soldiers had been discharged. Only the higher-ranking personnel were not given their freedom. The dismantling of the Dutch army and allowing soldiers to return to their homes to work and assist in rebuilding the country was promoted by the German authorities as a special act of favour by Hitler to the Dutch people. He was doing his best to win the favour of the Dutch and promised freedom, provided they did not resist the German authority.

And so, with a seemingly gentle approach, the five years of German occupation of the Netherlands began.

22. Living Under German Occupation

"There is nothing which so certifies the genuineness of a man's faith as his patience and his patient endurance, his keeping on steadily in spite of everything."

~ *Martin Lloyd-Jones*

After the capitulation of the Netherlands and the escape of the Dutch Royal family and the Cabinet, Hitler appointed Dr. Arthur Seyss-Inquart, a prominent Austrian Nazi and lawyer, as Reichskommissar. For the next five years, he would be responsible for administering the affairs of the Dutch nation on behalf of, and in the interest of, his German master. He reported directly to Hitler and, from all accounts, they had mutual admiration for each other.[27]

The leader of the Dutch Nazi party, Anton Mussert, was severely disappointed that he had been overlooked as the Dutch leader, having for many years fostered leadership dreams for himself. However, he overcame that disappointment and became a close ally of Seyss-Inquart, who gave him the responsibility of ensuring the compliance of the Dutch citizens. Mussert relished this recognition. The Dutch Nazi party grew very quickly to more than 100,000 members and enjoyed the full support of the German leadership who had banned all other political parties, thus making Mussert a powerful figure feared by many.[28]

In his inaugural speech held on the 29th May 1940 in Parliament's Ridderzaal, The Hague, Seyss-Inquart outlined his vision for the Netherlands and its citizens. He acknowledged that the five-day war was unfortunate, but necessary, and with that behind them, claimed now was the time to rebuild and work together. He assured them that he did not wish to interfere in their lives or freedom. He recognised the close ethnic bond between the German and Dutch races and how they should be natural allies:

> *We rejoice in the bond of blood that binds us as people. We are delighted with your children and would like to see your boys all become energetic and strong men and your girls happy mothers of large families.*
> *We did not come here to cripple your national characteristics, to ruin your land or to take away your freedom. We do not have imperialistic desires for this country, nor do we wish to force on your country and people our own political thoughts.*
> *The Dutch people can through cooperation and focus on the common destiny we share, ensure that the freedom of this land and nation, is maintained and guaranteed for the future.*[29]

These words contrasted sharply with their actions. The Germans wished the Dutch to embrace and welcome the invader and deny loyalty to their own Queen and country. If the Dutch citizens all became NSB members and joined the

German war effort they would no doubt be fine. But embracing Nazism meant denying allegiance to their Queen and supporting an ideology that was ungodly, hateful and violent towards many minority groups like the Jews.

Mum wrote in her diary that the Germans started with nice words and good deeds including the act of discharging all the soldiers. However, she writes, they were simply trying to blind people to their reality. In her shop some customers would say: "They are not that bad. Just look what they are doing!"

On many fronts, life seemed to have some semblance of returning to normal, for some even the allusion of a bright future. The Germans pushed to have Rotterdam rebuilt into a modern city, to have the war damage restored as soon as possible and to have everyone in the workforce. They also launched into the construction of airports and defence positions throughout the Netherlands. This was done to provide them with a better position to attack and defend against the British. One major airport in Leeuwarden, where construction commenced in August 1940, employed thousands of men.

Unemployment had been high before the war. In 1936, 475,000 people had been unemployed and while this dropped a little due to the military mobilisation it was still a major issue for the nation. Now, with the rebuilding and with Germany's drive behind it, unemployment was predicted to be a thing of the past.[30]

The Dutch media reported this in glowing terms and ran many photos showing the Dutch embracing the German presence. With Germany winning across all battle fronts and feeling charitable, Seyss-Inquart announced, in June, a special holiday and learning opportunity in Austria for 6,000 Dutch kids between the ages of eight and 14. Some 6,735 children from all over the Netherlands applied to take advantage of this attractive offer and spent two months in Austria. Once again, the media celebrated the occasion and gave it extensive coverage.[31]

Newspapers, too, had to comply with the censorship of the German control agencies. Already on the 16th May 1940, one of the main Dutch newspapers, *Het Algemeen Handelsblad*, declared on its front page: *"From now on all control of this paper comes under the direction of the German Reichskommissar."* Understandably, the Germans used the media as its propaganda machine and ensured that all journalists and editors complied. This also meant that papers had to cover the German war efforts in a positive way, with the Allies being blamed for any mishaps. Blame for any bombs dropped on the Netherlands was directed at the English and this biased outlook would feature heavy in the newspapers.

For the first few months of occupation, the propaganda cycled through the Dutch papers worked very successfully for the Germans. Many Dutch citizens became complacent and accepting of what they saw as an inevitable occupation. However, in time, the actions of the Germans began to be countered by regular broadcasts from England by the Dutch Queen.

Officially, the Dutch citizens were not allowed to show any loyalty to their Queen nor listen to a daily broadcast she gave on the radio. Just that simple deed alone could lead to a two year jail sentence. Many became victims of these harsh penalties as the NSBs became more active in reporting anyone they spotted transgressing. Those with loyalty to their own country and Queen had to start watching their neighbours and guard themselves against possible NSB traitors.

While the Dutch were initially disappointed with the Queen leaving the country in their hour of need, in time they came to appreciate why she had to take that action: to preserve the Royal house and maintain the government. Many of the Dutch saw the Queen and the Cabinet stationed in England as the legitimate Government of the Netherlands. The Germans, who thought that the Dutch would simply embrace Nazism and become part of their growing empire, seriously misjudged the Dutch character. On the 29th June 1940, it was Prince Bernhard's birthday. This led to a spontaneous outpouring of Dutch support for the House of Orange. Flags flew, flowers and bouquets were left at royal statues throughout the country, people wore royalty badges and queued up in their thousands in The Hague to sign congratulation books.

The German leadership was most surprised and altogether unprepared for this nationalistic display. This was unfathomable to the Germans and completely unforeseen. They had convinced themselves that the Dutch and Germans were one. The strong and growing NSB movement in the Netherlands had underpinned that belief in their minds. However, the spontaneous Dutch action in respect to Prince Bernhard's birthday made them realise that perhaps the Dutch were not going to be so easy to manipulate and control after all. This awareness led them to introduce more regulations, harsher penalties and more intensive, comprehensive oversight.[32]

23. The Germans Tighten their Grip

"If you look at the world, you'll be distressed. If you look within, you will be depressed. But if you look to Christ, you'll be at rest"
~Corrie ten Boom

Already within a few months of the German invasion of the Netherlands on the 10th May 1940, Dad was finding it increasingly difficult to get the products required for his retail store. The Germans were shipping a lot of Dutch products to Germany which led to general shortages of products available to the Dutch. The Netherlands was seen as a country to plunder, to help fund and serve their war efforts. Everything was at risk of being possessed by the Germans. They would just grab a bike or car from a Dutchman, who simply had to acquiesce. Food products, horses, cows and pigs were being targeted. Nothing was safe.

On the afternoon of 8th July 1940, part of Sliedrecht, including the street where my parents lived, was bombed for the second time. Many houses were destroyed, and nine people lost their lives while more than 40 were wounded. There was utter chaos and panic. Mum, resting in bed at the time, in shock fled the house with the children. Windows were shattered and the internal furniture and fittings scattered everywhere.

Soon after an unexploded bomb was discovered; the area was evacuated and cordoned off. Dad had been exposed as he was outside at the time but was not hurt. They were forced to take temporary accommodation with the family of their shop assistant. Repairs had to be carried out, windows replaced, and the shop made operational again. Once this was completed the family moved back to re-open their shop and continue business the best way they could.

On the first day of September 1940 they were blessed with the birth of their third child, a healthy boy, whom they called Nicolaas (Niek). My parents had been very concerned for the welfare of this baby considering the trauma Mum experienced during her pregnancy, including the bombing only a few months earlier. *"This child had already experienced so much,"* wrote Mum. *"Shock after shock, tension and unrest. Yet the Lord heard our prayers and made everything well."*

Just over twelve months later, on the 29th September 1941 another daughter Janneke (Janet), was born. *"Despite the tension of the war,"* Mum wrote, *"They were now blessed with four healthy children."*

As the war progressed, things turned steadily worse for the Dutch citizens. Petrol was virtually impossible to get and, even so, you needed special permission to acquire it. Out of sheer necessity people reverted back to using bikes and horses. Coupons replaced money as the means to obtain some food produce already in June 1940. This use of coupons introduced by the occupiers gradually increased to cover all products, including dairy, meats, vegetables, fruit, and fish. Because of this, the Dutch citizens' access to food became either limited or, in many cases, restricted. The Germans controlled what each individual could buy for their sustenance. While the recommended daily intake for a person might be 2500 calories a day, under the coupon system, a Dutch citizen in 1941 only had access to 1800 calories per day and by 1944 it was set at 1437 calories per day.[33]

In April 1941, the Germans insisted that everyone hand in their radios. They had already taken this action in a number of towns where there had been evidence of citizens listening to Radio Netherland broadcasts from England. However, it now became illegal even to own a radio and possessing one carried a punishment of imprisonment.

Two months later, the Germans demanded everyone hand over their copper, nickel and lead products. Households had to hand in things like cutlery, vases, flowerpots, ashtrays and birdcages regardless of their sentimental value. Every household was affected. Then in September 1942, the Germans announced that they were taking possession of all the church and town hall bells throughout the country. Some 6500 bells were stripped from landmarks by the Germans and melted down to be used in the manufacturing of war hardware and weapons.

About the same time the Germans declared they urgently needed 100,000 bikes. They began randomly collecting them from parking stations and setting up roadblocks throughout the country taking possession of any bikes that the Dutch were using. Within a month, they successfully achieved half their goal, stealing 53,000 bikes from Dutch citizens who so desperately needed them as other means of transport was no longer available. Their loathing and hatred of the Germans grew with each incident like this.[34]

And so, as the German control tightened, life became increasingly difficult for the Dutch. Even more worrying, besides the material things that the Germans were plundering from the Dutch, was the mounting levels of violence and intimidation. Mum wrote in August 1942 that one evil action followed another. She witnessed raids and the capturing of families, the deportation of Jews and heard reports of a number of local men being shot for alleged treason. Young men were being rounded up to work in Germany. There was no more pretence by the German Reichskommissar that the Dutch would be granted their freedom. The Netherlands had become a place to extract whatever possible to assist the German war machine.

It appears as if Dad, despite the difficulties of the business and the challenge of making a profit, still had some access to funds during the war years. For his wife's 28th birthday on the 10th March 1943 he organised a horse and coach to pick up his parents-in-law, the Schuttes as well as Mum's sister, Sijgje, from Brandwijk to Sliedrecht so they could attend Mum's birthday. He also organised their return journey. The whole arrangement must have cost a bit of money for those days. It led to his adopted mother Miek, who thought the gesture was extravagant, to write that he really needed to be careful in these uncertain times. It is apparent that Dad did not have the same attachment to money and was keen to be able to assist his parents-in-law to attend his wife's birthday celebrations. Family get togethers were becoming rare and he wanted to make the birthday celebration a memorable and special event for his wife. Without this assistance Mum's parents and sister would not have been able to attend.

In March 1943, my parents' previous pastor from their hometown, Rev. C.P. Boodt, was arrested and sent to the concentration camp in Vught, located in the south-east of the Netherlands in the province of North Brabant. This truly shocked my parents. They had kept in close contact with him since they were married, and he had been a regular visitor, especially on their birthdays. Would he be able to survive, they asked themselves. His health was not strong. Mum wrote in her diary that many faithful Reformed ministers who had continued to speak up against the evils of Nazism were being arrested. The Germans were becoming more and more ruthless in stamping out anyone who refused to show allegiance to them.

Two months later, Dad received the news he had been fearing for some time. All the ex-service men were to hand themselves in and report for transportation to Germany to work in the factories contributing to the war effort. For Dad and Mum there was no choice – he would not give himself up and, subsequently, would have to go into hiding. So commenced the period of him being an '*onderduike*r' – 'going into hiding'. He joined a growing group of mostly men that were in the same predicament. In June 1943, 60,000 Dutch citizens were in hiding (including about 25,000 Jews), but by the end of the war, the number had grown to 340,000. They were mostly people fleeing from the Germans who would be arrested - and possibly shot - if found.[35]

Mum later recalled seeing the men of the town that did not escape into hiding rounded up and marched over the bridge near their home, on their way to the railway station. "It was such a tragic sight, seeing all those men there," she said. Young Peter, Mum's oldest son, who was seven at the time, was also deeply affected by the sadness of it all and, according to Mum, cried uncontrollably at the sight of those sombre and unsmiling men marching to the railway station.

24. In Hiding

"Greater love has no one than this, than to lay down one's life for his friends."

~ John 15:13 (NKJV)

By 1943 a whole network of Resistance fighters had formed in the Netherlands to assist those going into hiding from the Germans. Mostly, this involved them finding appropriate hiding places for each person, organising false identity papers, arranging food coupons, while at the same time avoiding detection. The Dutch NSB were everywhere and prepared, especially with the promise of a few guilders as reward, to inform the Germans of anyone they thought may be hiding someone or otherwise acting illegally. If a Dutch family, for example, were found to harbour a Jew, the retaliation was swift, with the outcome likely the immediate execution of the host family. The Germans showed no mercy and were ruthless in their determination to maintain control. During the last two years of the war it is estimated that the Germans summarily executed over 3000 Dutch citizens without trial or process.[36]

The *Alblasserwaard* district contributed significantly to the hiding and protection of those fleeing from German authorities. With its many small farms and outbuildings scattered throughout the region, it was ideally placed to provide a haven for those seeking it. However, they had to be doubly careful about NSBs as even the mayor of the district was a member. Many lost their lives due to the traitorous work of the NSBs.

During a 2017 discussion with a 90-year-old half cousin of my Dad, Arie Jan Verhoef, he recalled how the underground had been forced at times to execute traitors because they put so many lives at risk. He related how his Dad had endured a close escape once, when a traitor had told the Germans that the Verhoefs and other farmers in the district were accommodating refugees. Through their system of secret messages, the Resistance members were able to warn all the farmers of the impending raid, so they had time to hide the persons they were sheltering. That time, the raid yielded no people, but the Germans did find a number of radios which resulted in two months imprisonment for all the farmers that were found with them.

Arie Jan also remembered a man arriving once at their front door, someone who had been given a death sentence by the Germans. He was so weak and exhausted that he collapsed when they opened the door to greet him. He stayed at their place for the rest of the war and remained in regular contact with them for the rest of his life until he died at the age of 80. According to Arie Jan, there were many of these types of instances experienced and endured by those in the district.

However, there was also the other side of the story - the experiences of the spies or NSBs. Arie Jan claims that many people in the district today do not realise that their parents or grandparents may have been involved as spies during the war. He had recently been asked by the local historic society to partake in an interview about the war and the people involved. He refused because he did not want to reveal the truth about some people's actions during those dark times. He considered it best to just let it be and have the next generation think the best of their forefathers.

My parents never talked about having sheltered refugees or Jews during the war. My brother Niek, however, remembers a Jew visiting his school to talk about the war and he recognised him as the person who stayed in hiding at his parents' place for a while. He also remembers him visiting my parents from time to time, before they moved to Australia. It is quite possible that my parents, my mother in particular, would have taken people in from time to time while they were in transit. Those travelling long distances to get to a more permanent hiding place would be given a safe address to stay while in transit. Maybe my parents' home was one of those safe addresses where people seeking shelter could drop by for a period.

When Dad sought to go into hiding, he joined thousands of others in the same predicament. Within twelve months, some 250,000 additional people were hiding from the German occupiers, most because they refused to work for the Germans. Others were being sought for acts of alleged resistance and disloyalty. One of the national leaders of the Dutch Resistance movement, a pastor known as 'Frits de Zwerver' ('Frits the Wanderer'), was passionate about looking after those refusing to work and acquiesce to the Germans. "Not one person who refuses to work for the Germans should be refused assistance and shelter," he declared. "Whether it involves a thousand, ten thousand or a hundred thousand we should help them all. It is our responsibility as loyal Dutch citizens to stand by these people."[37]

There were basically three ways that people could go into hiding. One was to change identity and become either a family member of the host family or a worker at their farm or business. This then would involve creating false papers and ensuring that food coupons and all relevant documentation were in place.

The other way was to have the host family have someone stay in hiding in either a secret room in the house, the cellar or the attic. This meant that the person would have to remain out of sight at all times and also avoid discovery from curious neighbours. Food coupons for these people had to be either stolen or forged. Many of these host families were in constant fear of raids and searches by the German SS, particularly as there were so many NSB snooping around. That some 35,000 Jews did escape death in the Netherlands during those five years of terror is a testament to the bravery and compassion of many Dutch citizens who, at great risk to their own safety, extended hospitality and protection to those that were persecuted.

The third way that the resistance fighters assisted those fleeing the Germans was by finding strategic geographical locations throughout the country where they could be safely hidden because the terrain made it difficult to be found. This hiding of groups of mostly men in remote locations had the advantage that it did not put others at risk. The main challenge was to ensure that the people in hiding had access to food, as well as warmth and protection from the elements. Dad was offered this third option when he sought assistance from the Resistance movement to go into hiding.

With large numbers seeking hiding places it is surprising how quickly Dad was offered a place. The challenges and bravery required to find places for some 250,000 Dutch citizens, all under the watchful eye of the Germans and the NSB, was an enormous logistical undertaking. By mid 1943, it is estimated that some 45,000 Netherlanders had joined the Resistance forces and were actively assisting those that were fleeing the Germans.

Besides arranging safe places, the resistance fighters were also involved in sabotaging German activity, blowing up railway tracks or distributing illegal newspapers and printed items. At times, as Arie Jan related in 2017, the resistance fighters were called in to execute traitors who, through their activities, were responsible for the deaths of many loyal Dutch citizens. While in the early war years the resistance fighters were often working alone, without leadership, as the war moved on they grouped together into cells and were more formally structured under the direction and support of the London based Dutch Government. Prince Bernhard was given the responsibility, on behalf of the Dutch Government, to oversee the operations of the resistance fighters and so became the principal contact for them.[38]

25. Staying Undercover

"The cross is laid on every Christian. The first Christ-suffering which every man must experience is the call to abandon the attachments of this world..."

~Dietrich Bonhoeffer, The Cost of Discipleship

After receiving notification in May 1943 that, as an ex-serviceman, he was to report for transportation to Germany to work in the factories there, Dad set about finding a suitable place to hide and go underground. He was determined, whatever the cost, to avoid working for the Germans. He had a contact in the underground resistance movement, one of the local leaders, Mr. Klaas Feringa, whom he approached for assistance. Mr. Feringa was well known to Dad and his daughter, Froukje, had for a time worked and helped out in his shop. (Froukje was later, in 1947, to marry Eppo Groenewold. They migrated in 1957 to Australia and settled in Launceston).

Mr. Feringa arranged for Dad to move into the area known as the Biesbosch. Just south of Sliedrecht, this swamp land was an ideal hiding place with its maze of creeks, mud flats, reed buntings and bushes. Unless you were familiar with the area you would easily get lost in the extensive tidal wetlands and face, as many Germans discovered, the possibility of sinking down in quicksand. The Germans, predominantly, were frightened of the Biesbosch, so its inaccessibility made it an ideal place to hide people. Many found refuge there including ex-servicemen, resistance fighters, Jews and English pilots who had been shot down.

There were a series of old boats known as 'arks' that had, in times past, been built to accommodate seasonal workers that came to cut reeds. These arks provided ideal shelter for those fleeing the Germans. With five others, Dad ended up in one of these.

It was a difficult time for my parents. Mum had been told by Mr. Feringa that it was best for her not to know where Dad was, but he offered to take Mum's letters to Dad and would ensure that Dad received them. Living in cramped quarters with five others in the small confined space of an ark, with little to do, it was not long before boredom became a major issue for Dad. For someone who was always living a busy life, this inactivity was really hard to take. Over and above dealing with the arduous conditions, Dad also lived in constant worry for his family, having left behind a pregnant wife and four young children, as well as a struggling business that needed constant attention.

Mum, with no idea of Dad's whereabouts, was having difficulties of her own. Her employee and shop assistant of five years had left a few months earlier and she was having difficulty finding a reliable replacement. Then, shortly after Dad left, her new assistant became sick, so Mum had to cover for her as well. Besides these increased responsibilities, she also had to deal with a busy shop as all customers now had to pick up their milk quota from the shop as Dad was not around to deliver the milk to their homes. Mum had little down time.

When Dad left to go into hiding Mum was seven months

pregnant, so that would have progressively affected her ability to sustain the heavy workload. Besides running the business, she also had her four young children to look after. In June 1943, Dad's foster mother, Miek wrote to Dad's sister Marie, that Mum's brother had visited and found her extremely busy. However, Miek wrote, it is probably a good thing, because she has little time to worry or ponder on things.

Mum had become overwhelmed with the bookkeeping. A near neighbour, seeing Mum's distress, offered to come in every evening to help with the accounts. The German introduction of coupons to exchange for food also added to the complication of doing the accounts. How relieved Mum was with her neighbour's offer. It also meant that every evening she had company.

On the 2nd of August 1943, two and a half months after Dad had gone into hiding, Mum gave birth to a healthy girl whom she named Maaike (Mappie). The same day she sent a note to Dad, via Mr. Feringa, to advise him that all was well. An encouraging reply came back swiftly, already the next day. *"The Lord be praised,"* he wrote, *"I hope I will soon be able to see my daughter. Be of good courage."* Mum was overjoyed to hear so quickly from him and to have confirmation that all was well with him.

The baptism of children was encouraged by pastors to take place as soon as possible after birth. This was why the first four children were presented for baptism on the first Sunday after birth. Mum would then still be recuperating so Dad had presented all the first four children for baptism without the presence of Mum.

In the case of Mappie, however, Mum had to present her for baptism on her own. It was too dangerous for Dad to show himself, so Mappie had to wait until Mum was well enough to bring her to church for baptism. This meant that Mappie was baptised unusually late during those unusual times - three weeks after she was born.

Meanwhile, Dad was working out a way to catch up with his wife and see his newborn child. He arranged for Mum, along with baby Mappie, to travel to her brother Peet's place in Dordrecht where he would then meet them. So it happened that in October 1943, after four and a half months of separation, that they were reunited briefly again. What joy for them to meet again in good health and for Dad to see his two month old baby daughter for the first time!

By this time, Dad was getting restless and impatient to be doing something. The boredom and inaction were just getting too much. He thought that if he worked in another town where they did not know him, and kept a low profile, he would surely be safe. So, in November 1943, he took the courageous step of working for a baker in Barendrecht, about 20 kilometres west of Sliedrecht. He also found someone in the town who was willing to accommodate him. He was still in danger and had to remain undercover, so both his work and his accommodation had to be with people who were loyal to the Dutch Queen and not to the Germans.

There is no doubt that he was taking some serious risks leaving the safe haven of the Biesbosch and moving into a town where he could be easily stopped and arrested. Nevertheless, he took this risk and then took a further risk by visiting his family. Unexpectedly, one Saturday night Dad arrived at his home in Sliedrecht. It was late at night, so the children were in bed.

My parents felt that the children were too young to understand the danger of his situation and might inadvertently say something to their friends. Therefore, it was arranged that

Dad would stay out of sight of the children by spending the time in his upstairs bedroom and at certain times, Mum would allow the children to come into the bedroom while Dad hid in the wardrobe cupboard. He would then leave the door slightly ajar so he could see and hear them, without them knowing he was there. It was a tricky and risky situation, but they seemed willing to take the risk just for the sake of being together occasionally, and for Dad to be able to see the children.

He managed to come home most Sundays and spent the day under difficult conditions, hiding in his own house. However, after six months he noticed the Germans were increasing their checkpoints on the bridge crossings and it was becoming more dangerous for him to make the trip home from the bakery where he worked. So, what to do? Throwing caution to the wind he decided to stop working at the bakery and stay at home. This meant he had to hide in either the attic or his bedroom, as he still needed to be kept out of sight from curious neighbours and from his children.

According to Mum's later recollection, the house was searched a number of times by German soldiers looking for Dad. Jenny, who was about five at the time, recalls soldiers coming in to search one time when Dad was home. He had made a special hiding place in a cupboard under the stairs and when the soldiers came, he had enough warning to be able to get in there before the search began. Jenny recalls the tense situation and the relief when they left having not found him.

As time went on my parents must have realised the futility of not sharing the situation with their children, especially the older ones. Peter, the oldest, was certainly aware when Dad was home. Even Niek, who was under four at the time, recalls Dad coming into his bedroom after they were supposedly asleep, just to see them and tuck them in. When my parents became aware that they knew Dad was around they decided to talk and share with them the seriousness of the situation. They were then instructed to call Dad 'uncle' and impressed on them the importance of not talking about it to anyone.

However, after the raid, where Dad really had experienced a miraculous escape, he decided to move out of the house again. Raids were usually initiated because someone had given information to the Germans. My parents felt there were NSBs everywhere and were really anxious about the possibility of another raid. So, in about June 1944, Dad arranged to go and live with his sister, Lijsje, and her husband, Dirk, in Streefkerk. They had a farm where Dad could work, he thought, in relative safety. He kept this up for three months, until September 1944, when the pull of home became too much, and he decided to go back into hiding again at home. It was also the time when the Allied troops were pushing north from France and the southern part of Holland had already been liberated. Surely the war would soon be over, they thought.

For a further six months he remained in hiding at home, but from March 1945 he was confident enough to show himself on the streets and take on his normal work again for his shop. He reasoned that the Germans had their hands full with other, more pressing things than trying to round up ex-servicemen for work in Germany.

26. The Final Gasp

*"You can never learn that Christ is all you need,
until Christ is all you have."*

~ Corrie ten Boom

When Dad went into hiding in May 1943, it would still be two years before the Dutch were finally liberated on the 5th May 1945. During the course of those two years, the situation for the Dutch, including that of my parents, became progressively worse. The Germans were becoming more irrational and violent, food shortages were severe and essential services - like water and power - became totally unreliable. The Dutch had been mercilessly plundered by the Germans and, even towards the end of the war, farming produce, that was so essential for feeding the Dutch, was being transported to Germany.

While the situation on the ground was becoming unbearable, in the air above the Netherlands the war in the sky was intensifying and relentless. The Germans had built several airports and defence positions right across the country to strengthen its position against the Allies. To weaken the German defence, a constant barrage of Allied bombers would target key German defence positions and seek to destroy them. Any German troop movements or military installations were considered to be bombing targets by the Allies.

Unfortunately, the accuracy of the bombing was not like the pin-point accuracy we know today. There was much collateral damage and many Dutch citizens lost their lives through Allied bombing. While there were numerous instances resulting in small numbers of deaths and some houses damaged, there were also some major bombing incidents that caused hundreds of deaths.

Some examples of these were: On the 6th December 1942 the Allies successfully completed a bombing raid on the Philips Works at Eindhoven – however in the process a total of 148 Dutch civilians died from those bombs dropped. On the 22nd February 1944 the Americans bombed the city of Nijmegen in an attempt to destroy German defences before they could launch a land offensive to liberate the city. Over 800 Dutch citizens died in the attack, nearly as many as when the Germans bombed Rotterdam at the beginning of the war. On 3rd March 1945 the Allies tried to bomb a V-2 launching site in The Hague Forrest but missed the target and bombed the neighbouring city of Bezuidenhout instead, resulting in the death of a further 500 Dutch citizens. The same month, on the 21st March 1945 the Allies bombed and destroyed the small town of Doetinchem, killing about 130 Dutch citizens and wounding many more. Why the town was targeted remains a mystery.[39]

As described earlier, my parents also experienced Allied air bombing from close up in the early stages of the war. Other major events stand out for them. On 15th October 1944 Allied planes bombed a stationary train at the railway station just a few hundred metres from my parents' place. The train was loaded with horses destined for Germany. The train and horses were destroyed but, as was usual in these cases, some bombs dropped on nearby houses destroying them and killing their occupants. Despite the tragedy, the hungry citizens in Sliedrecht made sure the horse meat was not wasted, most of it finding its way into their kitchens.[40]

Then on the 8th December 1944, a few bombs fell in the residential area of Sliedrecht causing extensive damage but, fortunately, this time with no casualties. Then on New Year's Day 1945, there was another major attack in Sliedrecht, this time on its harbour. Again, residential houses were hit resulting in seven casualties. The bombings continued and, especially during the last months of the war, there was increased activity as the Allies tried to weaken German resistance sufficiently to provide an eventual entry point through which to liberate the Netherlands. They particularly targeted railways and harbours in an endeavour to stop supplies getting into Germany.[41] Regrettably, with each bombing the Dutch had to sustain collateral damage, with houses destroyed and lives lost. It is little wonder the Dutch lived in constant fear every time they heard a plane overhead.

My eldest sister, Jenny, born in 1939 was six at the time and remembers the fear well. She recalls how every time she heard a plane she would, with her siblings, rush to hide behind the organ for protection. It happened on a number of occasions that the force of the blast would shatter the front windows of the house and shop. Brother Niek, who was eighteen months younger, also has very vivid memories of those planes and bombings. He remembers the shattering glass and going outside and seeing a row of houses destroyed and carried that fear of aircraft overhead with him into adulthood. He admits that, even in his twenties and living in Australia, at night he pulled the blankets over his head for fear of a bomb being dropped whenever hearing a plane overhead.

Many Dutch citizens would have been affected in similar

fashion. The Dutch air space was, for the Allies, *en route* to Germany, so they used it as a thoroughfare for bombing missions in Germany. The Germans would respond with anti-aircraft guns and sometimes score a hit. During the course of the war, from both the Germans and the Allies, some 6000 planes were shot down over Dutch air space affecting about 20,000 airmen. Living in the Netherlands, you just did not know when a bomb might hit your street, when a plane might be shot down or when an airman might come knocking on your door seeking refuge.

Besides the incessant fear of danger from the air, my parents had to cope with diminishing food supplies with which to feed their growing family. In the winter of 1944/45, the Dutch faced a major food shortage. The German plundering and flooding of fertile areas to make the potential entry by the Allies more difficult as well as the constant bombing of distribution lines by the Allies – these all contributed to a disastrous and tragic period for the Dutch. It is estimated that more than 22,000 people died of starvation in the last winter before the end of the war.

With Dad having to remain undercover, Mum had to go to Dad's farming family to collect food. They were more fortunate than most because of these connections. Farmers were overwhelmed by thousands walking on the road asking for food and, heartbreakingly, were not in a position to accommodate them all. Mum writes in her diary how she tried to go every week, with a borrowed bike, to get some food. By close to war's end she admits, she had nothing to offer in exchange as the shop supplies had run out. This meant she just had to rely on the charity of friends and family. Nevertheless, each time she managed to secure some food. The portions had to be carefully divided and they were still always hungry. She wrote how the children fought over a few crumbs of bread that may have been spilt or dropped on the ground. Nothing was wasted. "It was a time," she stated, "that you felt totally reliant on God and when you prayed for and received your daily bread it really meant something."

Jenny remembers clearly the hunger they suffered and especially the lack of bread. Being the baby, Mappie would get more bread than the rest, so when she dropped some food, they all used to dive under the table to compete with each other to get it. Niek recalls Mappie getting the best food and, like Jenny, he also was ready to pounce on any food she dropped on the ground. Having, or not having, food was uppermost in everyone's mind as they lived with constant hunger. Food not normally considered edible or on the menu - like sugar beets and tulip bulbs - were now sought after and eaten.

Life was becoming incredibly difficult for the family. Electricity no longer worked and running water had stopped. They had a small tap in the cellar from which they could draw some water, but larger amounts had to come from the river across the road. For some light at night they relied on a bike battery but, to preserve it, they used it sparingly going to bed at 8.00 p.m. and rising at 8.00 a.m. when it was starting to get light. Cooking was also a challenge as firewood was sparse and hard to come by. The situation was getting desperate. Surely the war must soon end, they thought.

Some letters from that period written by Miek, Dad's foster mother in Brandwijk to his sister Marie in Amsterdam, have been preserved and give an indication of the stress that they experienced.

On the 10th October 1944, Miek described how the Germans came to seize a car from her neighbour and how they were whipping him and threatening to shoot him as he did not respond quick enough to their request. She then wrote:

> *They – the Germans - have impounded all the motor bikes and cars in the district and who knows what more they want – and this week all the farmers had to present their horses and carts for handover to the Germans. They even came in the night to steal and plunder and just do whatever they fancy. At Schutte's place* [my grandparents] *they shot and shattered the window in his small garden shed to see if there were any bikes stored inside. They then went through their vegetable garden and took all what was ready – the tomatoes and carrots.... There are constantly planes overhead and bombs being dropped. We just hope the Lord will spare us all for there is danger everywhere at present. How long will it still go on?*

On the 14th October 1944 she wrote:

> *P. Korenvaar and other farmers have had their cows taken from them. From Jansje van de Giesen who had eight milk cows they took seven. Suddenly they are no longer farmers. Isn't it terrible? Cows are getting slaughtered and pigs and poultry are all being taken away. When are we ever going to be free and what else do we still have to experience....? We have our suit cases packed and ready to leave at a moment's notice, but we really hope it won't be necessary because that would be just terrible.*

On the 8th November 1944 Miek wrote:

Yesterday the Germans planted bombs at the Dam Locks so they can flood the whole area before the Allies come here. Who knows what we still have to endure. Monday we were notified that 2000 refugees were coming this way - we were allocated four people.

The Allies were advancing but the situation remained horrendous for the Dutch with the Germans becoming increasingly more desperate and unpredictable.

27. Towards Freedom

*"You will reduce the noise of aliens,
As heat in a dry place.
As heat in the shadow of a cloud,
The song of the terrible ones will be diminished."*

~ Isaiah 25:5 (NKJV)

As the year of 1945 dawned, my parents prayed fervently for relief and freedom. It was nearly seven months already since the D-Day landing in Normandy and they had hoped that by now they would have been liberated. The Allied troops were so tauntingly close. They had liberated a few Dutch cities by this time and were stationed only about 20 kilometres south of Sliedrecht, on the south side of the Biesbosch, where Dad had previously been hiding.

There was a secret pathway through the Biesbosch which allowed people to travel between the occupied and liberated area. This became a valuable line of contact and exchange for the Dutch resistance fighters and their allies. Twenty one men volunteered to become regular Biesbosch-crossers to deliver crucial intelligence for the Allies and also to receive instructions from them, as well as receiving and taking back critical equipment and medicines. They assisted many Jews and English pilots across to the Allied side and to freedom. This perilous journey was undertaken by these renowned Line-crossers, as they became known, a total of 370 times in the six months before the liberation of the whole of the Netherlands. They were subsequently honoured and recognized for their bravery and persistence.[42]

With such close connections and regular contact with the Allies, confidence started to grow with respect to the imminent liberation. But, still, the citizens had to be careful. The Germans feared an uprising as soon as the Allies started making headway, so, to minimise that impact, decided to forcefully round up all men aged between 17 and 40, starting in Rotterdam. This served the purpose of providing necessary labour for their factories but also minimised the risk of mass uprising. So, on the 10th November 1944, the citizens of Rotterdam woke up to find the city surrounded by soldiers. There was no escape as each house was progressively searched for men. After two days, they had captured more than 50,000 men. The roundup was ruthless and anyone attempting to escape was shot.

This shocked the Dutch and anyone in hiding had to reconsider their safety measures. Hiding places throughout the country were reassessed and made more secure. Two weeks later the citizens of The Hague woke on the morning of the 21st November 1944 to also find themselves surrounded by soldiers and again a house to house search ensued. While more prepared this time, nevertheless, 13,000 men were rounded up in one day. Next came Delft, then Haarlem and a number of other cities. Progressively, the number of men found diminished as the underground had worked non-stop to warn people, inspect hiding places and improve them as deemed necessary so they would not be discovered so easily.

Nevertheless, between September and December 1944 approximately 120,000 men were dragged from their homes and hiding places and sent to Germany.

The transported men experienced horrendous conditions. The majority were immediately transported by train to Germany, packed in cattle cars with little food and just a bit of hay for bedding. When they arrived some three days later at their destination, they were taken to workplaces, most in factories where they were treated like slaves. Besides the deprivations and the resultant health impacts, they lived in constant fear of being bombed by the Allies who were especially targeting factories in Germany that were manufacturing war weaponry. Many would not return home again. In most cases, the families left behind were left in the dark as to their whereabouts and, in many cases, did not hear from them again until after the war.[43]

All this must have shocked Dad and made him doubly careful to remain alert and stay in hiding. The Germans were not yet slowing down their war effort, despite their eventual defeat seeming obvious. The Dutch were experiencing an enemy who was becoming more dangerous and volatile.

The Allies had to cross the Rhine before they could progress further, and this hurdle would take time to plan and execute. However, the news coming across was positive: my parents and all the Dutch citizens just had to be patient and not take unnecessary risks. Even so, many died during the last days of the war.

By March 1945, two months before the liberation, Dad decided that it was safe to emerge from hiding and started to get back to his work the best way he could. At least now he was in a position to help Mum and also travel to collect food and wood from his hometown, Brandwijk. Mum writes with some fondness of this time: "It was so pleasant to be together just as a family," she wrote. "If the times were not so awful, we would be enjoying ourselves."

It seemed Dad could now provide the unconditional support which she so valued. She had borne the responsibility for the family and business on her own shoulders for so long. Many times, the responsibility had made her physically ill. Now, at least, he was by her side and seemed to have no fear of capture any more. It was just a matter of surviving and getting enough food each day until the inevitable liberation arrived.

The food shortages now reached crisis point and was receiving international attention. In the cities young children were dying in the streets. The Allies were moved to action and negotiated with the Germans for a safe passage for relief planes so they could coordinate a food drop. This was agreed to, so from the 29th April to the 8th May 1945, plane loads of food – a total of 11,000 tons - was dropped on the starving Dutch citizens. Every day over 400 Allied bomber aircraft flew back and forth over the Netherlands at low altitudes of about 150 metres in agreed flight paths to avoid enemy fire. The operation termed Manna for the British effort and Chowhound for the Americans provided a welcome relief for many but, for others, it was too late.[44]

The Allies were progressing and had crossed the Rhine in three places. But they still had to fight hard to regain the territory paying a heavy price. Approximately 50,000 Allied soldiers lost their lives in the battle to free the Netherlands from the tyranny of Nazism. Then, finally, on the 5th May 1945, the surrender of the Germans was official. Freedom at last after five years of occupation! The joy of the Dutch knew no bounds. The Queen was welcomed back, and the Dutch government restored.

Dad and Mum could thank God that, as a family, they had survived those terrible five years. Many others were mourning lives lost or still awaiting news pertaining to the whereabouts of loved ones. My parents considered themselves blessed and could now look forward to planning for their future again.

On the 6th May 1945, just one day after the German surrender, my parents attended a Thanksgiving service in Sliedrecht led by Reverend P. Prins. The text for the sermon was Isaiah 25, verses four and five:

> *For you have been a strength to the poor,*
> *A strength to the needy in his distress,*
> *A refuge from the storm,*
> *A shade from the heat,*
> *For the blast of the terrible ones is as a storm against the wall.*
> *You will reduce the noise of aliens,*
> *As heat in a dry place,*
> *As heat in the shadow of a cloud,*
> *The song of the terrible ones will be diminished.*

After the service they all stood and sang the national anthem, 'Wilhelmus van Nassouwe.'

It had been five years since they could do this in freedom, without fear. You can imagine the emotion and gratitude my parents felt, both for the sermon and the singing of their national song.

28. The Cost of Freedom

"There are few die well that die in a battle."
~ William Shakespeare - Henry V.

The war was over for the Dutch, but the emotional, material and financial wounds were deep. It was estimated that nearly 250,000 Dutch citizens lost their life during those five years of occupation, representing 2.7% of the population. Compared to some other occupied nations this was extremely high. Belgium, with 88,000 deaths, lost 1.05% of its population and France, with 600,000 deaths, lost 1.44% of its citizens. Australia, with 40,400 deaths, lost .58% of its people while America, with 420,000 deaths, lost .32% of its population.[45]

While Australia and the Netherlands had similar size populations, the Dutch lost six times as many lives during the Second World War than Australia. Even in the First World War, where Australian soldiers suffered such massive casualties, losing 62,000 men and women out of a population of five million, the percentage of population lost was 1.2%.

The greatest percentage of Dutch casualties came from the Jewish community living in the Netherlands, who were decimated with only 35,000 surviving from 140,000 living in 1940. Most of those that did survive had been given shelter and hiding places by the Dutch. Of more than 100,000 Jews rounded up and sent to camps only a few thousand survived the war.[46]

The second largest contributor to the death tally involved those who had been corralled into German work camps, where about 30,000 Dutch citizens lost their lives. Mostly men, they had either voluntarily given themselves up or been forcibly rounded up to work in German factories. The conditions and deprivations suffered there, as well as regular Allied bombing, led to many deaths. Most of those who did return after the War were weak and sickly. Many would suffer long term illnesses and disorders as a result.

When analysing the Dutch casualty count, it is noteworthy that 22,000 died as a result of hunger in the winter of 1944/45, while a further 20,500 Dutch died because they were in harm's way, either through Allied bombing or from living in areas where some of the main battles were fought. Much of the Dutch territory had been converted by the Germans into a major defence line, with airports, bunkers and missile sites scattered and strategically placed throughout the nation to be used to launch attacks on England as well as withstand reciprocal attacks. The British were well aware of this and, consequently, were relentless in bombing strategic military positions. Five years of protracted attacks had resulted in enormous collateral damage.[47]

Then there were Resistance fighters, those harbouring refugees, or who refused to comply. They were sent to concentration camps, often to die. Finally, there were those who fought in the early days of the war or who joined the Allies to fight. A total of 250,000 deaths in a nation of 8.7 million people.

Besides the many casualties, the wounded, sick and starving, the Dutch landscape and many of its cities also lay in ruins. The Dutch had endured intense battles on their soil and the intentional flooding of large areas of farming country by the Allies and Germans. This, combined with the relentless and ruthless plundering by the Germans, resulted in the Dutch, after five years, being physically, mentally and financially spent. Added to this exhaustion was the immense loathing and disgust so many felt towards the thousands of NSB traitors who had made life so fraught with danger during those long, difficult war years. Numerous loyal Dutch citizens had lost their lives because of their traitorous deeds.

In the first heady days of liberation, Dutch citizens took out their frustrations and anger on the traitors by publicly humiliating them. Girls who had been known to fraternise with the Germans had their head shorn and tarred and were bundled together on carts and driven around the towns. My brother, Niek, still remembers this happening in Sliedrecht, recognising one of the shaved and tarred girls as someone who had worked for Mum in the shop for a time. The family had indeed been fortunate. While Dad was hiding and Mum was assisting other people who needed shelter, she had for a time, employed a young lady who was sympathetic to the Germans. This was someone who could have easily betrayed them if she had procured knowledge of Dad's whereabouts or of others passing through. No one had been safe from the NSB and they obviously came in all sorts of disguises.

But the time for justice had arrived. Members of the Dutch Resistance, under the direction of Prince Bernhard, were given the responsibility of maintaining law and order and seeking out the NSBs so they could be brought to justice. There were some 300,000 registered NSB so a massive manhunt was orchestrated to round them up as quickly as possible. Prison camps were hurriedly assembled to house the 130,000 that were arrested. They received no sympathy and experienced in their arrest and treatment the full-scale antipathy that the Dutch held for them.[48]

A total of 154 NSB received the death penalty. Many successfully appealed against their death sentence, but 39 of them were executed, including the founder and leader of the Dutch Nazi party, Anton Mussert.[49] Dr. Arthur Seyss-Inquart, the Austrian Nazi and lawyer who had been the Dutch Reichskommissar during the five years of German occupation, and remained a close associate of Hitler, was arrested and sent to trial in Nuremberg. He was found guilty and sentenced to death on the 16th October 1946.

Meanwhile, Queen Wilhelmina worked hard to ensure there would be no leadership vacuum once the Germans surrendered. For the Dutch, she had been a tower of strength during occupation and even now, they looked to her to provide leadership. Her decision to flee to the safe shores of England five years earlier had been vindicated as this helped preserve the Crown and Government. From the safety of her vantage point, she had been able to provide much needed encouragement and solid leadership, and was now in a position to ensure that an interim Government could be formed until such a time as an election would be feasible.

On the 2nd May 1945 she moved back to the Netherlands, initially to the town of Breda, which, by then, had been declared safe by the Allies. Three days later, following the unconditional German surrender, she addressed the nation on the radio. After recognising and thanking all the brave men and women who never gave up their fight for the nation's freedom, as well as the enormous effort and sacrifice paid for by the Allies, she went on to say:

We all await now the great task, which we thankfully can now do together in unity but which we have to start without delay. Under the oppressor we have found ourselves again as a nation, our identity as Dutch people has been reawakened.

Let us all tackle the task at hand, driven by an inner strength, understanding our duty and obligation to those who paid the ultimate price and who are no longer with us.

Fellow citizens let us keep our sights on the future, so we, under the blessing of God Almighty, may rise again.[50]

"Rebuild and repair" became the national catchcry. But this was no easy feat. There was no money and a large proportion of the population had bare cupboards and no food. Thousands in the cities were starving and needed urgent relief. To overcome this immediate crisis, the Allies had to fly and ship in more food. A mammoth effort was undertaken to ensure that the people could eat again.

In this giving of aid, the Queen played an important role; she was a strong and forceful negotiator who worked hard to ensure the needs of the people were properly assessed and addressed. She travelled extensively throughout the country, meeting people and giving comfort and encouragement as necessary. At this critical time in their history the Dutch were certainly fortunate to have a Queen who was able to provide such stability, strong leadership and direction for the nation until such time as the political processes could be put back in place.

A year after the liberation, on the 17th May 1946, the Dutch had their first national election for their House of

Representatives. The interim Government that had been provisionally appointed by the Queen had fulfilled its role and a democratically elected Government could now form.[51]

During this early period after the war, my parents also struggled to survive. While they battled to keep the business going, food remained scarce and, often, they had to do without basic necessities. Miek, Dad's foster mother, wrote in August 1945 to Dad's sister Marie that Dad came looking for potatoes as he could not buy them anywhere, despite holding coupons for them. Because of the shortages of food, the coupon system that was introduced by the Germans had been maintained. Miek makes the comment in the letter that there was little improvement in conditions in the three months since the end of the war and "that everything was still in a mess." However, as Mum wrote in her diary, at least they were no longer living in fear.

Nonetheless, the business was becoming a challenge for Dad. Besides the difficulty of still dealing with coupons and the ongoing food shortages, he was concerned by new regulations introduced for milk and dairy products. All milk now had to be pasteurised so Dad could no longer deal directly with the farmers but had to buy milk from the milk factory. He also was forbidden to manufacture butter and butter-milk, but, again, had to buy it from registered producers. All this gave him little flexibility to set prices and control profit margins.

This was all exacerbated by the fact that Dad was still owed a lot of money by his customers. During the difficult war years many could not find the money to pay for milk and cheese products, so, after the war, Dad also had to deal with collecting old debts. This was not his strength. According to my eldest sister, Jenny, Dad was too good-hearted and allowed customers to accumulate debts for far too long. When he did try collecting what was due, customers simply stopped buying from him to avoid increasing debts. This, in turn, meant a drop in regular clientele.

During the war, when everything was in crisis, the modus operandi had been one of survival. No profit was made and instead Dad had to subsidise losses to keep the doors open. After the war, however, Dad assessed the long-term prospects. He needed a viable business that could expand, make profits and provide for his growing family. He was slowly starting to realise that this business was not going to do that for him. Because he now had to get all his produce from the factory, he felt like he was working for them rather than for himself. It was not long before he was considering other options.

29. The Call of a Glorious Gospel: Rev. Boodt

"I can forgive a man for a bad sermon, I can forgive the preacher almost anything if he gives me a sense of God, if he gives me something for my soul, if he gives me the sense that, though he is inadequate himself, he is handling something which is very great and very glorious, if he gives me some dim glimpse of the majesty and the glory of God, the love of Christ my Saviour, and the magnificence of the Gospel. If he does that I am his debtor, and I am profoundly grateful to him."

~Martyn Lloyd-Jones

Two months after the liberation of the Netherlands, my parents received the devastating news that Reverend C.P. Boodt had passed away on the 22nd June 1945. Freed from the Bergen-Belsen concentration camp by British soldiers he was so weakened that he died a few months later. He left behind a wife and seven children. Already in the early 1930s he gained a national reputation as he warned against the dangers of Nazism and how it was so totally incompatible with Biblical truth.

After his 1943 arrest, he continued to preach and witness in the camps at great personal danger to himself. He suffered beatings and punishments, but nothing could deter him from remaining faithful in his calling to proclaim the Gospel and the hope of salvation. Many could later testify, with thankfulness, of the spiritual encouragement they received while detained in the camp, through Rev. Boodt's example and messages of faith. His friends from the camp later organised a relief type of sculpture to be created, an artistic representation showing him huddled together with others in the concentration camp surrounded by people listening to his every word of spiritual encouragement.

The news of his death deeply saddened my parents. He had been their pastor and mentor when they were at an impressionable young age, he had given them catechism instructions, they had together professed their faith in the Church where he was minister, and he had also officiated at their wedding. Rev. Boodt had instilled in them a deep appreciation of what it meant to live by faith every day. They were particularly taken by his faithful stand against the evils of Nazism, despite the danger and cost this afforded him. He had called for steadfastness in the struggle against a regime that attacked the very fundamentals of Christianity. He saw it as a spiritual battle and was relentless in his endeavour to fight that fight at every opportunity, using the words of Scripture as his tools. "How could a Christian in all good conscience just give himself up to work for and support such an evil regime?" he asked. He encouraged resistance and the harbouring of those that needed protection.

In his own house, he harboured Jews and even after he was captured, his wife, at great personal risk, continued showing hospitality to those who were in danger of losing their lives, including Jews. He had been a powerful preacher who had drawn large numbers to his church, especially young people. Many of his listeners found him a devoted preacher, one whose faithful exegesis and interpretation of Scripture really spoke to them during calamitous times. Due to such preaching many were compelled to resist Nazism and became convinced that their calling was to work as Underground warriors.

It was amazing that he was able to preach unhindered for as long as he did. It was not until the third year of the war - in January 1943 - that he was arrested. He was assured of his continued captivity when, at the first interview, he told his captors how evil Hitler was and how Hitler would one day also have to face the judgement seat of God. He later wrote to his wife that he thanked God that he was given the courage to say that. Some time after, he was given the chance of freedom if only he signed a declaration which agreed to his silence and refusal to preach against the Nazi regime. Despite his great desire to be back with his wife and seven children, he refused to sign. He felt called by God to continue proclaiming His Word at every opportunity and he could not, in good conscience, be silenced.

He was taken to camp Vught, located in the province of North Brabant near the German border, where he was interned for about 18 months till September 1944, when he was transferred to Germany to the camp known as Bergen-Belsen. There he was still able to joyfully experience, despite his desperate condition, the liberation by the English soldiers on the 15th April 1945. What the British found in the camp were 60,000 starving and seriously ill people crammed together without food, water or basic sanitation. Many were suffering from typhus, dysentery and starvation. Despite the British giving urgent medical attention and hospitalisation to many of these desperate individuals, a further 14,000 of these freed prisoners would die over the next months. Rev. Boodt was to be one of them.

In the camp, he had been busy providing spiritual support and encouragement to other inmates who were lost in despair. Every Sunday he organised clandestine services behind the barracks. People from all denominations came together at great personal risk to share and confess their common faith and reliance on Jesus.

When Rev. Boodt heard from his prison about the church struggles and divisions that were raging within the Reformed Church, he was totally perplexed. How could they possibly be fighting amongst themselves when the core values of Christianity were being attacked from all sides by the demonic Nazi regime? In the camp he was experiencing the gathering of true and faithful Christians that cast all the divisions aside because of the common enemy and the danger they all faced. For Rev. Boodt, it was a beautiful experience of unity and he would wish that those outside the camp would strive for the same unity.

In 2020 I met two of Rev. Boodt's daughters: the youngest, Richtje Zuideveld-Boodt, born in 1942 and the oldest daughter, Alice van der Kerk-Boodt. Alice still remembers when their family lived in the manse next door to my mother's family in Brandwijk. At 16 years of age, Mum had worked one day a week in the Boodt household. In 2020 all seven children of the Boodt family were still alive and enjoying relatively good health. The eldest, a son, became a pastor and moved to Canada. Another daughter migrated to America. Their mother Richtje, died in 1998 aged 90. Their mother never remarried and as a widow had the responsibility of bringing up her seven children single-handedly.

Alice and Richtje explained how their mother kept the memory of their dad and his faithful commitment to Christ alive in a very positive way. They got to know him, and appreciate him personally, through her many references to his deeds and actions. Their mother harboured no bitterness and had been totally supportive of her husband's stance. Despite having opportunities for release, she understood why he felt called to continue preaching the gospel in prison. As he wrote to his wife from prison in October 1943: *"It is about Christ and his Kingdom. Not about us or our lives. Jesus said if you are not prepared to leave your father or mother - or even lose your own life - you cannot be my disciple."*

The children of Rev. Boodt have donated a lot of their father's papers and letters to the museum at Camp Vught. In May 2020, at the 75th commemoration of the liberation, the camp planned to put together a special exhibition and presentation in memory of Rev. Boodt. His leadership and principled stand is to be recognised and shared with today's generation.

30. Church Life

"We have come to a turning point in the road. If we turn to the right mayhap our children and our children's children will go that way; but if we turn to the left, generations yet unborn will curse our names for having been unfaithful to God and to His Word."
~ *Charles Spurgeon*

Rev. Boodt was not the only Reformed pastor that paid the ultimate price. More than 30 pastors from the Reformed Churches in the Netherlands died as a result of their principled preaching and witness. Many others went into hiding to avoid arrest. A number even became national leaders of the underground movement.

Already at its 1936 Synod, the Reformed Church of the Netherlands (RCN) had declared that Nazism and membership of the NSB was not compatible with church membership. One of the church leaders, Professor K. Schilder, a prolific writer and editor of a weekly paper, *De Reformatie*, used every opportunity to underpin and reinforce that message. He had a large following amongst the membership of the RCN who enjoyed his articles. As a consequence, many members of the Reformed Churches took a very strong principled stand against Nazism.

This principled approach had a deep impact on the way the underground resistance went about their tasks. Their motivation was based on the deep religious conviction that what they were doing was in obedience to the will of God. Analysts and historians of the Dutch underground movement have found that, in contrast to some other nations where the motivation was purely driven by hatred against the Germans, the Dutch resistance had strong religious overtones. Many groups called on God in prayer when meeting or starting an action and would analyse what they were doing in light of what God's will revealed to them in Scripture.[52]

When the Germans invaded the Netherlands on the 10th May 1940, it did not take the Germans long to realise that many pastors across the country were warning their members against the dangers and unscriptural foundation of Nazism. Prof. Schilder and his anti-Nazi writings came to their explicit attention so on the 22nd August 1940, they arrested him and made the publication of *De Reformatie* illegal. He was released just over three months later on the 6th December 1940, on the proviso that he would cease all writing and publishing.[53] At this point the Germans were still trying to be amenable in the hope that they could convince Dutch citizens to cooperate and so live in 'freedom'. After all, they saw the Dutch as being of the same Aryan race and of pure blood.

However, it was not long before Schilder received word that he was again being sought by the Germans. To avoid arrest, he went into hiding, which as it turned out, had a major impact on the Reformed Churches during this period. Again the churches were holding a synod, this time convened during the years 1939 to 1942, and enlivened discussions ensued with regard to various issues of doctrine and Schilder's presence there would have been of great benefit. He was, after all, the Professor of

Dogmatics at the Theological Seminary in Kampen.

The Reformed Churches were established in 1892 when two groups, the Doleantie and Secession merged. Both had previously separated from the Government-sponsored Dutch Reformed Church. The Secession movement had done this in 1834. It was acknowledged that there were some variations in their doctrinal understanding of the covenant, common grace and election between the two groups, but they did not see that as an impediment to merge and become the one church. This thinking and tolerance for the sake of unity prevailed until the 1930s when a group began agitating for acceptance of just one particular interpretation of the covenant and the meaning of baptism. Schilder had been writing and expanding on these subjects and challenging Abraham Kuyper's interpretation on the aforementioned topics which were now being pushed by his followers. Schilder's writings caused a huge reaction by the followers of Abraham Kuyper, led by his son H.H. Kuyper, who did everything in his power to protect the reputation and doctrinal interpretations of his father.

The 1936 Synod decided to appoint a committee to investigate and report to the next Synod in 1939. Shortly after the 1939 Synod was convened, war broke out and it became difficult to get everyone together. It was generally assumed in the churches that common sense would prevail, and the Synod would be deferred until after the war. After all, the country was in turmoil and many people were in constant fear of their lives. Two thirds of all the congregations and consistories appealed to the Synod not to proceed with discussions on the doctrinal matters until peace in the nation was restored and everyone was able to attend.[54]

Despite copious overtures for postponement directed to the Synod - from regional synods, 21 church classes, consistories and individuals - it was to no avail. There was a small core group of leaders, led by Professor H.H. Kuyper, who seemed to have inordinate control and who pursued their own agenda. They seemed to have little respect for following protocol, listening to people, and working in the best interests of all church members.[55]

As an editor, Kuyper was able to continue publishing a weekly paper called *De Heraut* during the war. This was in contrast to Schilder, who had been forced to close his publication. This gave Kuyper an ongoing platform to expound his views and consolidate his influence. Kuyper had refrained from directing any criticism at the Nazis and had, as related earlier, shown contempt for the resolution of Synod 1936 which condemned membership of the NSB. By contrast Schilder, and many others, saw it as their duty to awaken in people the need to resist the evil intent of Nazism - and risked their freedom and lives in that process. It appears as if these two professors had very contrasting world views.[56]

Synod 1939 was reconvened a number of times and ran for a total of four years, until 1942. This was totally in conflict with the Church Order which stated that Synod should be convened every three years. This group of people became like the supreme governing authority of the churches. They made a ruling on the meaning of baptism and the doctrine of election and declared that the children of believers are to be considered as regenerate until the contrary is evident. This, they argued, would become clear as the person grew to maturity and accepted Christ.[57] There was, therefore, a focus on regeneration rather than on the surety of God's promises.

The meaning of the 'covenant of grace' as something God worked throughout the generations was lost in this interpretation. The tolerance that had previously accepted varying views in the churches on this difficult matter of doctrine for nearly 50 years was now gone and only one view was allowed to prevail. Anyone who refused to subscribe to this ruling was to be suspended. And this was in the middle of the war where many were fighting for their very survival!

Schilder had the strong Biblical view that baptism is a sign and seal of God's covenant and that we do not need to doubt God's promises. Parents who lost their child in infancy could have the firm assurance that their child was an adopted child of God, confirmed with the promise to eternal life. Unfortunately, however, as he was in hiding, he had not been in a position to attend Synod to put this case forward.

Looking at it today, the arrogance of the leaders led by Kuyper's son was quite incredible. What were they possibly thinking? What was their motivation? Were they driven by power and was Schilder seen as a competitor? There certainly was little or no evidence of the fruits of the Spirit amongst the church leaders. Synod rules regarding meetings were frequently broken. In light of these infractions, for Synod to also insist on the adherence of its decisions just gave no recourse, or way out, on the basis of principle and conviction. Of course, it was going to lead to a schism, particularly once the Synod started deposing those who refused to accept what they now declared as doctrinal truth. It was church hierarchy at its worst.

31. The Liberation: Seeds Sown for the Free Reformed Churches

"Blessed be the Lord, Who has not given us as prey to their teeth. Our soul has escaped as a bird from the snare of the fowlers; The snare is broken, and we have escaped."

Psalm 124:6-7 (NKJV)

After the Synod, which ran for four years until 1942, another Synod was convened already in 1943, in order to handle all the appeals and to clarify their positions on the doctrines of election and the covenant. Synod's response to the appeals and questions confirmed what everyone had feared: there was no turning back or attempt to compromise. All churches received communication from the Synod stating that they must reaffirm the Synod's doctrinal interpretation. The communique also insisted that all elders and pastors subscribe to this declared doctrine.

Thousands of church members and pastors were deeply saddened by these developments. The church they had loved and worshipped in their whole lives now seemed determined to cause schisms and deep doctrinal divisions. Most church members did not want to leave and had been hopeful that common sense and goodwill would prevail. But in this, they were severely disappointed.

Soon news came through that ministers were being suspended or denied the right to be ordained in the first place, as was the case for a nephew of Professor K. Schilder, young H.J. Schilder. He had successfully completed his candidate exams but, at the classical examination, could not give an undertaking that he would abide by the synodical pronouncements. With that, he was then barred from taking on the office of pastoral ministry. Shortly after, on the 23 March 1944, Prof. Schilder was suspended both as professor of the Kampen Theological Seminary and as emeritus minister of Delfshaven. Meanwhile, whole consistories that disagreed with the Synod decisions, as well as individual office bearers, were discharged from office by the Synod without reference, as required by the Church Order, to the local regional classis.

Heightened frustration with the situation meant something had to be done. There were cautions issued against leaving the bond. On the 11th August 1944, a meeting was called by a group of professors and ministers in The Hague, inviting all concerned persons to come and discuss these issues. Over 1200 people turned up from all over the country. The organisers had not counted on so many and had to, at the last minute, change venues to accommodate them all. Dad was also able to be present despite still being in hiding. No doubt this would have applied to many of those present, but the issue at hand was so pressing that risks undertaken to attend were deemed necessary.

K. Schilder was also present. In July 1944, he had received official word from the Germans - through his brother, A.

Schilder - that the German authorities were no longer seeking him and he was free to attend to his church duties. This was a remarkable development. After having been forced underground for over three years, he was suddenly given complete freedom.[58] What was the German motivation for this? They certainly were not inclined to support the church from which they already had incarcerated so many of its leaders.

It has been suggested that they were quite happy to see the church involved in serious doctrinal disagreements. With the leaders of the church busy with doctrinal disputes, they reasoned, they would be less inclined to spend time fighting and warring against the Germans. It appears that they were setting the stage for the Reformed church to tear itself apart. Just the fact that 1,200 men could attend a public meeting without the Germans raiding the event speaks volumes in itself. Elsewhere, they were rounding up men daily and transporting them to Germany. The Germans were extremely efficient and obviously well informed about anything unusual: with NSBs everywhere there is no way they would have not known of this major gathering.

At the The Hague meeting, K. Schilder presented a document titled, "A Deed of Liberation and Return." This document clearly outlined how, according to Article 31 of the Church Order, Synods could not procedurally hold their statements and actions as binding. In proceeding this way, they were in conflict with both God's Word and the Church Order. The meeting gave those present a clear sense of their responsibilities and outlined for them the best way forward.

Just two days later, on the 13th August 1944, the Church of Bergschenhoek, after a meeting between consistory and all members, decided to liberate themselves from the Synodical decisions. This would be the first church to do so. The meeting was led by the consistory chairman, Mr. L. Schoof.

(In 1958, Mr. Schoof migrated to Launceston, Tasmania with his wife and eight children where he joined the Free Reformed Church of Launceston. One of his children, Maria Jacoba, was in 1966 to become my darling wife.)

The consistory emphasised to the congregation that while they did not wish to break from the bond of the Reformed Churches, they could not accept the Synod edict on doctrine regarding election and covenant.[59]

The following week, on Sunday the 20th August 1944, the Bergschenhoek consistory invited the disposed Professor, Dr. K. Schilder, to lead the Church service; it was to be his first service in a Liberated Reformed Church. His text for the service was 1 Corinthians 4 verses 6-7.[60]

> *Now these things, brethren, I have figuratively transferred to myself and Apollos for your sakes, that you may learn in us not to think beyond what is written, that none of you may be puffed up on behalf of one against another. For who makes you differ from another? And what do you have that you did not receive? Now if you did indeed receive it, why do you boast as if you had not received it?*

The reaction of Synod to the Bergschenhoek meeting was swift and decisive. On the 4th September the letter from Synod delegates declared that the individuals forming the schismatic consistory of Bergschenhoek were no longer considered members of the Reformed Churches, and that the Church of Bergschenhoek was no longer part of the bond. Furthermore, the Classis of Rotterdam would be requested to accommodate those that wished to remain 'faithful' and not follow the direction of the schismatic consistory.[61]

Despite the best attempts of many to maintain unity and seek compromise there was no opportunity left open by the determined convenors of the Synod. In the following year, many churches followed Bergschenhoek's example and freed themselves from the yoke of synodical hierarchy. They maintained the name 'Reformed Churches' as they considered themselves the continuation of the true and faithful church. For clarification they added the word 'liberated'. In the early years after the Liberation, they were often referred to as "Article 31-ers."

The first annual report of the Reformed Churches Liberated published in June 1946 shows there were a total of 216 churches and 77,300 members. This represented about ten per cent of the Reformed Church membership. It had been a grassroots movement that gained momentum. K. Schilder played an increasingly important role in leadership and encouragement. He became a leading professor at the newly instituted Theological Seminary in Kampen and a prolific writer in '*De Reformatie*' paper, which he reinstated after the war.[62] He was well-loved and respected within the newly established Church community and had a lot of influence. My parents followed his writings closely and, like many of our Australian church founders, had most of his published books on their shelves. My parents always had a photo of Schilder displayed somewhere in their house indicating the warm regard and respect they had for him.

The majority of the church members of Sliedrecht, where my parents attended, also joined the Liberated churches. However, as was the case in many places across the country, not all members could agree. In some cases, the majority did not wish to join the new movement, and so those who did had to liberate themselves and establish a new, separate church with often very small numbers. In Sliedrecht, discussions took place for at least a year, with many meetings held and papers outlining both positions of the argument passed around.

Finally, the majority decided to go with the liberation while those that did not agree could leave and join a neighbouring Reformed Church. These were difficult and stressful times for church members, and it was not something that anyone had been seeking. At a personal level, the split caused divisions in many families as well as the breakup of friendships. On a church level, it caused disputes and legal challenges particularly around the legal ownership of church properties.

My parents were now part of a smaller but very committed and dedicated federation of churches. Within a few years, this federation grew to about 100,000 members and established its own Theological Seminary, primary and high schools throughout the country. Such was the enthusiasm and commitment amongst its members that they formed their own daily newspaper, the *Gereformeerd Gezinsblad* and their own political party, the 'Gereformeerd Politiek Verbond' (GPV).

In 1963, Piet Jongeling became the first GPV member of the National Parliament. He became a well-respected member of parliament and served there till his retirement in 1977. He was also a prolific author of Christian youth books written under the name Piet Prins. Many of these books were later translated in English and could be found on the bookshelves of many migrant families.

When the first Free Reformed Churches of Australia were instituted in the early 1950s its founding members all came from this newly formed federation of churches. They came bearing with them that strong church commitment and determination to serve God in their newly adopted country.

32. The Post-War Years

*"Things don't go wrong and break your heart so
you can become bitter and give up.
They happen to break you down and build you up
so you can be all that you were
intended to be."*

~Samuel Johnson

After the war, things were taking a long time to improve and Dad was getting increasingly concerned about the long-term prospects of his business. He was starting to look at other options including the possibility of going back into his trade, baking. He had a growing family – Mum in the meantime had given birth to me, Gerrit Jan (Harry), named after Grandfather Schutte, on the 20th March 1946, so now there were six mouths to feed. At the time of my birth Peter was 9, Jenny 8, Niek 6, Janet 5 and Mappie 3. Mum wrote how I grew like a 'cabbage' which was so different than those children who had been born during the war. Mum still complained about the shortages and the coupon system for food but, nevertheless, acknowledges that no one was starving anymore.

After several months Dad raised the possibility of migration with Mum. This received short shrift – no way would she think of migrating, particularly in light of then having to leave her elderly parents behind. But migration was being talked about in many families. The frustration with the country's slow recovery and the uncertain future - the Dutch had suffered five years of war and, prior to that, some ten years of economic depression - drove many, including my Dad, to look at other countries and other opportunities. With the housing shortage, the Dutch Government was also actively promoting and encouraging its citizens to leave for distant shores.

After having received a firm rebuttal from Mum, Dad decided to get serious about buying another business, preferably a bakery. Following some discussion, it was decided that they would first sell their house and business and then look for something else.

Just over two years after the end of the war, in August 1947, they sold their business and home to a young couple about to get married. Part of the sale agreement was that my parents could remain in the house with the young couple until they had found and bought another residence and business to move into. This meant my parents with their six children had to use the four upstairs rooms and the attic while sharing the downstairs kitchen and toilet.

There was an acute housing shortage in the Netherlands, so the new owner was quite happy to have found a business with a house as part of the deal. The housing crisis forced many couples at that time to live with their parents for years, and others simply delayed marrying until a house could be found. The housing shortage was a strong motivation for many young couples to migrate to another country and, with government support and encouragement, many did.

On the 14th September 1947, the new owners took over the business. They were due to get married in a fortnight, so had agreed not to move into the house until after that day. In the late hours of the next night, the 15th of September, Mum gave birth to her seventh child, a daughter they named Maria Elizabeth (Mieke). It all happened so quickly that they didn't even have time to get a doctor so Dad had to attend to the birth as best he could. It was only after the baby was cared for, and wrapped in a blanket, that he left Mum to get a doctor.

During Mum's convalescence period, which in those days meant staying in bed for ten days after giving birth, the children all had to be distributed among family and friends. Brother Niek clearly remembers those occasions and would always be taken to stay with Auntie Miek in Brandwijk. For him, it was great to go there as she used to spoil him and allow him to go to the nearby shop to buy things he fancied. There must have been some mutual love because Miek wrote to Auntie Marie after Niek had stayed for a period, "He is such a sweet boy."

Two weeks after the birth of Mieke the family all moved into the upstairs section of the house. They converted one room into a lounge and had all the children, except the two youngest ones, sleep in the attic. The main inconvenience was that they had to share the kitchen downstairs for cooking with the new owners, Mr. and Mrs. van Leiden, who had now settled in and were operating the business, including the shop.

The shop was one aspect Mum did not miss. The commitment and hours spent there had been relentless and she now appreciated the more relaxed pace. She retained the services of a maid, Riek Versteeg, who had been with her for two years. Now, without the shop, Mum was in a position to spend more time with her children. My oldest sister, Jenny, recalled in 2016 that in Sliedrecht she was mostly cared for by the maid, as Mum was always busy in the shop.

One day, when Jenny was 8 years old, she was possibly

feeling this lack of attention from Mum and decided to go and visit her Opa and Oma Schutte in Brandwijk. Along with her sisters, Janet and Mappie aged 6 and 4 respectively, she wandered off for the 10-kilometre walk to Brandwijk. They reached their grandparents, who no doubt were surprised to see them. They didn't receive the best of welcomes – they were given food and drink and promptly told to go straight back home! So back they went, eventually arriving to find a frantic Mum who, sick with worry, had been searching everywhere for them. Talking about it in 2016, Jenny remembers the occasion and the stress it caused her parents and herself as an eight-year-old. For her it had simply been a wish to see her grandparents, yet no one ever looked at that positive aspect of it. As the oldest, she was held responsible and was severely reprimanded.

With the business sold and money in the bank, Dad went hunting for a bakery business. While doing this he found temporary work with a bakery in Dordrecht, about 10 kilometres from home. Together with a business partner, Jan Blankestijn, he eventually bought a run-down bakery in Oosterbeek near Arnhem and about 90 kilometres east of Sliedrecht. It would mean no longer living in the Alblasserwaard. Dad had met Blankestijn during the war while hiding from the Germans in the Biesbosch. About ten years younger than Dad, he was married and had one child.

Why he chose to go into partnership is a mystery. Dad had the capital, business experience, and was a qualified baker, whereas his partner, also a baker, had no capital nor experience. It appears Blankestijn may have come across the bakery and offered to partner with Dad to buy. He must have convinced Dad that it was too good a deal to pass up. Dad himself writes that the business was in steep decline but had strong potential for building something substantial. The husband of Dad's sister Lijsje, Uncle Dirk, strongly advised him against going ahead with it. He didn't trust Blankestijn and was concerned Dad might end up losing his money.

However, Dad was determined to go ahead. So, on 5th January 1948, the business was settled and the two families moved into the house that was purchased as part of the business. The bakery, shop and home were all incorporated on the same premises. My parents moved upstairs and the Blankestijns with their one child took the ground floor. Mrs. Blankestijn took responsibility for the shop, so Mum did not need to be involved with that. Mum did, however, help keep the bakery clean and wash the baking trays. The long hours worked by the men did not give them any time to do much more than baking.

Dad was now back working extremely long hours, which he had not done since his youth. In a letter to his sister Marie, written just a month after he started, he admitted to not being home one evening since starting. The day started 4.30 a.m. in the morning and continued through to 1.00 a.m. the next morning. On Fridays he worked right through the night while Sundays was spent mostly in bed, sleeping.

Meanwhile, Mum lost her reliable maid, Riek, who came over for a few weeks to help clean up, but did not want to move away from her family in Sliedrecht. My parents decided to try without this help. It appears that money was now tight, so it can be assumed that Dad must have put it all in the business. The business definitely needed additional capital to improve it. They installed a brand-new oven boasting the latest technology. But the pressure to pay for it seems to have been enormous, as they avoided employing an additional worker despite the growing turnover and the ridiculous hours they had to work to keep up with the demand. So, it was not an ideal scenario. Mum, caring for seven young children, without assistance and expecting another child, and Dad so busy that the family never saw him. How could this go on?

Mum was starting to worry about Dad's health. He was overdoing the work hours but even when in bed, he was restless and could not relax. In addition, living on the premises and sharing the house with their partner was starting to play on her nerves. Some other accommodation had to be found. Living at the bakery was not sustainable nor compatible with a healthy family life.

On the 14th March 1949, 15 months after taking on the new business, another healthy girl was born whom they named Willy after Mum. Despite all the pressures and disappointments they were experiencing, they saw each child as a gift from God. "The Lord be praised," Mum wrote in her diary. As was customary, Dad presented the baby the following Sunday in church for baptism. Mum was still recuperating at home so remained home. The service was led by Prof. K. Schilder.

In contrast to the Sliedrecht church, where most members of the 'mother' church joined the new group, in Oosterbeek the situation was different. Here the majority of members decided to stay within the traditional bond while only 70 members withdrew themselves to institute the Reformed Church (Liberated). Their withdrawal left this small group with no church building and no pastor, so it was a special privilege when they were visited by Prof. Schilder, the highly regarded church leader, to lead the services for the day.

The additional child highlighted the urgency of arranging other accommodation. A house had to be found. Four months later, in July 1949, they found what they were looking for - a spacious house with a large backyard just down the road from the bakery. The investment in the business was reduced to get back some capital and a loan was needed. Nevertheless, they could now live together as a family with more room and privacy. For Mum, it was an absolute relief. However, Dad's hours remained relentless, and the family still saw little of him. Mum said they saw less of him now as he only came home to sleep.

Dad wrote to his sisters that the business was going well, with the turnover climbing. However, the long hours and the difficulty of accessing money was starting to take its toll. He found it difficult to reconcile the lack of money with the increasing business and growth in customers. From a rundown operation when they started to a modern and bustling business there should have been good profits accumulating but, alas, that didn't seem to be the case. Dad did not control the daily takings or do the banking – that was all done by his partner's wife. Where was all the increased income going to? Dad was starting to become worried and realised that the situation could not continue. In April 1950 the partnership with Blankestijn was dissolved and Dad was paid out. While he lost a lot of money in the transaction, he claimed that the settlement was sufficient for him to be able to pay off the debts. He had come to the conclusion that it was better to cut his losses and move on.

But what to do now? He no longer had the resources to buy a business so he needed to find employment. But with eight children, and one on the way, he was under pressure to get a well paid job. The long hours in the bakery had burnt him out and he now started looking for a steadier nine-to-five job. Those were offered in factories around the country, so he applied and was able to secure a job.

Within six months, he tried more than four different factory

CLOCKWISE FROM TOP: Bastiaan Kleijn (father of Klaas Kleijn); Cornelis Verhoef (father of Jannigje Verhoef); Lijzebeth Kleijn-Verhoef (mother of Klaas Kleijn); Klaas Kleijn; Jannigje Kleijn-Verhoef.

LEFT: Extended family at the wedding of Klaas Kleijn and Jannigje Verhoef.

1. Unknown
2. Cornelis Verhoef (brother of Jannigje)
3. Janna Verhoef-Spruijtenburg (wife of Cornelis)
4. Pieter Verhoef (brother of Jannigje)
5. Maria Elizabeth Verhoef-Tukker (wife of Pieter)
6. Maria Cornelia Verhoef (half sister of Jannigje)
7. Unknown
8. Unknown
9. Wout Tukker
10. Niesje Kleijn (sister of Klaas)
11. Arie Verhoef (half brother of Jannigje)
12. Annigje Arie Verhoef (half sister of Jannigje)
13. Willem Blom (married Annigje Arie in 1915)
14. Marinus Jan Verhoef (half brother of Jannigje)
15. Maria Jantje Verhoef (half sister of Jannigje)
16. Cornelis Verhoef (cousin of Jannigje)
17. Bastiaan (Saan) Kleijn (cousin of Klaas)
18. Janna Kleijn (sister of Klaas)
19. Unknown
20. Unknown
21. Unknown
22. Teunis Pieter Terlouw
23. Unknown
24. Cornelis Kleijn (brother of Klaas)
25. Mijnsje Spruijtenburg (wife of Cornelis)
26. Jan Leendert Kleijn (brother of Klaas)
27. Unknown
28. Unknown
29. Aart Maat (brother of Dingena Maat)
30. Fop Kleijn (brother of Klaas)
31. Willemijn Kleijn-De Bruijn (wife of Fop)
32. Adriana Kleijn (daughter of Fop & Willemijn)
33. Bastiaan Kleijn (father of Klaas)
34. Klaas Kleijn
35. Jannigje Kleijn-Verhoef
36. Cornelis Verhoef (father of Jannigje)
37. Dingena Verhoef-Maat (stepmother of Jannigje)
38. Jan Cornelis Verhoef (half brother of Jannigje)
39. Janna Cornelia (Keet) Verhoef (half sister of Jannigje)

ABOVE: The house in Streefkerk where Klaas and Jannigje lived. This photo was taken in 2019.

BELOW: Niesje Kleijn, the foster mother of Lijsje Kleijn and the sister of Klaas Kleijn.

ABOVE: Photo of the three siblings taken shortly after their mothers' death. From left: Marie, Lijsje and Cornelis. On the back of the photo is a handwritten caption saying 'moederloze kinderen' (motherless children).

ABOVE Verhoef Family picture taken in 1923.

Back Row: Pieter Verhoef, Cornelis Verhoef, Annigje Blom-Verhoef, Willem Blom, Jan Cornelis Verhoef, Nicolaas Klein, Maria Cornelia Klein-Verhoef, Janna Cornelia (Keet) Verhoef, Maria Jantje Verhoef, Marinus Jan Verhoef.

Front Row: Maria Elizabeth Verhoef-Tukker, Janna Verhoef-Spruijtenburg, Cornelis Verhoef, Dingena Verhoef-Maat, Lena Maria Verhoef-Bos, Arie Verhoef, Maria Verhoef-Bongers.

ABOVE AND BELOW: Display of equipment used at the St. Joris Gasthuis which were in use during the internment of Klaas Kleijn.

ABOVE Marie, Lijsje and Cornelis as young adults.

LEFT: Jennikke van Veen—Schutte, mother of Willempje.

BELOW LEFT: Willempje Schutte as a young girl.

BELOW RIGHT: Gerrit Jan Schutte, father of Willempje, at one of his regular duties—sharpening farm cutting blades.

LEFT: The house where the Schutte family lived is to the left of the church. They lived at the rear of the house.

BELOW: Cornelis Kleijn and Willempje Schutte on their wedding day.

CLOCKWISE FROM LEFT: Pieter and Miek Verhoef, foster parents to Marie Kleijn; Pieter and Miek Verhoef with Cornelis Kleijn; Cornelis Kleijn with two fellow soldiers in the army; Cornelis Kleijn with his Auntie Miek Verhoef.

Geen kaas zoo fijn als van Kees Kleijn

Thans voor Uw bonnen
fijne oude Boerenkaas f 1.- per pond

De Zuivelzaak
Kleindiepstraat 9

ABOVE: Cornelis and Willempje Kleijn in front of their shop.
LEFT: Advertisement for the shop, "No Cheese is so fine as that from Kees Kleijn".
BELOW: Cornelis Kleijn and an assistant on a milk delivery run.

ABOVE: Cornelis and Willempje Kleijn in front of their shop with their two oldest children, Peter and Jenny.

BELOW LEFT: Military attestation from the Geref. Kerk of Sliedrecht for Cornelis Kleijn 6 months before the Second World War.

BELOW RIGHT: Reverend Boodt.

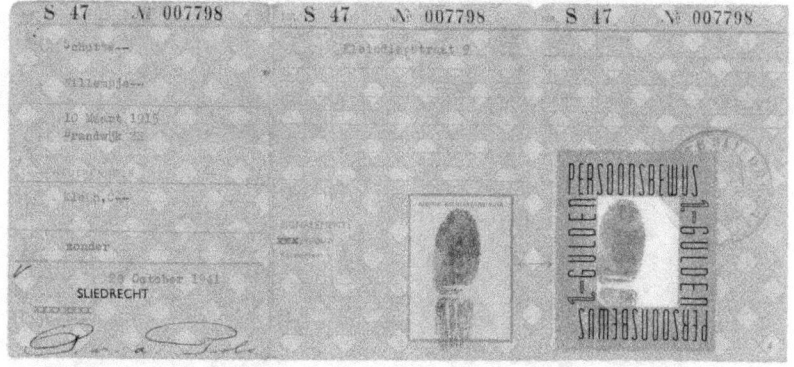

ABOVE: ID Card for Willempje Kleijn during the Second World War.
BELOW: A drawing by Cornelis Kleijn of the ark where he was in hiding from the Germans, and a photo of a similar ark.

ABOVE: The Johan Van Oldenbarnevelt on which the Kleijn family travelled to Australia.

BELOW: Ticket for the passage to Australia.

ABOVE: Photo of the Kleijn family before migration. From left to right: Jenny, Janet, Harry, Willempje, Kees, Pieter, Mieke, Niek, Willy, Cornelis and Mappie.

BELOW LEFT: Cornelis and Willempje Kleijn with Cornelis' sister Lijsje, saying farewell on board the ship.

BELOW RIGHT: Willempje Kleijn and Mrs Bijl on board the ship to Australia.

ABOVE: Members of the fledgling Free Reformed Church of Armadale waiting in Fremantle for the arrival of Rev. Pels and his wife.

LEFT: A form of assurance of accommodation for the Kleijn family, signed by Daniel Bosveld.

BELOW: Reverend Pels.

ABOVE: The first accommodation for the Kleijn family in Australia on Abernethy Road, Byford, showing the isolation in contrast to their life in the Netherlands. The photo was taken in the 1970s.

BELOW: Harry Kleijn in front of Fallon's Place.

ABOVE: Peter, Harry and Niek working on their weekly job of preparing firewood for the family.

BELOW: The motorbike used to transport the family, and an article that appeared in the newspaper reporting the traffic offense. In the sidecar were Mieke, Willy and Harry.

Four Go To Church

"Four people on a motor cycle is rather many—even when they are going to church," the magistrate (Mr. T. Ansell, R.M.) said in the Perth Traffic Court yesterday, when he fined Alan Cornelius Kleyn, of Roley-road, Armadale £4 for having carried more than one passenger. Kleyn was alleged to have told the police that he and his family had been going to church.

ABOVE: Willempje Kleijn holding Susan with from left, Kees, Arthur and Harry.

BELOW: Cornelis Kleijn with Harry, Kees, Arthur, Mary and Susan.

ABOVE: Janet holding Kees, Willy, Mappie holding Arthur, Harry and Mieke.

LEFT: Susan, Willy, Mary and Margaret.

BELOW: Willy on her wedding day with Cornelis and Willempje.

DUTCH CHURCH GROUP BEGAN 300 YEARS AGO

By Douglas Macdonald

FIVE Dutchmen, who worked at local brickworks, recently resigned from a trade union on religious grounds. They belong to the Free Reformed Church of Australia.

Few people in Western Australia had heard of this church until the resignations brought it into the public eye.

Around Armadale and Kelmscott are a number of Dutch families. They are members of this little-known religious group which has its origins in Holland.

Although it has only slightly more than 400 members, this is not just a small peculiar sect—nor is it a new church. Its origins go back nearly 300 years.

Based on Calvinism, the Reformed Church is similar to a Protestant church founded throughout Holland in 1618, after the country broke away from Roman Catholicism.

This original church ended when the French invaded and occupied Holland in 1795, and enforced Roman Catholicism. When they left the country in 1813, Holland formed its present Presbyterian Church, which had the king as its leader.

Several groups left the Presbyterian Church about 1837 and later united to form the Reformed Church of Holland.

Today, this church has about 500,000 members in Holland. The rest of the population of 10,500,000 is almost equally divided into Roman Catholics and Presbyterians.

After World War II a group left the Reformed Church because of a difference of opinion over two articles of faith. But this group kept the same name, being similar in most of its beliefs.

Members of this group who came to Australia began the Free Reformed Church of Australia, adding the word "free" to differentiate themselves from the Reformed Church of Australia, which was related to the original Reformed Church of Holland.

The congregation in the church at Armadale started in 1951 with three families. There are similar churches in the United States, Canada, South Africa and Brazil.

This week an elder of the church, Jack van Leewen, an Armadale orchardist, emphasised that the members of the church tried to join in the Australian way of life. He said that the church was not a Dutch community and most of the members over 16 years of age had recently been naturalised.

They had their own church school and most other religions—which catered for children up to 12 years old. All the teaching was done in English, and there was only one hour a week spent talking in Dutch. Language was one of the difficulties for the older people. But they were learning quickly and at present had one service a month in English.

Because there was no minister at Armadale, the elders read to the congregation sermons sent from ministers at Albany and Launceston, Tasmania.

The church was not a killjoy as some people imagined, van Leewen said. They drank beer and would have a drink in a pub. But they were against spending the whole evening drinking in bars.

They celebrated parties at home, although they were against dancing, cinemas and gambling.

In Holland, where there were many unions, many members of all the Protestant churches belonged to the Christian National Trade Union.

This union had members from all trades, but acted with Christian principles in all disputes. Although other unions existed for each trade, there was no compulsory unionism and no preference given to union members.

ABOVE: One of several articles that appeared in the West Australian regarding the union issue.

BELOW: The newly constructed family home on Third Avenue, Kelmscott.

ABOVE: Cornelis Kleijn working in his piggery.

RIGHT: Cornelis and Willempje Kleijn in 1988.

ABOVE: Cornelis and Willempje Kleijn with their children, grandchildren and a great grandchild on their 50th Wedding Anniversary in 1986.

BELOW: A reunion of the three siblings in Australia 1994. From left, Cornelis, Lijsje and Marie.

ABOVE: Cornelis and Willempje Kleijn in front of their unit in the Fair Haven Retirement Village on their 60th wedding anniversary in 1996.

BELOW: The gravestone in Karrakatta cemetery.

jobs, but just found it too difficult to maintain focus. Boredom crept in very quickly. Factory work was just not for him. He then tried door-to-door selling, which was in vogue at the time. When he started with two suitcases full of clothes, he first visited all his friends and relations and had good sales. However, trying the same round some weeks later it was a different story. Then he tried selling other door-to-door products, but nothing seemed to give him a steady income. Success eluded him. Thoughts of migration were creeping back into his mind.

On the 30th September 1950 another healthy son was born whom they named Cornelis (Kees) after Dad. Now they had nine children to feed and clothe. They saw his birth as a great blessing from God, but at the same time Mum writes in her diary about the difficulty of making ends meet with a large family. She calculated her weekly costs should be around 100 guilders but with Dad, who at this time was working in a bakery again, only earning 42 guilders per week and with a weekly child endowment from the government of 20 guilders, the total income was far short of their needs. As a mother, who felt acutely responsible for ensuring the children could be fed and clothed every day, she started thinking that maybe migration needed to be seriously considered. She wrote in her diary:

> *During this period, we talked and thought a lot about migration. Many people are migrating because they see so little prospect for the future in Holland. There is massive unemployment as well as overcrowding. I had never given it any serious thought as it would be terrible for my Mother. But I have had to come to the realisation that with a large family it is so hard to earn*

the level of income that we require.

She had found the last twelve months extremely stressful. Nothing seemed to be working for them anymore. Had they made the wrong decision going into partnership with Blankestijn, an unbeliever, she asked herself, and was God now punishing them? She acknowledged that nothing happens by chance and that God visits his children with difficulties for their own good, to bring them closer to Him. This was how they both saw their current situation and they made a commitment to think carefully about any future planning. All future decisions needed to be prayerfully considered and made with the goal to serve God and to live to His glory and honour.

Jenny, my oldest sister, then 11, remembers this time well. Speaking to her in 2016 she said:

> *Money became increasingly tight. I was embarrassed with some of the things I had to wear. Knitted gloves made from old socks, for example. I could sense the stress in the family. We had the cabbage that was grown in our garden on the table every day. Once a week we had a bit of horse meat. I remember the vegetable vendor coming past the house and I begged Mum to buy something I saw on the cart – but, no, she couldn't afford it. Things were extremely tight.*

Brother Niek, 10 at the time, had similar recollections. Speaking to him in 2017 he said:

> *After Dad left the bakery, he tried all sorts of things – salesman, factory work – you could see he wasn't very happy. He didn't know what to do. Nothing was*

working out for him. I delivered papers for a while and was even going house to house for Dad, selling hair clips. At the end of the year Dad asked me to go past the clients, as was tradition, and to knock on their door and wish them a Happy New Year. They then give you a tip. As a child you had more chance to get a tip than Dad would. One year I collected 64 guilders. That was big money and was I proud when I could give that to Mum.

Shortly after Kees' birth in September 1950 Mum relented, albeit reluctantly, for Dad to make enquiries and investigate the possibility of migration.

33. Preparation and Departure

"Trust in the Lord with all your heart, and lean not on your own understanding: in all your ways acknowledge Him, and He shall direct your paths."

~Proverbs 3:5-6 (NKJV)

Once Dad got Mum's support for the idea of migration, he didn't waste any time to follow through to make enquires. The possibility of migrating had been on his mind now for over three years and his subsequent experience in work and business had not diminished his commitment for trying elsewhere. His preference was South Africa. He saw the advantages of a Christian country with a strong Dutch heritage as well as established Reformed Churches. However, on enquiry, after passing on information about his own experience and background, he was advised that he could not come into South Africa. More bakers were simply not needed there.

For the Dutch considering migration, Canada was by far the most popular destination. During the period from after the war to the end of 1949, already 16,000 Dutch citizens had moved to Canada. This compared to 5500 to South Africa, 9000 to the United States and only 2600 to Australia.[63] Some of the popularity for migrating to Canada can be attributed to the fact that Canadian forces had liberated the Netherlands from the war and many warm relationships had developed with many of them. They were seen as the people that came to their rescue in their hour of need. They also had extended hospitality to the Queen's daughter, Princess Juliana, and her family during the war when, for safety, it had been considered best for her to live outside of England where her mother was. So, Canada and the Canadians were relatively well-known and loved. Its geographic location was also closer to the Netherlands compared to that far-away continent, Australia.

My parents, though, considered Canada too cold. Dad had never enjoyed the Dutch winters, particularly when he had to be out in the weather in the early mornings delivering the milk. And it appeared that Canada was even colder than the Netherlands. So, Dad then focused his attention on Australia as the next option. Australia was seen as a land of growth and opportunity. Dad went to Arnhem, the largest city near where he lived, to make enquiries. A booklet Dad was given stated that there was a massive shortage of workers in every possible trade and industry and that nobody would have any trouble getting a job. There were over 100,000 registered job vacancies in Australia that needed to be filled. The country was underpopulated with only eight million people and was predicted to grow to 25 million.[64]

Security of employment was at the forefront of Dad's mind after his experiences over the last years. The high unemployment in the Netherlands was not easing and the prospects were still dismal. So, the information he was gathering gave him some hope that Australia might be the place to go to. But what about church? Already in April 1950, Canada had established the first Reformed Church and others were quickly following. However, there was no word on this from Australia. Prof. K. Schilder, writing in *De Reformatie,* warned potential migrants going to Australia about the need to be discerning about the churches they joined as many of the established churches in Australia were not following confessions and Scripture as the Reformed members were committed to doing. In the concluding paragraph, Prof. Schilder wrote:

> *Overall, you can see that migration often means that children are exposed to dangers that the parents, before their departure, just had no idea about.*

In April 1950 Mr. D. Bosveld from Velp, on the other side of Arnhem, advertised in *De Reformatie* about his intended migration to Australia. Dad contacted him and from then on, they corresponded regularly with each other. The Bosvelds, with 14 children arrived in Fremantle on the boat, *Johan van Oldenbarnevelt,* on the 4th October 1950. He was met there by the Slobbe family who had arrived in Australia some 18 months earlier, on the 13th January 1949. There were now in Perth, Western Australia, a known total of 21 adults and children who came from the Reformed Church (Liberated) in the Netherlands.

It didn't take long for them to conclude that they could not join an established church in Australia but would need to institute a Reformed Church (Liberated), based on the same confessions and Church Order that the church had espoused back in the Netherlands. Each Sunday they held services together, in the morning at Bosveld's place and in the afternoon at Slobbe's. After three months they decided it was time to formally institute a church in the Armadale area on the outskirts of Perth, Western Australia, where they both lived. They were confident more people would soon arrive and then there would be an instituted church to welcome them. So, on the 25th Dec 1950 the two families together formally instituted the Reformed Church of Armadale. Mr. D. Bosveld was nominated as the single elder.

They sent the notice of institution to all the addresses they had, including the Dutch Church media, migrants already living in Australia and to a number of Dutch Churches. It was hoped that this would stimulate interest in those thinking about migrating to Australia and to encourage them to move to the Armadale vicinity.

In the issue of *De Reformatie* of the 13th January 1951 the following notice appeared under the headline "Church Instituted in Australia":

> *On the 25th December 1950, after prayer and scripture reading of Isaiah 66 verses 1-13, the brothers Bosveld and Slobbe instituted the Church of Armadale. The necessity of this was explained by one of the brothers. There are no churches in Australia, according to the information gathered, where we could go and become members of. The Free Presbyterian is considered closest to us, but they now have contact with the church in the Netherlands that we have been liberated from. Truth and faithfulness do not change with distance, so we have found them to be not a friend, but an enemy instead.*
>
> *We cannot look at our small numbers but in faith we have instituted the Church that maintains the truth of Scripture and confessions as well as the Church order. Because we desire to be the Church of our Lord Jesus*

> *Christ in Australia, we propose to hold the services in the language of the country. We have adopted the name Reformed Church of Armadale. Brother Bosveld has been chosen as elder.*
> *Correspondence address:*
> *Mr. A. Slobbe*
> *Mr. D. Bosveld*
> *P.O. Armadale, West-Australia.*

This confirmation of a church in Australia was just what my parents had been waiting for. Furthermore, the letters they were receiving from the Bosvelds were so positive and encouraging. They loved living in Australia and would never consider going back to the Netherlands. With their large family, they had no problem making ends meet; and, for both Mr. Bosveld and the older children, there was no shortage of work. They offered to help in whatever way they could, including making sure there was a house available when my parents arrived in Australia. Mum started corresponding with Mrs. Bosveld who filled in more information about family life and the general style of living.

All this gave, particularly to Mum, a lot of encouragement. So much so, that she came to strongly defend and back Dad's interest to migrate. She had heard a lot of criticism voiced by many members of the family, including her own Mum and her husband's two sisters. From then on she became very vocal in justifying their decision. Some of her letters that have survived from that period clearly reflect that. On the 25th March 1951 Mum wrote to Dad's sister, Marie, who was working as a midwife in Indonesia and who had indicated to my parents her objection to them migrating. Mum wrote:

> *We totally disagree with your objections. The Lord guides our paths and if we are obedient to His Word, we can be assured that He will not desert us even if we live in another country. After all, the whole world is the Lord's. If Kees [my Dad] can't fulfil his calling here in being able to care for and support his family, then surely we cannot just ignore that and so eventually just rely on charity. He is currently still working with a baker but that is only temporary and there is no other work here for someone who is nearing 40. Holland is too overcrowded and that is why people have to migrate. We have contact with people from Velp who have moved to Australia and those people write to us to say just come here, we will help you with everything including housing. Is that not a sign that God is busy with us to prepare a place for us there? They are people of the same faith and there is already a church instituted there.*

Some family members remained convinced that migration was the wrong thing for my parents to undertake, but most accepted it as inevitable. Especially after my parents were getting such positive news about the growth of the church in Armadale and the offers of support from the Bosveld family. Already in June 1951 Mr. Bosveld had secured a house for when they would eventually arrive. The house plan was shared amongst the family and they all agreed it seemed a spacious house, but it lacked an attic which was a feature of virtually every house in the Netherlands.

Six months after the institution of the Reformed Church of Armadale, the membership had already grown to more than 60 from just 21 in December 1950. It was decided to increase the consistory by one elder and a deacon. This led to the ordination of Mr. H. Terpstra as elder and Mr. A. Slobbe as deacon on 24th June 1951. They joined with the previously appointed elder Mr. D. Bosveld to form the consistory of now three members.

Two months later, on the 12th of August the Reformed Church of Armadale extended a call to Rev. G. Janssen who was serving the Reformed Church of Leeuwarden in the Netherlands. While he was unable to accept the call, it nevertheless demonstrated the commitment of the Armadale church members to have a pastor and teacher and their desire to be led.

In the period since the institution in December 1950, my parents had been busy getting all the formalities and required approvals for their big move. It involved getting passports, passing health checks, booking tickets for the boat, selling their house, organising and packing the container and then disposing of all the excess goods that they could not take with them.

Mum wrote in her diary that it was 18 months of uncertainty and tension, as they didn't get their final approval until just two weeks before their impending departure. Initially, they had booked to leave in April 1952 but during scheduled health checks in The Hague in January three of the children came down with jaundice, so it had to be cancelled. Their departure was rescheduled to a month later but then it took another two months for the health results and final approvals to come through. What a relief! If they had missed the boat in May, they would have had to wait another 12 months as Mum was six months pregnant on the proposed departure date on 9th May 1952. Any time later and she would not be allowed to travel.

Settling all the financial affairs and paying for all the costs associated with the trip proved no easy task for my parents.

PREPARATION AND DEPARTURE

The bakery partnership had been such a disaster. Even after settling all their affairs they were still short of money and had to borrow some additional funds from Dad's sister to settle everything. So, from a privileged youth and the recipient of a substantial inheritance at 21, Dad, at 39, was on his way to Australia with no money except that little bit he had borrowed from his sister to assist him until he had found work and income in Australia. My parents, however, still considered themselves blessed, with nine healthy children and the opportunity to start a new life in a new country.

They also left behind them the tragic events surrounding Dad's parents. In the Netherlands, the issue was hard to avoid and was spoken about often, especially in Brandwijk where the events took place. My parents had always been concerned about the stigma surrounding the situation and the effect this would possibly have on their children. Up to the time of migration, they had only confided to Jenny the true situation regarding the demise of Dad's parents. Jenny, as a young 12-year-old girl, had reacted in shock and had for a while displayed a fear of Dad. The horror of it all was just too much to absorb for such a young girl. Now, as they were leaving the shores of the Netherlands my parents made a conscious decision to put the tragic event behind them and not to share it with any of their children. They hoped that by living far away in Australia their children would be protected. They would not have to cope with being connected to such an emotional and sad event or suffer from any possible stigma resulting from it.

The final departure and farewells were not easy, as can be expected. Australia was a long way away and through the eyes of people in 1952 it appeared unlikely that they would ever see each other again. Beside the bonds of family, they had developed strong friendships in the small Oosterbeek church where they worshipped. These farewells were difficult and emotional. In the district Church paper of the Reformed Churches dated 3rd May 1952 it was reported under the heading "Immigration":

> *Shortly, on the 9th May Brother and Sister Kleijn with their nine children plan to leave on a boat to faraway Australia. This is for our small church a big loss. After the Church service on Sunday evening, members stayed together for a final farewell. The chairman of Consistory, brother G. Bouwmeester, speaking on behalf of the congregation, gave the departing family words of encouragement and farewell. The congregation was then asked to stand and sing for them Psalm 121 verse 4:*
> > *All evil strikes at you in vain;*
> > *The Lord will keep your life*
> > *Secure in woes and strife.*
> > *When you go out, when you come in*
> > *The Lord will fail you never*
> > *But keep you safe forever.*
>
> *After the singing, the Chairman presented to the family Kleijn a book authored by Professor Holwerda. Brother Blokhuis was then invited to also speak a few words to the departing family. He expressed the wish that they may experience the Lord's rich blessings in their new country. Members were then all given an opportunity to personally wish the immigrating family best wishes and farewells.*

During the last week in the Netherlands my parents, with a few of the younger children, stayed at Mum's parents' place, the Schuttes in Brandwijk. They would not be seeing the family off at the boat in Amsterdam, so the farewells were made at their home. Mum's Dad was 76, her Mum 74 - both elderly and realistic about not seeing each other again on this earth. Mum wrote that, while it was a very memorable time, words could not describe the pains of the farewell. Particularly with her mum she had a very close bond. They would faithfully correspond to each other every week until her death in 1957. None of these letters have survived as Mum considered them too personal and made a point to destroy them all decades later when she moved into the Fair Haven Retirement Village.

At the boat to farewell them were Dad's two sisters, Marie and Lijsje, as well as two of Mum's sisters and two of her brothers. The night before they had all stayed in Sliedrecht at Mum's youngest sister Sijgje's place, where friends and family all had the opportunity to bid their farewells. While some family members still had difficulty accepting my parents migrating, they all went out of their way to extend to them their best wishes and God's blessings in their new country. Dad's sister, Marie, who had spent several years in Indonesia, had come back from Indonesia on the boat, *Johan van Oldenbarnevelt*, the same boat my family were sailing to Australia on. She had timed her return so she could still meet and say farewell.

My older siblings were not so much affected by all the emotion of the farewells and were excited about the prospect of going on a boat to another country. Niek related in 2017: "We just couldn't wait to get on the boat. We were so excited." Jenny also saw it as one great adventure and even made up a poem which she set to music and sang many times. Speaking about it in 2017 she now cringes at the thought of how insensitive she must have been to my parents' emotions. Here she was singing at the top of her voice about the joy of going to Australia while my parents and, particularly Mum, was trying to come to terms with the impending final farewells.

Jenny's song compiled just before departure:

> *We are going to Australia!*
> *O, that will be a long journey.*
> *We are not going to Canada,*
> *But heading away from the Atlantic Ocean.*
>
> *Oh what Joy! O what Joy!*
> *That we in our young youth*
> *May with Dad and Mum*
> *Go to Australia.*
>
> *Packing we do all day long.*
> *Till the evening when we are exhausted.*
> *But in the morning, we start again with new energy*
> *And continue the whole day through.*
>
> *School we have already left*
> *For learning is not now a priority*
> *Australia is now number one*
> *And we want to make sure that remains.*
>
> *Finally, we can begin the long journey.*
> *We have said our farewells to all the family*
> *Waving goodbye as we leave the shores*
> *For we are so, so happy.*
>
> *We all enjoy good health.*
> *As we leave the Dutch soil*

With eleven of us we stand on deck
To leave our native lands.

The Netherlands receives our final farewell
That will be accepted with gratitude
And we hope that our native lands
Will remain in our thoughts and minds.

We now have English to learn
That we will certainly not try to avoid.
But first we will sing with feeling
The Wilhelmus van Nassau.

Original Dutch wording

Wij gaan naar Australia
O, wat is het een lange tocht.
Wij gaan niet naar Canada,
Maar om de Atlantishe bocht

Oh, wat vreugd, O wat vreugd!
Dat wij in ons jonge jeugd,
Met mijn vader en mijn moe,
Gaan wij naar Australia toe.

Inpakken, doen wij de ganse dag,
s'Avonds zijn wij t'al weer zat.
s'Morgens beginnen we met nieuwe moed.
Zo zijn wij de hele dag weer zoet.

School hebben wij al afgezet,
Want nu leren is geen pret.

Australia, staat bovenaan.
En dat laten wij niet ontgaan.

Eindelijk beginnen we de lange tocht.
De familie hebben wij al opgezocht.
Zwaaien komt er ook nog bij,
Want wij zijn, wij zijn zo blij.

Wij zijn allemaal gezond.
En verlaten Neerland's grond.
Met z'n elven staan w'aan t'strand.
En verlaten ons Vaderland.

Nederland krijgt de laatste groet,
Dat doet Neerland heus wel goed.
En dat Nederland getrouw
Ook nog aan ons denken zou.

Wij moeten ook nog Engels leren
En dat gaan wij heus proberen.
Maar eerst zingen wij getrouw
Het 'Wilhelmus van Nassau.'

The *Johan van Oldenbarnevelt* sailed out of Amsterdam harbour on Friday the 9th May 1952. Dad was 39, Mum 37 and their children were: Peter 14, Jenny 13, Niek 11, Janet 10, Mappie 8, Harry 6, Mieke 4, Willy 3 and Kees 18 months. They moved into two cabins on the boat – a six berth and a four berth - one for the females and one for the males.

34. On the Ocean

Those who go down to the sea in ships,
Who do business on great waters,
They see the works of the Lord,
And His wonders in the deep.
For He commands and raises the stormy wind,
Which lifts up the waves of the sea.
They mount up to the heavens.
They go down again to the depths.
Their soul melts because of trouble.
They reel to and fro, and stagger like a drunken man.
And are at their wits' end.
Then they cry out to the Lord in their trouble.
And He brings them out of their distresses.
He calms the storm
So that its waves are still.
Then they are glad because they are quiet;
So He guides them to their desired haven.
Oh, that men would give thanks to the Lord for His goodness,
And for His wonderful works to the children of men!

~Psalm 107:23-31(NKJV)

When my parents migrated to Australia in 1952, they joined a record number of Dutch citizens doing the same thing that year – leaving the Netherlands to find a better future elsewhere. Nearly 50,000 people left the Netherlands in 1952, of which 15,000 went to Australia. This compares with 37,000 Dutch citizens leaving the Netherlands the year earlier, in 1951, and 38,000 leaving the following year in 1953. They all went with the blessing of the Dutch Government which was proactive in encouraging its citizens to leave the country for better economical climates. They had set up offices across the nation to assist potential migrants with information and, in many cases, with subsidies as well. The Dutch Government also had to ensure that once a Dutch citizen wanted to migrate there was the transport available to do so.

To that end, the Dutch Government set about converting troop carriers to service the route to Australia. In 1948 the *Volendam* and the *Sibajak* were commissioned for this purpose. Then, in 1950, the Dutch Government chartered the *Johan Van Oldenbarnevelt* on which our family embarked on the 9th May 1952. This ship, over its faithful years of service till 1963, is estimated to have transported in excess of 50,000 Dutch citizens to Australia. Between 1940 to 1963 it made a total of 44 voyages from Amsterdam to Australia, docking in Fremantle, Melbourne and Sydney.[65]

Constructed in 1929, she was then the largest diesel-powered liner ever constructed in the Netherlands. Initially, she plied the seas between Indonesia and the Netherlands and had a capacity of 770 passengers travelling in four classes. Before the Dutch Government chartered the liner in 1950, she was converted to a one class liner with capacity to carry 1400 passengers. The *Johan van Oldenbarnevelt* was considered far more comfortable to travel on than either the *Volendam* or the

Sibajak and also had a reputation of providing excellent facilities and food. For its Dutch passengers, who had left a country where for many food had been scarce, the meals served on the ship were considered to be an absolute luxury.[66]

My parents were also struck by the size and the range of facilities available. Mum wrote in her diary:

> *The Johan van Oldenbarnevelt was an amazing sight. I had never seen anything like it... There was a large washing facility for us to use, with hot and cold water, wringers and separate ironing rooms with electric irons. Also, separate bathrooms, with a special baby section, as well as a swimming pool, a sport deck and more. Every cabin had a small table and a few chairs as well as cupboards for storage. It was all beyond my imagination.*

There were also good facilities to keep children occupied. There were three areas for children of different age groups to play: 0-3, 4-8 and 9-11. These areas had special playground equipment to suit the respective ages as well as staff to supervise and care for the children between the hours of 8 a.m. to 7 p.m. Parents did have to take responsibility for taking their children in to the dining room for mealtimes but, otherwise, they could relax and leave the care of the children to the crew.

Initially, Mum had hopes of having a relaxing time with everything virtually provided for, including meals in the dining room and cabin service. No doubt, after 18 months of stress and uncertainty as well as having just gone through the emotions of farewelling parents, siblings and friends she would have been physically and mentally exhausted and was now looking forward to a period of rest.

However, within a few days she was struck with sea sickness which progressively got worse. She had to seek help from the ship doctor and was, especially during the last two weeks of the journey, confined to her bed. In a 2017 interview, Niek didn't recall Mum ever leaving her room. "Dad used to take us to meals each time," he said. "We would get together first in the six-berth cabin where Dad would lead in devotions before we went to have our meal in the dining hall. But Mum never joined us there."

Jenny has similar recollections. At 13 years of age, and being the eldest daughter, she was kept busy looking after the children, changing nappies, cleaning up after vomiting from seasickness and so on, as Mum was seasick all the time. Jenny had been so looking forward to this great adventure but then got no time to enjoy herself at all. She has memories of just being busy for the whole four weeks of the journey.

The older boys, on the other hand, could move at will across the whole ship and had a great time. Niek, who at 11 was supposed to be in his designated children's area, quickly decided that this was not for him. He made out as if he was 12 and no longer qualified to be there. He loved having the full run of the ship, exploring and meeting new friends. All my older siblings also remember the delicious food served up for each meal. After the very standard fare of cabbage, potatoes and an occasional bit of horse meat that they had been getting at home, the variety and the amount of food they had on the ship was for them a feast every time.

Also on the ship was one other family from the Reformed Church (Liberated), Mr. and Mrs. Bijl with five children. The Bijls came from Pernis, just south of Rotterdam and were also going to Armadale. Aware of each other's presence through the church media, they sought each other out soon after embarking.

This initial meeting and sharing the boat trip together was to lead to a lifelong friendship. On Sundays they worshipped together, reading sermons in one of their cabin rooms. Many other times during the voyage, if they weren't struck down by seasickness, they would seek out each other's company.

As for the journey itself, after the first day at sea, the ship stopped at IJmuiden for loading final supplies and then crossed the English Channel to stop at Dover. Crossing the channel, the family already got the first taste of ocean sailing with the rocking ship and inevitable seasickness. Leaving Dover, the next day, and crossing the Gulf of Biscay the seas were even rougher and more than 50 per cent of the passengers, including most of our family, suffered seasickness. It was only day four and not an encouraging start to a four-week trip.

From the Gulf of Biscay, the ship passed the most western point of Spain, Cape Finisterre and then on past Cape Saint Vincent, the most southern part of Portugal. There was some beautiful scenic coastline on this route and every time something special was spotted an announcement would be made over the ship's loudspeaker to give everyone an opportunity to see these marvellous sights. Once the ship turned into the Mediterranean Sea, the weather seemed calmer and, for a number of days, there was some respite from seasickness so the family could enjoy the scenery as well as the food again. The coastline of Algeria and Tunisia was also a sight to behold. It appears that the ship kept fairly close to the coast, as the land was clearly visible.

Ten days after departing, on the 19th May, the ship pulled up at Port Said. Passengers were given an opportunity to disembark for the day and explore the town. It was also an opportunity to post any letters or cards to loved ones. Mum took the opportunity to send a card to her family and no doubt also some letters, but they have not survived. Her card reads:

> *Dear family. How are you all? We are doing well here. Sunday, we suffered from seasickness but by Monday we were already a lot better. The boat is excellent. The food and service is just fantastic. We have just passed the Island of Malta. A beautiful sight. We have met some good friends on board - the family Bijl from Pernis. They are also going to Armadale. We have held a Church Service together. Well folks – best wishes and greetings from Kees, Wim and Children.*

At Port Said the ship was surrounded by merchants in their little row boats, trying to sell their wares to the passengers. It was a noisy and colourful sight with a lot of yelling, gesturing and bargaining going on. Once an agreement had been made to purchase, money would be placed in a small tin and passed down via ropes to the seller. The seller would then tie the product purchased to the rope that was then pulled up by the buyer. Despite all the chaos there was a lot of exchange going on.

Dad decided to go ashore with some of the older children. Jenny went with him and despite her general recollections of the voyage being so negative, having to be busy all the time, she remembers this day out with Dad with a lot of fondness. "It was so much fun, and Dad was also so happy and enjoying himself that day," she said in 2017. "It was a real adventure in that strange country with all those strangely dressed people."

The next day the ship passed through the Suez Canal and into the Red Sea where it passed Mount Sinai. It was becoming extremely hot and uncomfortable. With no air-conditioning on board all the fans were on full blast to try and provide relief.

On the 23rd May, 14 days into the journey, the ship stopped at Aden, Yemen, where again passengers had the opportunity to disembark. It was still very hot and uncomfortable; the place didn't look attractive and the ship had arrived towards the evening, so it meant going out at night in the dark. Dad decided to stay on board and not avail himself of the opportunity.

After Aden the ship pointed into the Indian Ocean with the next stop being Fremantle, Western Australia. Two days into the Indian Ocean the passengers were warned of forceful winds and rough conditions. The ship lurched and plunged all day long. Not many escaped seasickness.

The lurching of the ship caused the food to slide off the tables at dinner time. Nothing was stable. This went on for a few days and then, despite the severity of the storm having passed, the ship nevertheless continued its constant rocking and rolling with the waves in the open sea. Mum was now totally bedridden and quite ill, not being able to eat. The doctor put her on a special diet and had even suggested she might have the baby there. How they looked forward to stepping on land again. Each day became a countdown to the longed-for destination.

Finally, four weeks after leaving Amsterdam, on the 6th June 1952, the *Johan van Oldenbarnevelt* docked at Fremantle wharf. What joy! Simply to be able to step on solid ground and not have that constant movement of the ship under you. Mum felt immediately better when on shore. They were warmly welcomed by members of the Armadale Reformed Church and everything was organised for them. Temporary accommodation had been arranged for the entire family until such time that the container could be taken off the ship and delivered to the house that had been rented for them to move into. It was anticipated that this would take about a week.

35. Australia in 1952

"We must populate or perish. We must fill this country or lose it."
~Arthur Calwell,
Foreign Immigration Minister, 1945-1949

My parents arrived at Fremantle in June 1952 at a time when the Australian Government was making it very clear in Australia and abroad that migrants were most welcome. While the Dutch Government was intent on encouraging as many of its citizens as possible to emigrate elsewhere, the Australian Government, after the war, was driven by the slogan, "Populate or Perish," developed by the first Minister of Immigration, Arthur Calwell. The 1942 Japanese bombing of Darwin and Broome, and the imminent threat of invasion by the Japanese, had reignited the age-old fear by the Australians of the 'Yellow Peril'.

While the war with Japan was over and won, in the 1950s there still remained an acute sense of insecurity and fear of the 'Asian Hordes'. Calwell verbalised these sentiments when he said in one of his most renowned ministerial speeches:

> *We must populate or perish. We must fill this country or lose it. We need to protect ourselves from the yellow peril from the north. Our current population of*

> *7,391,000 (about one person per square mile) leaves a land as vast as Australia unprotected.*[67]

In August 1948, Calwell, as Immigration Minister, had written a letter to the media where he spelled out his views on the need for migration:

> *I want 20 million people in Australia. And I want them in my lifetime. At present we only have seven and a half million – less than the population of greater London – spread over a continent as big as the United States of America. The way I look at it is that, if we do not populate Australia quickly with people of our own British stock and Europeans of our choice, we may get 20 million sooner than we think, 20 million invaders. And another light will have gone out in the British Commonwealth. We are grimly determined that this will not happen...*
> *We need more people because:*
> *Australia must be strengthened if she is to continue as a stronghold of British democracy down under where the wide Pacific meets the Indian Ocean.*
> *The enormous untapped resources of our Island continent must be developed for the good of the British Commonwealth of Nations as a whole.*
> *We cannot preserve Australia as an exclusive paradise for the lucky few, while the Asian continent, which sits on our northern doorstep, teems and overflows with people hungry for living space. If the British will not help to fill up Australia, other and nearer races will - and by force.*[68]

While Calwell was Immigration Minister for only just over four years – from July 1945 to December 1949 - he laid the groundwork for Australia's post war migration that was to radically transform Australia. Calwell had been working on developing a blueprint for immigration already since 1942, shortly after the Japanese bombed Darwin. He was passionate about the need for Australia to grow its population as a matter of urgency, so when he was appointed as Australia's first Immigration Minister in 1945 he immediately began implementing his vision of welcoming newcomers not only from Britain but from continental Europe as well.[69] He was a strong supporter of the White Australia policy and the need to ensure migrants integrated into society. So, no Asians or Africans were allowed entry but, he said, "people of our own British Stock and Europeans of our choice."[70]

Besides the British, whom he hoped would represent most migrants, he specifically mentioned the Americans, Baltics, Dutch and Polish as the most favoured migrants. In the six years between the end of the war and 1951, Australia welcomed 590,000 new migrants, of which 22,000 came from the Netherlands. In 1952, the year my parents arrived, a further 128,000 arrived, which included 15,800 Dutch migrants. In the 1961 census there were 102,000 Dutch born citizens in Australia, representing 5.7% of the total number of Australian citizens born overseas, which was then 1.77 million. The total population of Australia had grown to 10.5 million, from 7.5 million in the 1947 census.[71]

As can be gleaned from Calwell's comments, he was loyal to the British and saw Australia as squarely part of the British Commonwealth. After all, some 95% of all white people living in Australia at that time were descended from the British Isles. In the 1947 census, less than 2% of the population came from other countries like Italy, Germany, Greece, Poland, America, China, Japan and India. Australia and all its institutions were very British. From a population that nearly all originated from the Mother country England until the late 1940s, Australia now had to cope with the influx of thousands of migrants from different cultures, languages and experiences as well as having different loyalties. Many came to Australia driven by economic necessity or as refugees from their own country, and they came to a country where they were now part of the British Commonwealth and where the Queen of England was the Head of State.

For many migrants this took some getting used to. They were still loyal to their old country, which might even have had a history of wars with England. My parents, particularly my mother, remained very loyal to the Dutch Queen who had meant so much to them during the war years. The Dutch historically had never developed a close association with England and had over the centuries even competed and fought over some of its colonies and trade routes.

Fresh in their memory, too, were the Boer Wars (early 1900s), which remained a point of contention, with many Dutch citizens taking the Boer's side. Australia had enthusiastically supported the English and some 16,000 volunteered to go and fight there with them against the Boers. The Dutch saw this whole affair as driven by imperialistic English greed and claimed it was the English that introduced to the world the first concentration camps where a total of 27,927 Boers had died – 4177 women, 22,074 children and 1676 men. It was a terrible affair that affected both the Boers and the Dutch for generations.[72]

Now these thousands of new migrants, with their varying loyalties, needed to learn the intricacies of the English language, express loyalty to the Queen of England and embrace everything British. This was not always easy, and many hung on to their old traditions and language while at the same time integrating as best they could. However, migrants from the same countries did often seek solace in each other's company. This led to the formation of many clubs, be it German, Dutch, Italian, Greek and others which became popular meeting places, as well as providing support and encouragement. It was also a place where they could maintain their culture with foods, song and dance.

When my family arrived in June 1952 at Fremantle to settle in Western Australia, the State had a population of only 600,000, with 330,000 living in the Perth Metropolitan area. The economy predominantly relied on sheep, beef and wheat farmers, with the mining sector dominated by gold. Forty five percent of the state's population lived outside the Perth Metropolitan area. Kalgoorlie was by far the biggest city outside Perth, with a population of 22,000. Bunbury came next in size with a population of just 10,000.

With more than 12 million sheep, the state's economy was said to be riding on the sheep's back. Wool far exceeded any other commodity in export value to the state, with wheat coming in second and gold third. Pastoralists also made a substantial contribution to the welfare of the State. The total cattle population was 850,000.

Trams were then operating in the Perth streets and remained till 1958. Perth had not experienced a building boom since the late 1800s and early 1900s, so most buildings dated from these gold rush days. The building boom of the 1960s was yet to come. The tallest structure, the MLC building, was 10 storeys high.

Our family moved into the Shire of Armadale-Kelmscott, 35

kilometres south of Perth. Mr. Daan Bosveld had secured a house for our family on Abernethy Road, Byford. The Shire at the time consisted of the towns of Armadale, Kelmscott, Byford, Roleystone, Bedfordale and Karragullen and had a total population of about 5000 people living in some 1400 homes spread across this vast district.[73] Armadale had over recent years become the main commercial centre for the district, overtaking Kelmscott which had prized that role in the earlier years of settlement.

The Armadale township had developed and flourished particularly after the Armadale railway station had opened in 1897. Jull Street, initially just a track that connected the railway station with the Narrogin Inn, became the main street along which retail shops and businesses developed.[74] By the 1950s the main enterprises were comprised of: the Railway Hotel located opposite the Railway station on the north side of Jull Street, Blackburn's Bakery, the Chemist operated by Mr. D. Morgan, Armadale Electrics, and, on the corner of Jull Street and Third Road, the Bank of NSW. On the other side, opposite the railway station, was the Post Office, Harrison's General Store, the Doctor's surgery, Armadale Butchers, the Newsagent on the corner of Third Avenue and, on the opposite corner, the Armadale Kelmscott Co-op.[75]

It was a typical small country town that provided most of the necessary needs of its residents. Only occasionally would one venture all the way to Perth to buy something special, like a complete clothing outfit or furniture. It was also a town that was so small that practically everyone knew each other and where most had British background.

The weekly paper, The South West Advertiser, covered the district all the way from Victoria Park down to Mandurah and Pinjarra and, in it, each district was allocated space for its own local news. Armadale had its own allocated page and here the local reporter would cover all the personal and shire events of the previous week. If someone from Armadale was taking a holiday, even to Mandurah, it was reported on. The local teacher, Miss Turner, boarded a cruise ship to England in 1951 for a six-month holiday and her farewell was an occasion that got extensive coverage in the newspaper. It was considered a big event to take a trip back to Mother England in 1951 and the whole town would be informed of the occasion.[76]

The Armadale residents were proud of the historic luxury accommodation that the Narrogin Inn provided and the newspaper would regularly list all the guests that had stayed there during the previous period. Many came from the Perth suburbs of Peppermint Grove, Dalkeith and Wembley as well as some from overseas. It was considered a place of choice by the wealthy.

The Armadale town centre and the Narrogin Inn, located on the foothills of the Darling Ranges, provided a picturesque setting, particularly in springtime when the area would explode into a proliferation of beautiful and colourful wildflowers. In addition to the natural scenic landscape, large sections of the slopes of the Darling Ranges were covered with grapevines as major wineries had been established there. On the flat areas of Armadale, about five kilometers east of the Darling Ranges, orchards and gardens had been developed. The soils proved perfect for horticulture and gardens and so the Armadale district morphed into a food bowl for the State. All this added to the beauty and attractiveness of the district.

With the extensive clay deposits in the district, two major brickworks had been built in the Shire, the Armadale State Brickworks and the Cardup Brickworks. Combined, these two brickworks provided the bulk of Perth's brick needs and was by far the largest employer in the Armadale district.

It was into this small well-established Armadale community that Dutch migrants started arriving in large numbers during the 1950s. With little knowledge of the English language and mostly limited financial resources they moved, many with large families, into any home that was available. For the largely British-born Armadale residents, it was a completely new experience for them to welcome people from another country with another language and culture to their district.

What was happening in Armadale was occuring across all of Australia in the 1950s as migrants from all over Europe poured into Australia. What was unique in Armadale was that the migrants who came were predominantly Dutch, drawn there because the Slobbe and Bosveld families had instituted the Reformed Church of Armadale and had gone out of their way to make that known amongst people from the same denomination in the Netherlands. Many considering migrating in the Netherlands then chose Armadale as their preferred destination.

36. The First Days in Australia

*"Behold, how good and how pleasant it is
for brethren to dwell together in unity."*
~Psalm 133:1 (NKJV)

By the time my family arrived in Australia on Friday the 6th June 1952, members of the Reformed Church of Armadale had been proactive in both assisting potential migrants with information as well as extending a warm welcome and hospitality to those arriving. On the 10th January 1952 an Immigration Committee was formally instituted to ensure that a structure of support was put in place and that the work, as well as the costs, were borne by the whole congregation.

Before the institution of this committee, the Slobbe and Bosveld families, as the first migrants, had undertaken what was necessary to welcome new migrants, including the paying of rent for houses so that accommodation could be guaranteed. A year before we arrived, in June 1951, Mr. Bosveld had located and secured a suitable house for when we arrived.

Up until the formation of the Immigration Committee, the Slobbe and Bosveld families had outlaid 74 pounds in rent for migrant families. In today's economy that equates to nearly $3000 and, considering the weekly salary was about twelve pounds then, it was quite a commitment and outlay by the two families. However, they were determined to make sure that

Reformed people from the Netherlands would find a welcoming and supportive church community.[77]

Access to housing on arrival was essential if a family wished to move to a specific location. If no guarantee of a fixed address was obtained by potential immigrants, and if they still wished to migrate, they would then end up at one of the Government run hostels set up for that purpose. In that case, they had no choice of where to live, plus the conditions at the camps were very basic and the environment, with different nationalities placed together, was quite challenging.

At the first Immigration Committee meeting, held on the 10th January 1952, it was agreed that members of the Reformed Church of Armadale would be asked to contribute six shillings a month to the committee's work. It was also agreed that the Slobbe and Bosveld families would, in time, be reimbursed for the 74 pounds they had spent. Furthermore, it was decided to continue advertising in the Dutch church papers and encourage prospective emigrants to consider Armadale as their destination.[78]

A week before our family and the Bijl family was expected, the Immigration Committee met on Friday the 30th May to make final arrangements. Housing was finalised, arrangements were put in place to hire a bus to pick up the arrivals and a contractor was engaged to transport the luggage. The luggage of migrants that was packed in containers would not be accessible until a few days after the ship's berth. Until that was transported to their respective homes and unpacked, the immigrating families needed to be temporarily billeted out. Arrangements for this were put in place. Mr. Terpstra and Mr. van Leeuwen agreed to represent the Immigration Committee at the arrival of the new migrants in Fremantle.

And so it was that we and the Bijl family were welcomed by

Mr. Terpstra and Mr. van Leeuwen, together with a number of other members of the Reformed Church of Armadale, and transported to Armadale on the hired bus.

Mum was overwhelmed by the welcome and the hospitality extended to them. Everything was organised. They did not have to worry about anything. The bus dropped them off at van Leeuwen's place on Thomas Road, Armadale, where they enjoyed tea and refreshments and from where the whole family was billeted out to various addresses. Some of us stayed with the Terpstra family on Orton Road while others stayed with the Berkelaar family, who lived in the migrant house known as Fallon's Place, on Rowley Road. The de Vos and Visser families also lived in the same house. This migrant house was rented by the Immigration Committee as a temporary abode for families who did not, on arrival, have a permanent place. Mum, Dad and the three youngest children stayed with the Heerema family who lived within walking distance from the van Leeuwen family, where they had all been dropped off.

At long last, everyone was dispersed to their allocated place and Mum and Dad could settle down to spend a few days with the Heerema family until their container arrived. How they enjoyed being on land again, how beautiful and spacious the country looked and how wonderful to be so warmly welcomed by brothers and sisters of the same faith. They were now in a new country, far away from Holland and family, but nevertheless, they felt so at home with this welcoming and hospitable family.

The Heerema family had seven children, with one - eight-year-old Jacob - being seriously ill. They had also arrived on the *Johan van Oldenbarnevelt* some months earlier, in February 1952. Already on arrival, Jacob had suffered from severe earaches, which had become progressively worse.

Eventually, he was hospitalised and diagnosed with a severe form of meningitis which led to him losing his eyesight. It was a long and painful journey to recovery for Jacob, who spent nearly 18 months in Perth's Princess Margaret Hospital. During those 18 months, Mrs. Heerema visited him every day, travelling all the way from their home on Thomas Road to Perth. She would hitchhike to the Armadale train station to catch a train to Perth, from where she then had to catch a bus to take her to the hospital.

So, while my parents were enjoying their hospitality, Mrs. Heerema would be away during the day to visit her son. However, as Mum wrote in her diary, she would be home in the evenings where they would all sit and chat in the lounge around a cozy, open fire. On their first day, a Saturday, Mum wrote her first letter to her mum, as well as receiving her first letter. This was to become a weekly routine for both of them. That first day, they also received a visit from some church youth which Mum describes as a lively and excited group. Despite being winter, the sun was out and Mum wrote about sitting outside all day, enjoying the sun. Only towards the evening did it get colder, so she then moved back inside. She soaked in the beautiful quiet surrounds, the nature and the mild winter weather.

Being a Saturday and their first day in Australia, church attendance the next day was at the forefront of my parents' minds. Mum was seven months pregnant and not in a position to either walk or bike. She needed someone to drive her and from their information, Mr. Bosveld was the only one in the congregation who had a motor vehicle. Church services for the Reformed people were then being held in a small 70-seat capacity church owned by the Armadale Congregational Church, located on the corner of Wungong and Rowley Roads in Armadale. It was about 12 kilometers from the Heerema residence.

This small weather-board, tin roof church was built in 1913 by the local Congregational community, but had for some years not been used for Sunday services. When the group of Dutch Reformed people in the district became too large to have their services in one of the migrant houses, they had approached the local leader and caretaker of the Congregational Church, Mr. Murray, to see if they might be able to rent the building. This was agreed to, so, from Sunday the 6th May 1951, the Reformed Church of Armadale conducted its services there twice every Sunday.[79]

However, the Congregational Union had other ideas for the building and had been making plans to transport it to another location. This set off a wave of protests from the local Wungong residents who considered it their building, as they had both paid for it and built it. They organised a petition and got 107 signatures, including many from the Dutch migrants who had an interest in using the church every week. The Congregational Union strongly objected to the Dutch signing the petition as they "acknowledge no affiliation with the Congregational denomination and gave little evidence of any desire to join in worship of the district in general."

The Wungong District Progress Association met to discuss this response from the Congregational Union. The South Western Advertiser reported on this meeting:

> *The Association considered the Dutch Community has every right to participate in the petition, more especially as the Congregational Union rents them the church to hold services in their own language because they have not yet assimilated sufficient English to*

> *combine their services with those of the English speaking residents, but had agreed to cooperate with the committee...The Union was asked to accept the names of the Dutch community as parties to the petition. Mr. F.J. Newman informed the meeting of discussions he had had with representatives of the Dutch community who had intimated their willingness to cooperate in every way for the benefit of the district. Mr. Newman said he felt that these people would be a great acquisition to the district when they had mastered the English language.*[80]

The Association met again a month later, when they tabled correspondence from the Congregational Union which said that they had decided to leave the building as it was for the time being. It was a victory for the local community and, also, for the Dutch community, who could continue to use the Church for Sunday services. At that meeting, held on the 3rd June 1952, the president Mr. Franklin welcomed three Dutch members present.[81] We arrived three days later so, by that time, there was no longer any uncertainty about the Sunday worship services continuing in the Wungong Church.

However, for Mum to be able to attend, Dad had to bike to Mr. Bosveld to ask whether he would be willing to pick up Mum the next day and take her to church. The Bosvelds lived on what was then North-South Road No. 1, now known as Hopkinson Road. They were located close to the Rowley Road intersection. Dad was looking forward to catching up with the Bosvelds as they had been corresponding with them for several years, and it was due to them that they had decided to come to Armadale. Dad took a Bible with him which he had purchased for Mr. Bosveld, at his request, in the Netherlands. My parents had been surprised and a bit perplexed as to why the Bosvelds were not among those who welcomed them in Fremantle.

Unbeknown to my parents there had, in recent times, been some negative developments in the church. Mr. Bosveld was a driven person with a very strong and uncompromising personality. Some members did not always agree with his aggressive and forceful approach to things. In addition to this, some also questioned the legality of the church institution when just the Bosveld and Slobbe families were present. This issue was not resolved until much later when, in 1958, it was agreed by the Armadale consistory that the official institution date would be recorded as being the 24th June 1951, when an additional two office bearers were elected and from when the first consistory meetings were held. Before that date, Mr. Bosveld had been the one and only office bearer, so no consistory meetings had been necessary.

The fact is, that the notice of the first institution, held on the 25th December 1950, had been widely publicised in the Dutch church papers and resulted in many families, including my parents, making that crucial decision to go to Armadale. The timing was critical as many families in 1950-51 had been making firm plans to migrate. So, while the institution on the 25th December 1950 might have been somewhat irregular, there had been a strong commitment of faith by both families involved to establish a church without delay. As they declared in the public notice at the time, "We cannot look at our small numbers but in faith we have instituted the Church that maintains the truth of Scripture and confessions as well as the Church Order."

Mr. Bosveld felt increasingly targeted by slander and gossip, to the extent that he felt uncomfortable continuing in the office of elder. On the 23rd April 1952 he resigned from the office. On the 25th May 1952, less than two weeks before we arrived in Fremantle, two new office bearers were ordained - Mr. S. van der Laan as elder and Mr. J. de Vos as deacon. The functions were then established, with Mr. van der Laan as Chairman, Mr. Terpstra as the secretary and Mr. Slobbe as treasurer.

After his resignation, it appeared as if Mr. Bosveld withdrew himself from most of his roles within the church because, just two days later, on the 25th April 1952, he also resigned as member of the Immigration Committee. This was work he had been so passionate about and invested so much energy and resources into, promoting and welcoming new families to the district. Consequently, his resignation meant he was not present at the meeting held on the 30th May when they discussed the welcome arrangements and accommodation for my parents and the Bijl family. Nor was he then present to welcome the families in Fremantle.

When Dad visited Mr. Bosveld on the 7th June 1952, a day after his arrival, he had heard some rumours about the conflict and the situation, but had chosen not to enquire into it. They were simply happy to be welcomed by so many church members and did not want to engage with possible undercurrents and disagreements. So, with an open mind he visited the Bosveld family.

Dad was not disappointed. He was warmly received and offered whatever assistance he required and, of course, Mr. Bosveld would make the detour on Sunday to pick up Mum so she could attend church. So, the next day, the 8th June 1952, they attended the church service of the Reformed Church in Armadale held in the Wungong Church hall. It was a special day for them as Mum wrote in her diary:

> *So we met all the brothers and sisters at the church. Mr. Terpstra, the elder, led the service and read the sermon. What a wonderful blessing that also here, on the other side of the world, there is a church of the Lord with the same confession and faith as the congregation of Christ in Holland. The Confession and the Law were read out in English.*

The total membership was now about 130 and growing with each boat arrival. In the last six months alone it had grown by some 60 members. They came from all areas of the Netherlands, from the northern province of Groningen to the most southern province of Zeeland. Some of these provinces even had their own language and culture, as well as distinct character traits. Historically, there had always been a lot of rivalry between the provinces in the Netherlands and they were not always on the best terms with each other. However, it hadn't previously affected anyone personally that much because, while in the Netherlands, they didn't live together, and each was patriotically proud of their own province. Traditions in church life also differed somewhat from one province to another, particularly with regards to the liturgy and Order of Service. While the confessions and doctrine were the same for the one federation of Reformed Churches-Liberated, the experiences in the worship services could vary considerably.

Now here were these new migrants in Armadale, hailing from all over the Netherlands with such varying characteristics and personalities, most of them headstrong, independently minded and stubborn and with no church governance experience – none of the 130 members had served in a consistory before – and still trying to establish a Church where unity and love towards each other was paramount. On top of that, many were in the process of rebuilding their lives after experiencing hardships, traumas and deprivations in their old country. No wonder there were conflicts and testing times!

Humanly speaking, it seemed an impossible task for such an eclectic group of people to form a bond as brothers and sisters working together to serve God and the Church. They would face many challenges and disagreements and, in hindsight, it must be considered a miracle of God's grace that the Church did survive and grow.

37. A Home and Work

"All changes, even the most longed for, have their melancholy, for what we leave behind us is a part of ourselves; we must die to one life before we can enter another."

~Anatole France

Mum got her first taste of hitchhiking on the following Monday, when Mrs. Heerema agreed to take her to Armadale to see the doctor. Mrs. Heerema could make herself understood in English while Mum did not yet understand a word, so she really needed someone to come with her. As she was finding out, whenever she needed something, nothing seemed too much and nothing was a problem. Offers of assistance were always instant and spontaneous.

So, Mum met Doctor Carl Streich in Armadale who checked her out and tentatively booked her in to the Armadale Hospital in about six weeks' time, when she was due. She was used to having the birth at home and was not looking forward to spending ten days in a hospital with staff whom she could not understand.

The following day, on Tuesday, the container was expected to arrive at the house on Abernethy Road in Byford, so Dad left the Heerema's residence early to be there when the truck arrived. During the past two days, it had been raining relentlessly so, when he arrived at the house, he found the driveway from the road to the house flooded. The flat land had no runoffs and water was accumulating everywhere. Furthermore, the land and particularly the driveway had become boggy and unstable.

The truck with the container arrived about midday and, despite concerns about the stability of the driveway, the driver took a chance and drove through the flooded and waterlogged driveway. As could have been predicted, the truck became bogged as soon as it left the solid road. Despite all attempts, the truck refused to budge and needed additional assistance. Soon, some local farmers came to their aid with their tractors, but it proved to be no easy feat to get the truck back on the solid road. All afternoon they laboured with planks, shovels and tractors to unbog the truck and it wasn't till 6.00 p.m., just on dark, that they finally succeeded. But what to do with the container? There was no choice but to drop it off at the side of the road. The unloading would have to be done manually and the goods carried by hand down the 200-meter-long flooded driveway to the house. That would be the challenge for the next day.

The Bosveld family heard about their plight and offered to help. On the next day, three of their oldest boys came over to assist. Dad walked to the house from the Heerema's residence with the children but Mum, also keen to see the place and participate in getting it ready, followed Mrs. Heerema's advice: "Just start walking with one of the young kids and the first car that comes past will pick you up." This is then what she did and sure enough, within a short span of time after starting to walk, she was indeed picked up. But Mum, confused about directions, as she hadn't been there before, couldn't speak a word of English so the driver missed the turnoff. After some time, it became obvious that they had passed the location so the driver stopped at one of the farmhouses and asked if they knew where this new migrant family might be moving to. This farmer did know and gave proper directions, so Mum, after some detours, was eventually dropped off, in pouring rain, at the roadside of the house on Abernethy Road. Her first impressions looking at the house must have been dismal. There was water everywhere – the house appeared to be sitting on an island. Like everyone else, she had to wade through the water to get to her new home. She wrote in her diary, "at least it was dry inside."

The Bosveld boys, with their positive attitude and willingness to help, made a strong impression on Mum. Later she recalled how the eldest boy, Daan, just picked up a whole bed from the container, set it on his back and walked the entire distance to the house with it. They were used to hard and robust work. By the evening of that day most of the container had been emptied and everything placed in the house as best as could be. My parents had taken very little furniture from the Netherlands, mainly beds, bedding and clothes plus some items that were particularly dear to them. There was just the one bike. In the house and in the yard outside they found some boxes and crates they could use as chairs. The container itself was made of wood and, over the next few weeks, Dad, in his spare time, would use it to make some additional wardrobes, cupboards and tables. The house had no cupboards or built in wardrobes.

The weatherboard house had timber floors and a tin roof. Inside the walls were timber frames covered in plaster board. It was small by Australian standards with a lounge, kitchen, two bedrooms and a bathroom that had the bath removed and was used by the family as a bedroom. There was a small front verandah, and from this the front door opened into the lounge. At the rear there was also a small verandah which was partially enclosed, and here the laundry trough was located. The kitchen had no sink and just one tap that was located near the ground above a water drain grate. The toilet was outside in a separate outbuilding, but it had no toilet seat – just a very rusty bucket that fell apart when they tried to move it to empty it. The windows had no curtains but as my eldest sister Jenny said at the time, – it did not matter anyway, because there were no neighbours. They lived far enough away from others to be out of sight. There was a kitchen stove and an open fireplace in the lounge. There was no electricity and water came from two water tanks that sat just outside the house, but both leaked badly.

It was a house in need of some care and attention. However, on the bright side, the family now had a home, and could all come together again. Later that week, the owner's wife, Mrs. Peverett, came with a new toilet seat, a copper to boil the clothes, as well as some chairs and tables. She also assisted getting some firewood together so the open fire and stove could be lit. She proved to be very helpful and tried to assist wherever possible. However, her shabby appearance and willingness to just take on any menial task like collecting wood was a shock for my parents. In Holland, a farmer's wife was a respected person who would maintain a certain standard and dignity. With Mrs. Peverett there was none of that and, while they were the owners of extensive landholdings in the area, including several houses, her appearance in no way reflected any status or wealth. My parents got their first taste of Australia's egalitarianism.

In the meantime, Dad needed to find work. When he left Holland he had been assured that work would be readily available. From his initial enquiries, however, it became apparent that unless you were a tradesman, who were all in high demand due to the housing shortage and the increasing building activity, you could not so easily find a place, particularly if you didn't speak English. Mr. Heerema, who was working at the Cardup Brickworks, advised him to initially seek work at the brickworks until he became more fluent in the language which then would allow him to seek other possible opportunities. This was a real disappointment for Dad. He had not come to Australia to work in a factory. In fact, he had spent the last years in the Netherlands going from one factory job to another and had not enjoyed the experience at all.

However, he did need work urgently and didn't have the luxury to wait around for a possible position in a bakery to come up. So, taking Mr. Heerema's advice he visited the Cardup Brickworks. The day after moving into their Abernethy Road house Dad biked to the Cardup brickworks to enquire about possible work opportunities. Cardup Brickworks was situated at the foot of the Darling Ranges about four kilometres south of the town of Byford. This company had recently expanded with the addition of four new kilns increasing its production capacity from six million bricks a year to 11 million. It was, therefore, also on a recruiting drive for more workers, so Dad's timing was perfect – he could start the next day. And not only him but they were also happy to employ Peter, my eldest brother. At 14, the legal age to be able to leave school in Western Australia, it had been decided that he should go straight into the workforce.

So, while in the Netherlands he had been a talented student and would most likely have continued some form of further study as his cousins that stayed in the Netherlands did, the impact of the emigration for him was that he went straight into employment at 14 years of age and didn't receive any further formal education.

Instead of waiting until the following Monday, already the next day, on Friday the 13th June, exactly a week after arriving in Fremantle Dad and Peter became employees of the Cardup Brickworks. As they only had one bike, Dad had to carry Peter on the back of his bike to and from work each day. It was about a 10-kilometre ride and, with winds as well as the uphill slope towards the Darling Ranges, the bike riding took a lot of effort and energy. After a week Dad managed to buy two more bikes from his first salary, so at least Peter could cycle himself from then on.

They found that with their salary, which was eleven and a half pounds for Dad and five and a half for Peter, they could easily pay for their daily needs as well as set some aside for future purchases. To the Netherlands, Mum wrote that the combined salary equated to about 150 Dutch guilders a week. In the Netherlands, Dad had only been earning about 40 guilders a week, which was never enough to cover essential needs. Now Mum could write to her family that she no longer needed to worry about finding money to feed the family as the salary was more than enough. The news they all got in the Netherlands from my parents was very positive and optimistic. While none of Mum's letters to her Mum have survived, Miek, Dad's foster mother, lived in the same street and she would visit Mum's parents, the Schuttes, whenever a letter from Australia arrived. In turn, Miek would write to Dad's sister and her fostered daughter Marie, relating to her what she had learnt about my parents from those letters from Australia. Many of Miek's letters have survived and so are a great source of information about this time.

It is obvious that Mum was determined not to have her

mother worry and wanted to affirm the validity of their decision to migrate. So, she could write that Dad had work at a high salary, twice what he could earn in the Netherlands, that church life was positive with new members joining all the time and that soon they should have their own pastor. As can be expected, letters gave a very filtered version of what life was really like. Even the house was described as spacious and suitable for what they needed.

It is hard to imagine how my parents really felt coming from the Netherlands, where they had lived in a town which had all the necessary facilities like power, water and heating and where they could walk down the street to do their shopping. Here there was no power, an outside bucket toilet, no kitchen sink, no curtains, no neighbours and no opportunity to go just for a simple walk because there was water and mud everywhere. For Dutch people, who take so much pride in cleanliness, just trying to keep things clean must have been a challenge in the wet and muddy surrounds.

My older siblings recall how, Mum particularly, was extremely unhappy in this house. She was home bound because of the water and the house had no sense of what the Dutch call *'gezelligheid'* – cosyness, which in Holland was very important as Dutch women are extremely house proud. She was also shocked by the seeming callousness of the farmer. A young cow had become bogged in the mud just near the house and had died as a result, but the farmer just left it there as the body decayed and, of course gave off a terrible odour. This was just unthinkable behaviour for someone coming from the Netherlands, where cows were such a precious commodity.

But her biggest worry was how to get to the hospital when their baby was due. Nights she lay awake, listening to the rain pelting on the tin roof and wondering how she would navigate the long-flooded drive and get to the hospital in Armadale. Something had to be organised. The worrying was getting too much so eventually Dad decided to talk to Mr. Bosveld about the situation.

They came up with an immediate solution. As Mr. Bosveld had a vehicle, she could come and live at the Bosveld residence during the last week so she could be driven to the hospital when she went into labour. Mrs. Bosveld would then come to our house during the day, to look after our family. She had older daughters who would look after hers. So, here was a mother of 14 children prepared to come over every day, just so our household could continue without too much disruption.

Mum did not want to have the children billeted out with different families again, as she was concerned about the impact it would have on them, particularly the youngest ones. To her mind, they had already experienced enough disruption during the last months since leaving the Netherlands. In an interview with Mum in 2002, she still remembered with gratitude the assistance and support extended to her by the Bosveld family. "Nothing was too much for them," she said. "In the early period we had a lot to do with them. At the time the hardest thing was the isolation and the uncertainty regarding getting to the hospital. I was able to stay there. Their friendliness was heartwarming and something you never forget."

38. Another Child and Another House

"Home is the nicest word there is."
~Laura Ingalls Wilder

For the family, things were starting to fall into a bit of a routine. Each weekday Dad and Peter were away at work, Jenny stayed home helping Mum till the new baby arrived and Niek, Janet, Mappie and I, all attended Oakford School. This left just the three youngest at home, Mieke, Willy and Kees.

Oakford School was located on what was then North South Road No. 2, now known as Kargotich Road, close to the intersection of Abernethy Road. Initially, we walked the three kilometres to get there but, within a few months, more bikes were purchased so we could share the bikes to get to school. The Oakford Primary School was a typical small country school with just one teacher covering the seven grades for about 30 students. When we arrived there on the morning of Monday the 16th June 1952, more than half of the students at the school were Dutch. Children from the Bosveld, Terpstra, Bergsma, Slobbe, Heerema, t'Hart, van der Laan and van Leeuwen families had all arrived before us and while some had already moved on, most were still there. Many of them could already speak a smattering of English so were given the task of assisting us, the newcomers, in becoming acquainted. My sister Mappie later wrote of her early experiences at the school for a commemorative booklet that was published in 1998, just prior to the school being demolished:

> *I have very fond memories of my time at the Oakford School. Even though I attended only for a short while (6 -7 months), my time there had a great impact on me. I was eight years old and in Grade Three when we left the Netherlands to travel by boat to faraway Australia. We settled a few miles from the Oakford School and that was where our schooling in Australia started. A one class, one teacher school, with approximately 25-30 students. Quite unique. As I didn't know the English language, I was placed at the Grade Two level. There were two of us in that grade.*
>
> *I have great respect for Mr. Wearmouth, our teacher, for the way he managed to teach us all, despite having such a variety of ages in students. We were like one big happy family. He had a special method of teaching us the language. Every day we would spend some time in a group around his desk and we were instructed to get things and do things. It was very effective, and it really didn't take us long to pick up the language.*
>
> *Something that made an impression on me was that students were barefoot. How on earth could they walk on the gravel, especially on the very hot days? ... Life in Australia was a bit scary for us. We had been told how dangerous snakes were, and what happened if a racehorse goanna attacked you, and about spiders which could kill you. The Oakford School had an outdoor toilet, the typical dunnies they used to have in*

> those days. Quite often we didn't dare to use the toilet because of the spiders in there. Even a snake was spotted in there at one time. So yes, it did happen on several occasions that we had 'accidents'.[82]

With Mum being totally homebound, Dad did the necessary grocery shopping on his way home from work. Having no knowledge of the English language certainly gave them some challenging moments in the early months, also with shopping. Dad didn't always come home with the things he *thought* he had purchased so the evening meals would dish up some interesting surprises. However, they were determined to learn the language. Evening English lessons were being offered by the local schoolteacher but, despite wanting to attend, for Mum this just proved an impossibility. She was heavily pregnant and had no means of transport. For her it would have to wait for a more opportune time.

In the meantime, she had to adjust and cope with a whole different environment than what she was used to. She had to wash clothes without the use of a washing machine, prepare food without a kitchen sink and she had to cope without electricity.

However, as mentioned before, as the first weeks went by her greatest concern and worry was how to get to the hospital when the time came. Some of her previous babies had arrived with less than an hour's notice. When Mieke arrived, Dad didn't even have time to call a doctor. In the Netherlands, that had not been such an issue because the doctor lived in the same village and could be reached by bike in a matter of minutes. Here in Oakford, she needed to be sure she could reach the Bosveld residence in a timely manner and then get to the hospital on time. These were things she never had to previously be concerned about as she had stayed home for the births of her other children in the Netherlands.

On Sunday the 27th July, six weeks after they had moved into the Abernethy home, Mum just felt too ill to get out of bed. The constant stress and worry of when to go to the Bosveld's place was just getting too much for her, so Dad arranged with Mr. Bosveld to pick her up so she could await the baby at their place. With rubber boots on, she was assisted in the walk through the water and mud to the Bosveld's vehicle parked on the road. The driveway was still not negotiable for a motor vehicle and had actually gotten worse with the constant rain since they had moved there.

Mum was warmly welcomed by the Bosveld family and was able to relax and rest knowing that here was a vehicle that could take her to hospital when the time came. From their house it was only a seven kilometre drive to the Armadale hospital. Meanwhile, Mrs. Bosveld took a five kilometre bike ride each day to look after our family while her eldest daughter cared for her little ones. Their hospitality, generosity and can-do attitude was overwhelming for Mum who had been at her wits' end with worry.

My eldest sister, Jenny, still vividly remembered this time when I spoke to her in 2017. She was 13 and had not yet been to school in Australia as she was required to stay home to help Mum until the expected baby arrived. So, during the nearly three weeks that Mrs. Bosveld ran the household during the day, Jenny was there to assist. She found Mrs. Bosveld a very committed and fastidious person, with very high standards of cleanliness. Carpets had to be lifted and dusted and hung outside. Nothing seemed to be too much, and cleaning, washing and cooking were all tackled with zest and energy. With Mum having lacked energy during the last months it appeared that Mrs. Bosveld's drive was a new experience for my 13-year-old sister.

Dad, in the meantime, each day did a ten kilometre detour on his way home from work to go past the Bosveld residence to visit Mum. The whole journey home for him then became a 20 kilometre bike ride. After six days passed, on Saturday evening, the 2nd August, Mum asked to be taken into hospital. She didn't want to wake the Bosvelds up in the middle of the night, so made the decision to have them take her that evening, despite not being quite sure when the baby would come. So, Bosveld's eldest son, Daan, dropped her off at the Armadale hospital. She was now on her own, could not speak or understand English and missed, as she was used to in the Netherlands, having Dad by her side. How she longed to have this birth over with and be back home again. But the birth did not happen immediately and she started to wish she had stayed home longer. She wrote in her diary:

> *On Sunday morning still nothing was happening...I felt incredibly lonely. The language is quite something... it requires a lot of patience if you don't understand each other, and not many people have the patience. I now wished I had stayed at Bosvelds as the baby could linger another week... I felt like having a good old cry, but that wouldn't change matters. I then found comfort in my Bible which I had taken with me....*
> *I went to bed at 11.30 p.m. and at 12.30 a.m. the baby was born. A strong healthy boy. I was so happy and grateful then.*

My parents called their 10th child Arthur.

It was a long period of convalescence for Mum. She was not

allowed to leave the bed for the first 10 days and would not be released to go home until the 12th day. As was the practice in those days, the babies were kept in a separate room and were only given to the mother at feeding time. So Dad and the children had no opportunity to hold the baby until Mum came home with him. This was vastly different to what everyone had been used to in the Netherlands, where the baby was part of the family from the time it was born.

While Mum was in hospital, there had been some further developments regarding housing. A farmer, Mr. Brian Tunney, had asked Mr. Bosveld if he knew of anyone who might like a rent-free house for a period till his son got married and moved into it. Besides being rent-free, the farmer also offered a cow that could be milked, as well as access to a chicken pen and fruit from the many fruit trees that were established. Furthermore, it was a more modern house with a generator connected to provide electricity. It also boasted a proper kitchen with sink and tap, a laundry with copper, a bathroom with a bath, three bedrooms, a lounge and front and back verandahs. It was just so much better than the current house on Abernethy Road. The only disadvantage was the location. It was situated on North South Road No. 3, now known as King Road in Oakford, another 5 kilometres further from church, school and work for Dad.

The problem was the timing for Mum and her ability to organise the logistics. However, the Bosvelds would not take that as an objection and offered to organise the whole move while Mum was in hospital. This was then agreed to. On Saturday the 9th August, less than two months after moving into the Abernethy house, all the older Bosveld boys, as well as some of the girls and Mrs. Bosveld, worked together with some of my older siblings to shift and set up house on King Road.

Using Mr. Bosveld's truck for the removals, everything was in place at the new house by the end of the day. It was neatly set up – Mrs. Bosveld made sure of that. Our own furniture was complemented by some chairs and cupboards that the farmer had left behind. In contrast to the previous home, here all windows had curtains. The house had that 'cozy' feel that meant so much to those coming from the Netherlands. The boxes and crates that had served as temporary seating and storage space could now be discarded.

Five days later, on Thursday the 14th August, Mr. Bosveld picked up Mum and young Arthur from the Armadale Hospital and brought her to their now new home on King Road. The children had stayed home from school for the day to be there to welcome her. The front verandah, which was laced with timber bats, had been decorated with wildflowers that the children had picked from the surrounding bush. They also all had bunches of these strange, but beautiful flowers to hand to Mum on her arrival. Mum wrote in her diary:

> *It was a real emotional homecoming after being away for nearly three weeks. What a joy and delight to have your children waiting for you like that to welcome you home. Then they all had to admire and touch the baby.*

39. Finding a Place to Call Home

"A home is a kingdom of its own in the midst of the world, a stronghold amid life's storms and stresses, a refuge, even a sanctuary."
~Dietrich Bonhoeffer

If my parents felt isolated in their house on Abernethy Road, their new house on King Road was, by far, even more remote and isolated from civilisation. The Tunneys, who owned the 200-acre property (80 hectares) had some 20 years earlier built a neat and comfortable home for the family to inhabit. In August 1952 they had decided to move into Armadale. With their eldest son Brian having marriage plans, the idea was for him to eventually move back to live and work on the farm. Until such a time as he was married, he would live with his family in Armadale and commute to the farm to work. Hence, the house was vacant and offered to our family as a temporary residence.

The house included various outbuildings that served as storage for machinery, a workshop and a hay and shearing shed. As was typical for those days, especially in the Armadale area, the Tunneys had established a vegetable garden as well as planted an assortment of fruit trees. The Tunneys were focused on running sheep but, later, when Brian took over, he built a dairy shed and concentrated on milking cows.

The road to the house was just a simple gravel track and the connection to North South Road No. 2 (now Kargotich Road), where the school was located, was also a narrow single lane track. Neighbours lived kilometres away. Opposite the house were hundreds of acres of natural bush where groups of wild horses roamed. It was outback Australia.

Brian Tunney, who worked the property each day, became a good companion and mentor to the family. He was also a very generous and giving man, who helped wherever he could. My family had access to all the vegetables in the garden and then also worked to keep the garden going. Mum even proudly wrote to Miek in the Netherlands that they were enjoying fresh vegetables from the garden each day and were now even enjoying Dutch lettuce that they had planted. It was so much softer and better than the Australian lettuce, she claimed. They also had a milking cow made available to them that Dad milked both morning and evening, so they had no shortage of fresh milk. As they had access to the chicken yards, they bought 20 laying hens. Within a short time they had plenty of fresh eggs.

The farmer, though, really felt that the family was not eating enough meat. For Australians, each meal must be accompanied by a large slab of meat and he witnessed that we rarely had any. For us it was like a weekly Sunday treat to have meat with a meal. He generously offered a whole sheep to us providing we slaughtered and prepared it. Dad was no butcher so he asked a member from the congregation, Mr. Berkelaar, whether he might be interested in taking on the job and, for the effort, he could take half the sheep with him. This was agreed to, so we ended up with half a sheep to eat. Yet another time, the farmer offered part of a young calf that he had slaughtered himself. However, some of the kids, including me, had been with him when he shot the calf as it was sucking from its mother. This caused a fair bit of trauma so when it was dished up to eat most of us could not touch it. Mum ended up making a soup out of it.

As Mum wrote to her family in the Netherlands, they never experienced any shortage of food in Australia. While in the Netherlands, feeding the growing family had been a constant concern and worry, in Australia they experienced abundance. Especially in this second house, most of the abundance came from the property itself, so they did not need to spend the hard-earned cash for which they had lots of other uses, including the urgent need to purchase a motor bike.

The biggest challenge living on King Road was the remote location and distance from all their essential points of contact. Dad and Peter now had another five kilometres of bike riding to get to work – a total of 15 kilometres, morning and night. Also, as summer was nearing, the roaring easterly winds would blow each morning and that made the trip doubly challenging. The eldest children - Peter, Jenny and Niek - were attending catechism classes and bible study evenings at the Wungong Church. This involved a 12 kilometre bike ride in the dark on gravel roads. As these classes were held Saturday night, they would often arrange to stay overnight at a family who lived close to the Wungong Church. The van der Laans on Thomas Road and the Bosvelds on Hopkinson Road became regular places for the three eldest to stay over. They would then reunite with the family at church the following Sunday morning. The younger children attending Oakford School also had to travel further now to get to school. With only two bikes some had to walk the six kilometres. More bikes were urgently needed.

Going to church on Sundays was a challenge for the family, particularly for Mum who could not ride the long distances on bike. During the first few weeks, she was taken by bike the few kilometres along the track to the Kargotich dairy farm. A milk truck would drive past each morning to pick up the milk. Mum was then able to take a lift in the milk truck to the Wungong Church. The milk truck, however, could not always be relied on as on one occasion the driver had already accepted hitchhikers before arriving at the Kargotich farm and so had no room left for more passengers. Despite walking on for over an hour in the hope of getting another lift, Mum eventually ended up at the van Leeuwen's Thomas Road residence where she stayed until someone from the church picked her up and took her back home. She also tried taking public transport a few times. A bus ran along Kargotich Road towards Armadale. Unfortunately, its route past the Wungong Church was scheduled for an hour before the church was due to start.

The lack of transport and the long distances were becoming a major stress and it was obvious that something had to be done. More bikes had to be purchased, as well as a motor bike for Dad, but this all these had to wait until enough money was saved. Fortunately, living on Kings Road with free rent and with fruit and vegetables, as well as milk and eggs all provided, proved a bonus. Within two months, by early November, Dad had enough money saved to buy a motor bike. A few weeks later he was able to supplement that with the purchase of a side car. What joy and relief! Now he could take the motor bike with Peter as a passenger to work each day. On Sundays, he would connect the side car, which enabled Dad to take three children as well as Mum. Travelling to church was now a lot easier and arrival there on time more certain.

Again, things settled down into a routine. With the purchase of the motor bike, less time was spent travelling to and from work, and there was more opportunity to visit friends and church members in the evening, as well as attend any church meetings. Dad's work, while not his preferred occupation, nevertheless gave him a generous salary for which he felt blessed and thankful to God. There was more than enough to feed and clothe the family and to be able to put something aside each week for future needs. After the motor bike, the next thing they chose to save for was a fridge. By early December, with the hot weather upon them, the need for a fridge became more evident by the day. In the Netherlands, they had had an underground cellar which had been used to store foods that needed to be kept cool. However, in Australia they found the heat far more extreme and the need for a fridge was obvious. In the interim they made do with what was known as a 'Coolgardie safe' - a wooden box wrapped in a hessian bag that was kept moist.

However, in mid-December, out of the blue, Mr. Tunney gave notice that his daughter would like to move into the house within the next month, so we would have to find alternative accommodation and move out. It appeared that his son Brian, who worked on the farm and was due to eventually marry and live in the house, was now no longer moving in but that, instead, his sister was going to make the farm her home. Speaking later to Mrs. Tunney Jnr, Brian's wife, it appeared that she never had any intention of moving into the house at all, but preferred to stay in Armadale. She considered the location too remote and had convinced Brian to make their home in town once they married.

Having to move out so quickly after just three months was a severe disappointment for the family, particularly taking into consideration the benefits they enjoyed living there. While the location had been a disadvantage early on, now, with a motor bike and side car, as well as bikes for each of the children, this obstacle had been largely overcome. Since coming to Australia in June, this was going to be their third move in just six months. How they longed to settle down and have a place they could call home.

It was at this time that the 'migrant house' known as Fallon's Place became available. For over two years now, it had been rented by the church Immigration Committee as a temporary home for incoming migrants who had no housing arrangement. When we arrived in June 1952 the house was home to three families: Berkelaar, de Vos and Visser. Some of us had stayed with the Berkelaar family for the first week after our arrival in June. In December 1952 both the de Vos and the Berkelaar families had moved out to more permanent accommodation. The migrant house was seen just as a transitionary home. However, the flow of migrants seemed to have slowed down by December 1952 so there were no immediate migrant families that were allocated to move in to replace the two families that had moved out. The Immigration Committee was paying three pound a week for the whole house and the Vissers, who lived in about a third of the space, were charged just one pound a week for the area they occupied.

With no migrants scheduled to arrive in the short term and with the two pounds a week shortfall, the Immigration Committee was happy to have our family move in and take up the space left by the two families for two pounds a week. So it was that, on the first Saturday of January 1953, we moved from the house on King Road to Fallon's Place on what is now the corner of Rowley Road and Hilbert Road, Armadale. A removal truck was hired and with all hands on deck, including several helpers from church, the move was completed and finalised in the one day. Mum wrote that it was an extremely hot day – such a contrast to when they'd moved into the first house six months previous, when it had rained relentlessly.

Fallon's Place was a large timber and weatherboard house with a tin roof built in the early 1920s when the area was settled under the Group Settlement scheme. This was a government sponsored program set up to encourage unemployed and unskilled British citizens to migrate to Western Australia and, with government assistance, take up virgin land to clear and cultivate. Launched by the WA Premier, Sir James Mitchell, after the First World War it led to vast areas of crown land being opened up for settlement, with the goal for WA to become self sufficient in food production. While there were some successes, particularly in the Harvey area with the dairy industry being established, many participants failed. The government abandoned the scheme in 1930.

With the Visser family living in a third of Fallon's Place, the section we occupied consisted of a large sleepout, two other bedrooms, a large country kitchen with a dining area and a combined laundry and bathroom. A wide-open verandah faced south. The bucket-type toilet was outside, with the bucket needing to be emptied and the waste buried each week. Water came from a well which was attached to a windmill and tank on a stand. There was no electricity, so kerosene fuelled Tilley lamps provided lighting.

The house was in a state of disrepair. The timber stud walls with timber cladding was riddled with white ants and many of the walls, as well as some sections of the timber floor were breaking down. My Mum used hessian coverings or curtains to hang over the walls to camouflage the damage done by the ants.

The house was built on a slight rise so it would not flood in winter. It stood on a 100-acre property, the north boundary being the Wungong River, which became a great playground and swimming area for us children. Besides the house, the property had a hay and machinery shed, a disused dairy shed, and a poultry run. Part of the dairy shed, which stood adjacent to the road, was closed off and converted by Peter to a bedroom for both him and Niek.

Within 12 months, the Visser family, with their four children, moved to their own house that Mr. Visser had built on Seventh Road, Armadale. We now had the whole house to ourselves, although there were some rooms that were considered uninhabitable. However, it did allow the older girls to have a separate bedroom from the younger ones who all slept in the same room.

The house was owned by Mr. McDaniel who lived in a brick house across the other side of Rowley Road on the property that now houses the Free Reformed Church of Darling Downs. He was advanced in age and lived with a male farm worker who also looked after him. Once a week, he would take his horse and buggy to Armadale to catch up with friends and do some shopping. While the property had previously been a dairy farm, Mr. McDaniel now just ran beef cattle.

Moving to this house meant that the children now had to attend the Armadale State School. Wungong Church was less than two kilometres away and Armadale six kilometres or 30 minutes on the bike. Mum wrote in her diary after having spent the day moving:

> *We sat on the front veranda for a while enjoying the beautiful evening and the view we have here. On one side we look towards the beautiful hills, covered with*

vegetation and for the rest we have a good view of pastures. We noticed immediately that we were living in a more inhabited area. We see more traffic and occasionally a bus comes past on its way to Perth.

40. Church Life

"The Church's one foundation
Is Jesus Christ, her Lord:
She is his new creation
By water and the Word."
~Samuel L Stone, 1866

When we arrived in June 1952 the Armadale Reformed Church, as it was then known, had a membership of about 130. Two ministers had been called, the Rev. G. Jansen on the 12th August 1950 and the Rev. W.W.J. van Oene on the 7th May 1952, but both had declined. As the church membership was growing fast with the influx of new migrants, and, as no one had any experience in church leadership, the need for a minister was pressing. The second half of 1952 continued to see a rapid influx of new migrants, most of them arriving on the boat *Johan van Oldenbarnevelt*. Dad wrote to his sister, Marie, in December 1952 that the church membership had grown to over 200.

With several new babies born the question of baptism became a point of discussion. The Church Order of the Reformed Churches stipulated that only ordained ministers could administer the sacraments of the Lord's Supper and Baptism. With the two called ministers declining and with no immediate prospects of a minister arriving, the issue of the adminstration of the sacraments became a vexing question.

The tradition by Reformed people was to have a newborn baby baptised as soon as possible. Back in the Netherlands, Dad would not even wait until Mum was well enough to witness the baptism and would present the newborn to be baptised on the first Sunday following the birth. Now, in Australia, his son Arthur, had no prospect of being baptised soon, unless some special arrangements were made. There was also the question of the celebration of the Lord's Supper. Reformed churches would generally celebrate this at least four times a year and, here in Australia, due to no minister being available to lead the services, no member had celebrated it since arriving in Australia. For some, this was now over three years.

The consistory decided to ask the Dutch mother churches for advice in this matter. In the second week of November 1952 a special congregational meeting was held to discuss the advice received - which was that the consistory, with the congregation, should decide whether they would appoint an elder to carry out this role. Both Dad and Mum were able to attend the meeting. Mum, writing in her diary about the meeting, stated that, while there was some hesitation at first, after some discussion, it was decided unanimously that Mr. H. Terpstra be appointed to administer the sacraments, until such a time as a minister arrived.

So, the following Sunday, on the 16th November 1952, more than three months after he was born, Arthur was presented to receive the sacrament of baptism. Also baptised that day were Martin Bijl, Peter Jongeling, Margaret Groenewold and Bert Groenewold. Mum wrote in her diary that day:

What a rich day that was, for the whole congregation

> *but especially for us. The Lord is so endlessly great and good, that also here, we could witness the sign of His covenant. It is He who will keep us and our children by His word and testimony.*

Three months later, on the 22nd February 1953, after all the church members had been visited by the elders, the Lord's Supper was celebrated. Mum wrote about this day in an article dated 27th March 1953 and published in the issue of 21st May 1953 of the Dutch Reformed daily newspaper the *Gereformeerd Gezinsblad*:

> *Words cannot describe the rich blessings we experienced on that first celebration of the Lords Supper here in Australia. Elder Mr. Terpstra had chosen a sermon on Psalm 84:1 & 2:*
>> *How lovely is your dwelling place, O Lord of Hosts. My soul longs, yes, faints for the courts of the Lord; my heart and flesh sing for joy for the living God.*
>
> *This text also really expresses the longing by this congregation. After a long time – three years for some migrants – we could sit again at the Lord's Table. For the first time here in Australia the Lord showed himself to us through the sign and seals of his broken body and shed blood... Our hearts were filled with joy and together with the composer of Psalm 42 we could sing:*
>> *But the Lord will send salvation.*
>> *I will sing and pray at night,*
>> *To the God of life and light.*
>> *He will in His mercy hear me.*
>> *And for evermore be near me.*

I am sure this Sunday will stay in everyone's memory for a long time. We could experience the riches in Christ again. Despite our sins and shortcomings, we could see again that Christ maintains His Church. May we always seek the Communion of Saints. We cannot live without the Church. We really need each other on the road that leads to eternal life.

No one should think that the church here in Australia is perfect. The battle against the devil, the world and our own flesh will be ongoing as long as we are here on earth. We could not leave this battle behind in Holland. It will accompany us all over the world.

Evangelising and witnessing to the Australian people also became a point of discussion. Occasionally, some Australian people would attend the church services and of course, with the entirety of the service being held in Dutch, the question raised was - shouldn't we move into using the language of this country? When the church was instituted in December 1950, Mr. Slobbe and Mr. Bosveld had issued a statement saying, "Because we desire to be the Church of our Lord Jesus Christ in Australia, we propose to hold the services in the language of the country." However, two years later that goal seemed far from a reality. With the constant flow of new migrants who had little knowledge of the English language, the pressure to maintain the use of the Dutch language in the church services seemed to dominate.

In a letter to Dad's adopted mother, Miek, Mum wrote in December 1952 about a recent incident where two Australians had attended and asked for a translated sermon which they received. She finished by writing, "But you see how necessary it is that we learn the English language so that in time we can hold our services in English." She then mentioned that she was, together with Dad and Peter, doing correspondence lessons to learn English.

On the evening of 26th December 1952 church members organised a special Christmas celebration for Australian children. The youth of the church were engaged to proclaim the Christmas message and to organise a series of Christmas songs. Peter wrote very enthusiastically about the event to his Auntie Miek:

> *We sang songs, read Luke 2 and ran the evening the same as we did in Holland but now all in English for the Australian children. We had more Australian children present than Dutch. It turned out to be a terrific evening.*

With the growth in church numbers, the Wungong Church, with only a capacity of 70, was fast becoming too small. An alternative venue had to be found. After enquiries with the Armadale Road Board the Lesser Hall in the Town Hall was made available for ten shillings a week. This became the place of worship for the Reformed Church of Armadale from early February 1953. The Wungong Church, however, continued to be used for catechism classes and Bible study evenings. For most church people, who lived around the Oakford/Darling Downs districts, including us, using the Lesser Hall did mean travelling further to get to church.

Finding a minister remained a top priority and, on the 31st March 1953, the Reverend Franz Frederick Pels, minister from Almelo, in the Netherlands was called. It took only two weeks for Rev. Pels to send a telegram which had that briefest but most welcoming of messages: 'Accepted your call'. What joy for the congregation. It was something they had all hoped and prayed for and now it was to become a reality – having their own minister.

It would, however, be another eight months before he and his wife could finally arrive from the Netherlands. On Thursday the 29th October 1953 most of the congregation were at the Fremantle Harbour to welcome their new minister with his wife. Then on Sunday the 1st November 1953 he was ordained by Mr. Terpstra, who could now also hand over his role in administering the sacraments to the newly installed minister. Rev. Pels moved into the manse which had been bought six months earlier on Robin Hood Avenue, in Armadale. Costing two thousand five hundred pounds, the house was situated on one acre of land. This area was considered large enough for a future school and church.

On 27th April 1954, five months after Rev. Pels' arrival in Armadale, the first Synod of the Australian (Reformed) Churches was held in the Wungong Church in Armadale. There was representation from the instituted churches of Albany, Launceston and Armadale. With Rev. Pels being the only minister present, he was appointed to chair the proceedings. There was agreement amongst the three churches to form a bond of churches in Australia, but there was some hesitation regarding what name to adopt. Reformed Churches that were connected to the 'Synodical' churches in the Netherlands had already been established in some districts in Australia, with one being in Tasmania. It was therefore considered necessary that another name be found to clearly distinguish itself from these churches and which clearly identified them as being part of the 1944 Liberated Churches. The Synod gave the churches time to finalise the name within the following three months. It still took more than twelve months before the three churches all agreed to the name Free Reformed Churches of Australia which was initially proposed by Tasmania. This was formally adopted and introduced as from the 1st of October 1955.[83]

In June 1954, following the retirement of Mr. Terpstra, Dad was elected as elder in the church. The consistory now comprised of the following: as elders, S. van der Laan, M. van Leeuwen, P. Bijl and C. Kleijn and, as deacons, J de Vos and P.H. Bulthuis. The Free Reformed Church of Armadale at this time consisted of 250 members.

41. Tragedy in the Netherlands

"We must build dikes of courage to hold back the floods of fear."
~Martin Luther King Jr.

The Dutch have a long history of fighting and overcoming water, and, those that live below sea level, which is about a third of the nation, are always susceptible to storms and dikes bursting, and then having their homes and land flooded. Some areas of the Netherlands are more than six meters below sea level. Even the historic and iconic city of Amsterdam was built on land that is two meters below sea level. The Dutch had, over the centuries, reclaimed large tracts of their country from the sea by constant efforts in building dikes, waterways and dams, and by draining and pumping. The total coastline of the Netherlands is 880 kilometers, but its dike network runs a total of 22,000 kilometres.[84] Built and then improved and reinforced after each flood, this whole system of water protection was most severely challenged in 1953.

Early Sunday morning, the 1st of February, the Netherlands was struck with one of the worst natural disasters in its modern history. The combination of a high spring tide and north-west gale-force winds of 100 to 120 kilometres per hour hit the coast and the extensive dam network built around the Netherlands to protect it from the seas was breached in many places. From 3.00 a.m. the dikes started to give way and, by dawn, a large part of southwest Holland was under water. The *Alblasserwaard*, where most of my parents' families lived, was also severely affected when, at 5.30 in the morning, the Noorddijk in Papendrecht was breached. The water force was so severe that the breach was 60 metres wide. Within a few hours water had found its way into most of the western part of the *Alblasserwaard*, including in Brandwijk where Mum's parents lived.[85]

The scale of the disaster was such that it became international news. My parents also became aware of it through the Australian newspapers. There were reports of hundreds of deaths and the international community was rallying to provide support and aid in the rescue of stranded people. Every day new reports came in, but how was the family? Concern for their welfare was at the forefront of my parents' minds. They were aware of the area and its susceptibility to flooding. After all, the *Alblasserwaard* had suffered from floods throughout its long history. My parents sought the company of church people and could talk and think of little else.

Henk, who was married to Mum's sister Marie, and with whom my parents had always been close, must have realised the anxiety my parents would have been feeling. So, on the Tuesday of that week, they sent a telegram that simply read: "Dad and Mum and family safe." What a relief this message was but it also posed more questions. Where were the parents? Had their house been destroyed? What about other family members from Dad's side? They also lived in towns that had been flooded. With no telephone they could do little but simply wait till they heard more.

On the Sunday evening of the 8th February, my parents joined other church members at the residence of the van de Veen family to listen to a Dutch broadcast on their radio. Few people had radios particularly with the range of being able to listen to something broadcast from the Netherlands. My parents were keen to hear first-hand, direct from Dutch reporters what the situation was like with the flooding. Also, the Dutch Queen Juliana was scheduled to broadcast that evening. It was something my parents didn't want to miss.

Later, in that second week after the flood, the first letters and more information started arriving. Mum's parents, the Schuttes had been awakened early Sunday morning and evacuated about 15 kilometres south to a town called Giessendam. There they stayed for the first week and were then able to move in with one of their daughters who lived in Sliedrecht. It took a full month before they were given the clearance to move back home. There they found that while the house had been flooded and there was a lot of cleaning up to do, nevertheless the structure had remained intact. Other family members from Dad's side had also been evacuated but while there had been extensive flooding throughout the western *Alblasserwaard,* the depth of the water was not as severe as experienced in many other parts of the country. The family was spared the loss of life or injury.

Mum wrote in her diary:

> *We can't be thankful enough that the whole family has been spared. If you hear how many people lost their lives, then in humbleness, we must bend our knees and thank the Lord for His protection. He is the One who controls the clouds, sky and winds. He commands and they obey His holy will.*

The final loss of life and property and general devastation was enormous. 1,835 people died and as a result more than 250 children became orphans. 100,000 people were made homeless. About 8000 farmhouses were destroyed with the loss of 20,000 cows, 2,000 horses and 3,000 sheep. The rebuilding cost of both private property and public infrastructure ran into the billions of guilders. The Dutch had been struck hard and as a result there was a unified bi-partisan, national resolve to make sure something like this could not happen again.

The Dutch Government conceived and constructed an ambitious flood defense system which became known as the Delta Works. The project was designed to protect the areas within and around the Rhine-Maas-Scheldt delta from North Sea floods. It comprised the construction of 13 dams, including barriers, sluices, locks, dikes and levees. Taking 25 years to build at a cost of over 5 billion dollars it acts as a barrier across the sea that can be locked down in case of severe winds and high seas.[86] This, then, effectively protects the whole country from the onslaught of the open seas.

The Delta Works is recognised as one of the seven Wonders of the Modern World by the American Society of Civil Engineers. Since this had been built, the Dutch have, in the main, been protected from any further flood risk.[87] Floods that had plagued the Netherlands from its early history and had defined it as a nation, particularly in the area my parents came from, would now be a thing of the past. There have been no serious floods now for over 65 years.

42. Settling in at Fallon's Place

"All is flux: nothing stays still."
~Heraclitus, Greek philosopher
(535 BC)

When moving to the migrants' house on Rowley Road, many things changed for the family. It was no longer necessary for any of us to stay elsewhere overnight because of the long distances to bike home in the evening, especially after Catechism classes and Bible study, and my parents could now extend that hospitality to others who were in that predicament. Fallon's Place was considered a handy stop-over for anyone passing on their way home, so it became a convenient drop-in place for anyone who was looking for a cup of tea and a chat. The youth club for 12 to 16-year-olds was launched at Fallon's Place and was often held there simply because it had room and was considered a convenient location for those living in the Oakford/Darling Downs areas. Sundays also became a very social time with my older siblings taking along friends between church services and church members often just dropping by. Sunday lunch regularly had more than 20 people around the table.

Peter changed jobs the week we moved into Fallon's Place. He had been offered a position working in the retail section of the Armadale Co-op. A lot of Dutch migrants shopped there, and the manager was looking for someone who could understand Dutch and translate when necessary. By this time Peter had a reasonable command of the English language and had a personality that was considered suitable for customer service. So, at the young age of just over 15 he was given the responsibility of serving and dealing with customers. From all accounts, he thrived in the position and became a well-liked employee that customers enjoyed dealing with.

Jenny, meanwhile, had left school the day she turned 14 (on the 25th February 1953) to help Mum at home. She had had very little schooling in Australia. When we arrived in Australia in June 1952, she had stayed at home to help during the period of Mum's pregnancy with Arthur. After Arthur was born in August, Mum became ill so Jenny stayed at home for another month till mid-September. She then enrolled in Oakford School but spent less than three months there before the school went into recess for the summer holiday. Then, after the holidays, she enrolled at Armadale High School but left three weeks later when she turned 14, this being the legal age to be able to leave school. Jenny enjoyed studying and was very upset about leaving school. Speaking to her about this in 2016, she related how she had rebelled and insisted on staying at school. Dad then gave her a stern talking-to and insisted it was her duty to come home and help Mum. So, she reluctantly relented. She stayed at home for about two and a half years until September 1955, when her next youngest sister, Janet, turned 14. Janet then left school and took over Jenny's place working for Mum.

In early 1953, when we moved into Fallon's Place, Mieke, who was then five years old, also went to school, so Mum just had the three young children at home: Willy, who was four, Kees, who was two and a half and Arthur, who was just six months. The six of us who attended the Armadale state school could all catch the school bus from Wungong Road, so there was now less biking and walking.

Vocationally, Dad was still seeking a way to switch back into the baker's trade. He had taken the job at the Cardup Brickworks because he needed the immediate income but had been told by other migrants that, once he could speak English, he should be able to find a career back in his trade. Six months after arriving in Australia he was confident of being able to make himself understood and he started keeping an eye out for a possible bakery job. In March 1953 he was accepted for a baker position in Cannington. However, it turned out to be a big disappointment. The early starting hours, having to work all through the night on Fridays, the inordinately long distance to travel and the generally negative atmosphere of the workplace, which included a lot of swearing and cursing amongst his colleagues, made Dad long to be back at the brickworks. There he had enjoyed a good relationship with his boss and colleagues, and a decent variety in his work. His boss at the brickworks had said he was welcome back if the bakery job didn't satisfy him. It took him just five weeks to leave the bakery and go back to the Cardup Brickworks. They welcomed him back and he was slotted into his old role without any fuss.

At Fallon's Place Mum enjoyed the additional contact with people and the ease with which she could now visit others. The Bijl family only lived about a kilometre away on North South Road No. 1. They had moved there after the Bosveld family vacated the house to move to their own house on Albany Highway, Armadale. Mr. Bosveld had bought a large tract of land there and had erected a temporary home which they had moved into while their larger family home was being constructed. Now Mum could easily exchange visits with Mrs. Bijl, which they did on regular occasions. Already, on the boat from the Netherlands, they had decided to stay in regular contact.

Now that Mum had more time she was able to get more involved in church life. She started writing articles about the church and the migration experience for publication in the Dutch Reformed newspaper. She took on the role of president of the Ladies' Bible study club when it was launched on the 12th August 1953. She also became more involved with struggling community members. As a youngster working for Reverend Donner and his wife, she had been mentored in being available and helping, wherever there was need. Mrs. Donner instilled in her the mindset of always thinking of others. This stayed with Mum so she would often get involved with families under pressure for any number of reasons. Many times youngsters from other families would be invited to stay over for a few days to give the parents a break, or else Jenny would be sent over for a few days to help them out. Despite having a big family, there always seemed to be room to accommodate others.

Learning the language, however, was put into the too-hard basket. Dad and Peter were learning it at work and particularly Peter, working in retail and dealing with customers, was very fluent in English by the end of 1953. Jenny, who had only spent a few months at school, was still struggling with the language. All the children who went to school had no problem at all and moved seamlessly to English. Being at home or visiting Dutch-speaking friends, meant Mum did not progress at all, despite some attempts at taking correspondence lessons. She did express the intention many times to learn but her limited contact with Australians and her own busy life with a growing family made it an impossibility for her. By the end of 1953 she was again pregnant and expecting her eleventh child

SETTLING IN AT FALLON'S PLACE

in April 1954.

At the previous house on King Road, Dad had been spoiled with having access to a cow for milking as well as chooks for eggs. He wished to maintain that also now on Rowley Road, so, within a short time, he bought a cow and some chooks. Shortly after, he also bought two young piglets for fattening. It was also decided to start a vegetable garden.

With all these purchases there was constant pressure on the budget. With the Visser family having moved out after a year, Dad became responsible for the total rent of three pounds. This was an additional expense because the previous house had been rent free. He had managed to buy the cow on instalments but then could not delay any longer the purchase of a kerosene fridge. Going another summer without a fridge was just too difficult.

Twice a day the cow had to be milked, the chooks had to be fed and watered, eggs collected, and the pigs had to be fed. Other chores included making butter weekly, the vegetable garden had to be attended to and, each Saturday enough wood had to be collected, sawn and chopped to keep the stove and open fire going all week. The Tilley and storm lamps needed to be fuelled up every day as well as be maintained. On top of that each week, the worst job of all had to be done - burying the toilet waste! There was no shortage of work for the boys in the family, who divided responsibilities for all of these between them. Niek was already starting to develop mechanical skills and Peter watchmaking skills so it wasn't long before they were both given work to do in their own areas of expertise. I was only 7 in 1953 and so was given the job of looking after the chooks and pigs. Several years later, when I was 12, I would be promoted to milking the cow each day.

The ladies in the house – Jenny, who in 1953 was 14, Janet,

12, and Mappie, 10, - were all kept busy in the house. Jenny was working full time at home. She recalled in 2016 how the weekly washing, in particular, was such a big job:

> *All day Monday and Thursday were allocated to washing. Everything was done by hand, with all the clothes boiled, then wrung out and then washed in the tub and wrung out again before hanging them out to dry. The whole process took all day. Then there was all the ironing etc.*

Added to this was the cooking, sewing and cleaning. Whenever there was spare time there were always clothes to mend or make. Nothing was ever thrown away or wasted. Jenny recalls getting gloves that were made from old socks. I remember my school bag being made by my mother stitching a few old rags together. Recycling and making do was the norm.

Nearly nine months after moving into Rowley Road Dad suffered a motor bike accident. It happened on a Sunday night, the 27th September 1953, when he was riding his motor bike after taking Jenny's friend, Trijntje Terpstra, home. He failed to take a corner on Rowley Road near home and the bike skidded off the road. While initially thinking he was okay he continued to experience severe pain in his shoulder, so Mr. Bijl, who happened to be visiting that evening, took him into Armadale to see a doctor. He was sent to Perth for x-rays which established that he had a broken collarbone. This meant that he could not work for six weeks. There would be no income as in those days there was no compensation available. However, as he wrote to his sister Marie, he was thankful because it could have been a lot worse than just a broken collarbone.

Peter, who had just turned 15, had learnt to ride the motor bike two weeks before. He became, as Dad wrote, the 'taxi driver.' He took the family to church on the motor bike with the side car, as well as to any other event Dad or Mum had to attend. There was no mention in any of the correspondence of the need for him to have a licence, which at his age would not have been available. It was quite common for youngsters to drive as soon as they could, even if they were not old enough to get a licence. Then when they turned 17, they would simply turn up at the police station, do a brief driving test, and go home with the required licence. By that time, a lot of youngsters were already seasoned drivers.

Dad's healing progressed without complications and six weeks later he returned to work. To supplement his income, he got a job fruit picking on Saturdays. Peter, who still worked at the Co-op all week, including Saturday mornings, joined Dad every Saturday afternoon in the fruit picking. It appeared that, in the early years in Australia, Dad always held out another job besides working at the brickworks. For a period, he worked evenings for Daan Bosveld on his Albany Highway property. Mr. Bosveld offered work to anyone with the ability to wield a pick to help cut out a large piece of the Darling Ranges so he would have a level piece of land to build his spacious family home. Many picks were worn out in this quest, one that was completed without the help of machinery. He also worked Friday nights at the Byford bakery for a while, which was owned by Mr. Bulthuis, also a Dutch migrant. It did mean that Dad was rarely available to do the chores at home, so these were all allocated to the children.

43. A Growing Family

*"Behold, children are a heritage from the L*ORD*,*
The fruit of the womb is a reward.
Like arrows in the hand of a warrior,
So are the children of one's youth.
Happy is the man who has his quiver full of them;
They shall not be ashamed,
But shall speak with their enemies in the gate."
~ Psalm 127:3-5 (NKJV)

The summer of 1953/54 felt particularly severe for the family with many days over 100 degrees Fahrenheit (37 Celsius). Being pregnant, Mum, too, had difficulty coping with the hot weather. Dad ended up purchasing a cooler to alleviate the situation a little. The house, with tin roof and no insulation, absorbed the heat very quickly and it wasn't until the sea breeze came late in the afternoon that some relief was experienced.

Mum wrote that she was particularly 'big' and found it difficult to get around easily during the last few months of her pregnancy. Riding on the back of the motor bike was also not possible during these last months of her pregnancy so Dad organised a taxi for her to go to church.

This time there was no stress or worrying for Mum about getting to the hospital. The roads were accessible, and the plan was to call a taxi when she was ready. However, when she was ready for delivery, on Good Friday the 16th April 1954, Dad couldn't get a taxi so ended up having to call an ambulance. Within an hour of Mum arriving at the Armadale hospital, Elizabeth Maria (Mary) was born. My parents rejoiced. Mum wrote, "The Lord has made everything well again. How rich we are, again a healthy daughter." With Reverend Pels now serving in the Free Reformed Church of Armadale, Mary could be presented for baptism without delay. In contrast to the Netherlands, however, Mum was present to witness the baptism.

The next baby, Suze (Susan), was born 15 months later on the 4th July 1955. She was also in the Armadale Hospital, where Mum stayed for 10 days. She still didn't appreciate being in the hospital and really didn't like the fact that Dad was not even allowed to be present at the birth and that the child was put away in a nursery, only to be given to her at feeding time. She often reminisced in her letters to the Netherlands about how having the baby at home was so much better and how then Dad was there, and the children could hold the baby very soon after birth. It seemed such a natural family affair for Mum, while in Australia it was such a sanitised occasion. They even tried to give her chloroform during the birth to ease the pain, which she had found most offensive. She wanted to be fully alert and awake to experience the joy of hearing the first cry of the baby.

Jenny had been full time at home helping Mum for nearly two and half years. She worked occasionally for a day a week for other church families when the need arose, as well as for a period of time with an Australian family as a way to learn English. Attending school for such a short time, Jenny had been at a disadvantage as far as learning the language went for at home with her parents the conversation was always in Dutch. In fact, Dutch was still the main language used by all the Dutch community members in church services, Bible study clubs and Catechism classes and in their conversations together. With the (still) constant flow of new migrants it seemed an impossibility to change to English.

While there was initial optimism to learn the language quickly, in time this faded into despondency, particularly by many stay-at-home mums like my mother. With frequent pregnancies and not being well physically, the motivation to learn the language was not there. This was increasingly a source of frustration as the children were, within a few years, easily conversing in English with each other. This meant Mum was excluded from the conversation around the evening dinner table and this was just not acceptable for my parents. The rule then became that the whole family had to speak in Dutch while at the family dinner table. The reminder to '*Hollands praten*' ("speak Dutch") became a regular refrain by my parents to the children at the dinner table.

When Janet turned 14, just two months after Susan was born, she left school to replace Jenny in the household working for Mum. The tradition that one of the daughters stayed home to help in the family was something that Mum had grown up with and continued in her own household. While Jenny had initially resisted leaving school to work for Mum, she grew used to it and found Mum quite relaxed to work for. Recalling that time in 2016, she said that Mum gave her time off and she had most nights free. However, she had found Mum very strict on dress codes and fashion. She always insisted that Jenny wore dresses or skirts and not pants.

Janet worked at home or helped out other families till Mieke, on turning 14 on the 15th September 1961, left school and took over from her. Mappie, born after Janet in 1943, was the daughter who could complete her Junior certificate – the first one in the family – and went straight into the workforce on leaving school at 15.

Janet had her hands full at home. As she recalled in 2020, Mum was unable to do the washing due to recurring skin issues and allergies to soaps, so Janet did all the washing and ironing. She also made all the beds each morning as well as cleaned and vacuumed, and bathed the younger ones. Then when Mum suffered bouts of illness, as happened shortly after Susan's birth, she even had the responsibility, at just 14 years of age, of looking after the whole family, including trying to get them all to behave and cooperate. There was virtually no break for her as, even in the evenings, she had to organise tea and coffee for everyone, including any guests who were there. Fallon's Place was an open and welcoming house for everyone. Janet recalls that especially on Saturday night there were virtually always visitors, with several of them sleeping over as well, particularly if they lived far away. Janet found it tough going, with few breaks and everyone relying on her to do the housework. Even on Sundays, when everyone else could sleep in, she had to get up early to make breakfast, serve the parents a cup of tea with Dutch rusks in bed and, after the church service, make sure everyone got their coffee and cake.

With the growing family it became a challenge to get everyone to church on Sundays. The motor bike and side car that Dad had purchased within six months of arriving in Australia, was limited to two passengers, one on the pillion seat and the other in the side car. For some time Dad had squeezed three children in the side car, but this had to stop after he was pulled up by the local policeman and was fined by the traffic court a total of four pounds for overloading. So, about six months after Susan was born, in January 1956, Dad stretched the budget, spending 20 pounds to buy a 1928 Dodge utility. It was a real vintage car with wooden spokes and a temperamental motor that needed to be started with a crank handle. Fortunately, by this time my brother Niek had developed some mechanical skills so he was able to make the necessary temporary repairs from time to time to keep the car running. It served as the church car for the next 18 months. It was then replaced by a 1936 Dodge sedan.

It was about this time in 1956, that Niek was admitted to the Armadale Hospital for an appendix operation. This was quite a common ailment experienced amongst many migrant families and doctors seemed to be quick to suggest that the appendix be removed. Peter also had his removed a few years later.

However, in Niek's case it developed into a serious health concern. After the operation, he became increasingly sick until, after five days he was diagnosed with a life-threatening infection and needed to be operated on without delay. A specialist was rushed from Perth and the family doctor, Dr. Bernie O'Brien, had to travel to our house on Rowley Road to get the required signature to do the operation. My parents were shocked at the doctor's sudden arrival at their front door and the urgent need for a signature so he could get back to attend to the operation with the specialist. How serious was it? Would Niek pull through the operation? Dad, no doubt, would have had flashbacks to his own youth when he had been critically ill with the same condition. They prayed earnestly to God that He would guide the doctor so that the operation could go well and that Niek would recover.

Dr. O'Brien rushed back with the signature of approval but, in his haste, was traveling too fast to navigate a corner in the road about a kilometre from Fallon's Place and consequently, rolled his car. Fortunately, he was not hurt and found other transport to get to the hospital to proceed with the operation. The operation was a success and Niek returned home following two more weeks in hospital. Still, he needed another six weeks to fully recuperate before returning to work. Mum wrote in her diary: "The Lord heard our prayers."

Niek recalled in 2008 that it was at this time, when he was off work for a period of nearly two months, that Dad also was off work for several weeks due to illness. With no social security and with the loss of two incomes, he ran out of money. Niek remembers the deacons of the church coming to visit and offering financial assistance. To his knowledge, this was the only time that the deacons' help was ever needed.

On the 7th March 1957 Mum's mother, Oma Schutte, died aged 80. She had been ill only a short time, but letters from family had warned that she may not live long. Communication with the Netherlands at this time was only via letter; there were no phones and the mail was picked up daily by one of us children from the Armadale post office. I still vividly recall that day when, as a 10-year-old, I picked up the mail from the Armadale post office after school and came home with that telegram announcing her death. Mum's outpouring of grief was instant and unrestrained. Dad was not home. Jenny, the eldest at 18 years old, was put in a position to console Mum in this sad and difficult moment the best way she could.

The passing of Oma Schutte hit Mum hard. Later, she admitted that it was then that the loneliness and the impact of migration really hit her. She had been very close to her mother and, since leaving the Netherlands, had corresponded faithfully with her every week. Now she was no longer there, it would leave a big gap for Mum, to which she had to adjust. They were not in a position to travel to the Netherlands to attend the funeral and share the grief with siblings and other relatives. This also made the process of grieving more difficult.

Two months later, on the 28th May 1957, the thirteenth child and eighth daughter was born. My parents called her Margaret because, according to Mum, her daughters thought that was a 'nice name'. The doctor assisting at the birth was a young Dr. Bernie O'Brien who had become the family doctor following the death of Doctor Carl Streich in September 1956. Dr. Streich had been the family doctor since he had been introduced to Mum by Mrs. Heerema a few days after she had arrived in Australia. He had been in the Armadale district since the 1930s and had been, by reputation and from all reports, an outstanding doctor for the district. Mum also had found him a "wonderful, caring and fatherly person."

When Mum gave birth she reflected on her own mother who also had thirteen children but who had to bury five of them. "How richly we have been blessed. They are all so healthy," she wrote in her diary. Each child was considered as a blessing by my parents. Speaking to Mum in 2002 after Dad had passed away, she said that Dad was excited every time there was a new child on the way and each one had been welcomed with gratitude. With him not having experienced a normal family life in his youth he valued a united family that cared for each other. He was particularly aggrieved when his children would fight amongst each other. He had so longed to grow up with his own siblings and simply could not understand nor tolerate intense disputes between his children.

When Margaret was born the family had been in Australia five years. Peter was now 20, Jenny 18, Niek 16, Janet 15, Mappie 13, Harry 11, Mieke 9, Willy 8, Kees 6, Arthur 4, Mary 3, and Susan 22 months. Three of the family were now in paid employment, one was at home helping Mum, five were at school and four, including baby Margaret, were at home. It was a busy family with 20 years of age difference between the youngest and the oldest.

Peter was working as a carpenter with Paul Bijl, who some years earlier had started his own building business. While Peter had enjoyed working at the Co-op for over two years, Mr. Bijl offered him a position with training in carpentry and building which he had accepted.

Jenny was a trainee nurse at the Royal Perth Hospital. After Janet took over her work with Mum at home, Jenny found a job in a grocery shop in Armadale but applied for nursing as soon as she was eligible. She was accepted in October 1956. This meant she was away from home all week as the trainee nurses all lived in the nursing quarters adjacent to the hospital.

Niek worked at a local dairy farm owned by Tom Cunningham, about a kilometre away from Fallon's Place. A year earlier, after leaving school at 14, Niek had secured a job with the Public Works as a trainee carpenter working on the construction of the Royal Perth Hospital. It was a long-term training program and during the first weeks he was simply the Billy Boy, preparing cups of tea and attending to the needs of his fellow workers. This did not satisfy him for long and soon he went looking for another job. He worked in a motor mechanic workshop in Byford for a period before finally accepting a position with the Cunningham Dairy.

44. Building Our Own Home

"It takes hands to build a house, but only hearts can build a home."

~Unknown

Dad had harboured ambitions early on to own his own home. Paying rent seemed like a waste of money but he had to first save enough money to buy a block of land. All of his spare cash in the first years in Australia were taken up buying essential things like bikes for everyone, a motor bike, fridge and cooler, as well as clothes and other necessities. Then he also had to pay back the loan he had taken out with his sister to fund their expenses leaving the Netherlands. He was able to do that within three years.

Furthermore, in addition to this there were also the church and school obligations. Already in 1953, with the formation of an Adults Association, a commitment was made to work towards the establishment of a Reformed school for the children. In December 1954, a School Association was formed with a membership fee set at one pound a week. Every adult Free Reformed Church member was encouraged to be a member of the School Association. The financial commitment then became one pound for the church, and one pound for the school. With Dad earning a salary of about twelve pounds a week, this commitment represented about 16% of his salary.

They saw this as a necessary commitment and never complained about it, but seemed happy to contribute.

Because of these financial commitments, no money was spent frivolously, and Dad sought to earn some extra income by finding work on Saturdays and evenings whenever possible. Working children were also expected to contribute the bulk of their income to the family coffers. Even before leaving school, most of the children would be working somewhere on Saturdays and after school. This money would then go towards some of their own personal expenses, like clothes and schoolbooks. And, of course, as soon as some money was being earned, a portion of it had to be given to the church.

For the children, there was no desire to move into our own home. While the house we lived in at Fallon's Place was badly eaten by white ants and was literally falling apart, this didn't worry any of the children. The house was spacious, there were outbuildings to play and mess around in, and, just some twenty metres from the house, there was a large winter water lagoon that was a great place to sail makeshift boats in winter. Along with all these bonuses, next to the house there was a massive sand pit that the younger children could be entertained in all day, building tunnels and all sorts of imaginative and dreamswept things. Then there was the 100 acres of surrounding land, bordered on one side by the Wungong River, which was a popular place to swim with family and friends. Across the river was bushland to wander around in and where rabbits could be trapped for consumption on the dinner table. For the children, it was an idyllic habitat and lifestyle. Peter and Niek had set themselves up in the dairy shed with their own room on which they had a carved timber sign hanging on the door with the words: "Our Happy Home." Here two beds were set up, as well as a desk where Peter could maintain his hobby of fixing watches. There was ample space and freedom for all to roam, live and play.

In 1956, after living there for about three years, the landlord decided to build a modern flushing toilet inside the house. This was a major improvement and convenience for the family. No longer was there a need to share potties and no one had to venture outside in the dark. Best of all, the chore of burying the full toilet bucket each week was no longer on the to-do list.

Two things that stood out as major issues while living in Fallon's Place was the fear of fire and of storms. In the heat of summer, the timber house, surrounded by tinder dry grass, was at high risk. After one of the church families lost their house to fire in Byford, the awareness of this risk was heightened. Once a 6-year-old boy boarding at our place for a few weeks was playing with matches outside and inadvertently got a grass fire going. Within a short time, the fire raced out of control. Fire fighters and the local surrounding farmers came with their equipment to fight the fire and managed to save the house, but the shed that had been stocked with hay was completely destroyed. Another time a summer fire swept through the area surrounding the house but, again, the house was saved.

Jenny, too, came close to burning the house down when she grabbed a bottle of what she thought was kerosene to help fuel the stove fire. Instead, it was petrol that exploded in flames when poured on the fire. Flames were everywhere and it would have been only a matter of minutes and the whole thing could have been out of control. Niek, sitting on the toilet, heard his sister's screams and ran out, saw what was happening and without hesitation grabbed a large pan filled with water and potatoes that was standing next to the stove and threw it over the flames. This slowed the fire sufficiently to get it under control and extinguished.

Then there were the storms. Nearly every summer evening the easterly winds roared relentlessly. The loose roof sheets would flap, the house would shake, and the noise was deafening. Inside the house, the Tilley lamps hanging from the ceiling would sway from side to side. In the sleepout, where most of the younger family members slept, the walls were just single sheets of corrugated iron and the dust and debris driven by the roaring easterlies would find its way through the open gaps. Many a time a full roofing sheet became dislodged. During one storm the whole verandah roof was lifted by the wind and folded on to the main roof. On another occasion, the ceiling collapsed in the main bedroom where the little one slept in a cot. Miraculously, the collapsing ceiling missed her. So, while the children were generally enjoying Fallon's Place, for my parents it became a safety concern. There was also fear that, one day, the whole house might collapse in such a storm.

So for Dad, besides his desire to own his own home as a sound investment as time went on, the condition of Fallon's Place became more precarious and there developed a sense of urgency to move.

In January 1955, two and a half years after arriving in Australia, Dad put down a deposit to purchase a five-acre property on Third Avenue, Kelmscott. Not able to pay in full the purchase price of five hundred pounds, the balance came through a loan with the Armadale New South Wales Bank. The blocks had recently been subdivided into five acre properties and, besides Dad, several other Dutch migrants also ended up purchasing some of these blocks. This included the van Leeuwen, van der Plas and Maring families. The Marings purchased a block directly next to Dad, so were set to become our neighbours.

Dad's plan was to pay off the block within a few years and

then start saving to build a house. He was loathe, at his age, to get a long-term loan. With the block now secured, serious planning could begin with respect to the house. First of all, the block had to be cleared and a water well dug. It wasn't long before the oldest boys, Peter and Niek, together with Dad (providing he didn't have other work commitments, which was often the case) would spend Saturdays working on the block, clearing the trees in the area where the house was to be built and to sink a well. Trees were axed at the roots and then taken down with pulleys slung from one tree to another. Once down, the trees were sawn into sections with a long two-man cross cut saw.

The well took about a year to complete. Digging by hand with pick and shovel, a concrete 1.5 metre high circular ring was placed into the hole to prevent it caving in. As the concrete circular rings sank into the ground another ring would be placed on top. As the well got deeper, pulleys were put in place to lift the buckets of dirt out of the well. At 3 metres, hard rock was encountered so gelignite was used to loosen the ground. This involved drilling a hole in the middle, placing a stick of gelignite into this, lighting the wick and then climbing in haste up the ladder out of the well before the explosion. This was a dangerous procedure with little room for error, especially as the well became deeper and the climb up the ladder longer. I was there many Saturdays and remember Jan Hollebrandse, who was courting Jenny and assisting us, just barely reaching the top rim a few times as the explosions went off. He had no fear and just shrugged the close shaves off with a joke. Finally, at 8 metres, the well was holding enough water so the digging could stop.

With water sourced and the building area cleared, serious planning could be undertaken to begin the building process. In the meantime, Dad had arranged with his supervisor at the brickworks that he be allowed to go through the brickworks rubbish tip each evening to collect bricks that could still be used. Slowly, over a year, he collected the bricks needed to build the house. They were progressively carted to the block – some 20,000 bricks free besides the cost of transporting them.

The other big expense was to be the roof tiles. Enquiries were made and it seemed feasible to make our own tiles, bringing further big savings. Some 50 tile metal moulds were purchased and from then on, for many months, Peter and Niek spent evenings stripping the moulds, making concrete mixes and pouring that into the moulds. Once dried, the tiles were stripped from their moulds and stacked. So, at 50 a night eventually the approximately 6000 tiles necessary were made.

By 1958 drawings of the proposed house were completed. It was going to be a large house that could accommodate the whole family. The front area had a spacious lounge with two large adjoining bedrooms and, on the other side, a massive country-style kitchen and dining room. Another bedroom ran off a small passageway. The back section of the house had two adjoining bedrooms, where you had to walk through one bedroom to get to the other. In the centre was a small, enclosed verandah that served as the rear entrance. On the other side of the verandah area was a large laundry, bathroom, and toilet. The laundry would have a wooden copper which would be used for all the hot water requirements, including personal bathing and the washing of clothes.

A lot of thought and discussion went into this final layout. But, then of course there was the question of how to fund such a large house. Mr. Bijl was engaged to assist in the process of costing and building. Despite the savings made on the bricks and tiles as well as deleting nonessentials like painting that could be done later, the cost was still such that Dad had to get a substantial loan from the bank. This was set to be paid off over eight years which, at the time, was considered a long period to be paying off a mortgage. Paying a mortgage meant that the household budget would need to be kept tight for those years and the whole family was engaged to assist in this quest to pay off this 'massive' loan.

With two children, Peter and Jenny, soon to be married, the household income would be considerably reduced, so that also had to be factored in. It meant the family, and Dad in particular, would be under severe financial pressure for quite a few years yet. The loan repayments were going to be considerably higher than what was currently being paid in rent. To save costs further, family members also became involved in the building project. Mr. Bijl's contract was on a cost-plus basis so any work done by others would help reduce the total outlay.

Upon setting out, the digging of the foundations was all done by hand by family members. When ready, Mr. Bijl laid all the bricks forming the foundation. Mr. Bijl, together with brother Peter, his employee, and at times Mr. Bijl's own children all worked on the house. They were a very multi-skilled team of workers that could tackle most of the skills required to build a house. The only outside people called in were the electrician, the plumber for the final connections and the roof tilers. Everything else, including bricklaying, roofing, flooring, ceilings, wall plastering, wall tiling, leach drains and gutters was done by Mr. Bijl and his team. Then 13 years old, I spent many days working on the site doing whatever Mr. Bijl put us to work on. He was a very effective organiser of workers and led by example. There was no tolerance for easing off or slackness. The pace of work had to be maintained throughout.

It was nevertheless a positive and happy atmosphere and I was certainly happy to participate wherever possible.

The manager of the Armadale bank who advanced the loan came to inspect the building, just before the roof tiles were due to be put on. Seeing the amateur handmade tiles, he was shocked. There was no way he could allow them to be placed on the house. Ultimately, he considered it would diminish the value of the building which, up to then was looking quite magnificent with nice brickwork and spacious layout. He advised Dad to get a quote from Bristile and have the roof covered with proper glazed clay tiles instead of the dull cement ones. This was a blow for Dad and the family who had put so much work into making the tiles. However, there was no alternative; more money had to be found and the house would end up covered with Bristile tiles. The bank manager certainly made the right call and it was appreciated later. At the time, though, it caused major angst and disappointment.

At the end of October 1959, the house was finally ready for the family to move in. How Mum was looking forward to that! She had lost confidence in the structural stability of Fallon's Place after some major storm incidents caused more damage. The lack of maintenance, and the unwillingness of the landlord to spend any money, had really led to the deterioration of everything, including the windows, doors and walls. With the dust and debris freely blowing through all the gaps it was becoming an impossible house to keep clean. Now she could move into a solid brick home that was well constructed and designed for the family. There was also electricity, so the Tilley and storm lamps could finally be discarded. As a further bonus, Mum could now also have an electric iron and an electric washing machine. What a difference that would all make!

Some of the children did not, however, share Mum's enthusiasm. Peter had enjoyed his own space in the dairy shed and was not looking forward at all to the move. He told Mum: "I'd like to stay in the shed, but seeing I'm building my own house and hope to get married soon I will not be long here anyway."

Nine months later, on the 29th July 1960, Peter married Zwannetta Zuidema and moved into his own house that he built on Seventh Road in Armadale. The other children, too, were less enthusiastic with the move. Five acres seemed such a small property compared to 100 acres, and Fallon's Place had a river to swim and play in, as well as lots of outbuildings to muck around in. The children had good memories of the seven years at Fallon's Place, also with respect to the social life it allowed. There had always been lots of people dropping by and it had been a convenient go-to place for many.

Despite the new house having been designed to house a large family, it still took a bit of juggling to fit everyone into the bedrooms. With Jenny having married Jan Hollebrandse six months earlier, on the 3rd April 1959, room still had to be found for the five boys, Peter now aged 22, Niek 19, Harry 13, Kees 9 and Arthur 7 - and seven girls - Janet, now aged 18, Mappie 16, Mieke 12, Willy 10, Mary 5, Susan 4 and Margaret 2. With five bedrooms, this meant that the five boys had two bedrooms to share and the seven girls also had to share two bedrooms leaving one bedroom for my parents. With guests also often staying over, the bedrooms were well used and sharing bedrooms gave lots of opportunity of talking well into the night, as often did happen.

The two milking cows had also been moved to the new property, so the tradition of milking the cows each morning and night by a member of the family continued. A milking shed and chicken shed were erected as well as a large garage which also served as a workshop. Slowly, over a period of some months, all the necessary outbuildings, water tanks and fences were put in place and the family got back into some routine and rhythm. Dad and Mum were extremely happy and grateful to be now living in their own house. It was seven and a half years since they had left the Netherlands. Four additional healthy children had been born since that time. One daughter was now married, and another son was due to marry soon. Despite the many hardships they had experienced along the way, they considered themselves blessed and were thankful to God for everything they had.

45. A Church in Strife

*"I believe in one, catholic and apostolic Church.
I confess one baptism for the forgiveness of sins…"*

~ *The Nicene Creed (325 A.D.)*

While the building and completion of his own house was a real triumph for Dad, on other fronts he had been struggling for a number of years. In June 1954 he had been appointed an elder in the Church. He, along with the others elected to that office in the Armadale Free Reformed Church had no previous experience on which to draw. They had been moulded by a terrible war and by what they considered to be the deceitful and disgraceful behaviour by the church hierarchy, which, in 1944, led to the liberation and the establishment of the Reformed Church Liberated. On top of that, they were all watching their pennies as they were trying to establish themselves in a new nation.

Mr. S. van der Laan, who served in the consistory at the same time as Dad, acknowledged in an 1997 interview that the early migrants from the 1950s were, by the very fact that they had sought to migrate, characteristically strong-willed and independently minded people. Added to that, they all came from different parts of the Netherlands bringing with them a variety of different customs with respect to church life. And then, with most of the consistory having little to no experience in the overseeing of church life, conflict seemed inevitable.

Reverend F.F. Pels, who had arrived in October 1953, was, on the other hand, an empathetic, gentle and compassionate pastor. He was a great shepherd and teacher, but had difficulty giving strong and firm leadership when it was most needed. He was also relatively young and inexperienced at just 34. Different members confronted him with conflicting advice and demands to which he had difficulty responding in a confident and clear manner. Worst of all, his personal integrity and honesty was questioned and attacked. This really cut him, emotionally, to the core. While he loved Australia and would have preferred to stay, the emotional drain and stress was just too much for him. Consequently, when he got a call to the Church of Huizen, in the Netherlands, he decided to accept it and left Australia on the 9th April 1957. He died just 9 years later in 1966, at the age of 47. Reverend P. Van Gurp, who was his colleague for two years while he served in the Albany Free Reformed Church, said in 2017 that Rev. Pels mourned having to leave Australia and never really got over the disappointment. It had affected his health; he aged prematurely and died a broken man.

When Dad arrived in Armadale in June 1952, he sensed immediately that there were some undercurrents and disagreements amongst church members. Mr. D. Bosveld was at the centre of one of these. He had been grossly offended when the institution of the Reformed Church of Armadale, formalised when just his family and the family Slobbe were present on the 25 December 1950, was challenged by the newcomers and deemed illegal and unconstitutional. These newer arrivals sought to formally reinstitute the church, after the election of three office bearers on the 24th June 1951. Mr.

Bosveld, being a forceful leader who had been the main driving force of the Church development up to that time, now found himself increasingly misaligned. In April 1952, just two months before we arrived in Australia, he resigned as consistory chairman and withdrew from most activities within the church. In 1957, he and some of his family relocated to Tasmania. The date of institution was finally settled in late 1958 – after the Bosvelds had left for Tasmania – when the consistory came to a consensus and formally recognised the 24th June 1951 as the valid date of institution. On that day, three office bearers were ordained and from then on regular consistory meetings were held. This, then, became the official date that was celebrated at various milestone events which commemorated the Armadale Free Reformed Church's institution.

The institution date was just one of the many issues that divided people. While there were, seemingly, no serious theological arguments, there were significant disagreements about the way consistory dealt with things and, with the bulk of church members all being very independently-minded, offence was soon taken when consistory made unilateral decisions that affected the rest of the members. There was a considerable breakdown of trust, respect and love for each other. Consistory was bombarded with letters of complaints; some of the letters were even co-signed by groups of people to drive the point home. As a consequence, consistory was kept extremely busy, responding and discussing all these problematic issues as they were tabled.

Mum recalled in 2001 how Dad would often come home from consistory meetings well after midnight and sometimes even past 2.00 a.m. during this particular difficult period. There was even one time when he still wasn't home after 2.00 a.m.

and she got so worried that she woke up my eldest brother, Peter, and got him to go to Armadale to see if Dad was okay. He came home at 4.00 a.m. that morning. Just three hours later, at 7.00 a.m., he had to turn up bright and early at the Cardup Brickyards to start his day's work.

Dad had a particularly difficult time during this critical, foundational period of the Armadale Church, while he was in consistory for the four years from 1954 to 1958. He had some empathy for Mr. Bosveld, as he had had such a positive experience with him, and this, in itself, put him in a difficult position. It was not in my Dad's nature to seek out conflict. Rather, he had in his life always gone out of his way to avoid it. And now, he was stuck in the middle of it. In a letter to his sister, Marie, in 1958, he described those four years in consistory as the worst, most stressful years in his life, which is something, considering the times of war and hardship he had experienced in the Netherlands. "We need a good pastor who can give sound scriptural leadership," he wrote, "and who can powerfully preach the Word. Only then can we expect repentance and reconciliation." No doubt he would have been thinking of his beloved Rev. Boodt, who had been able to bring the Word so powerfully that it moved people and changed behaviours.

In 1957 the division in the church had reached a critical stage where there was some agitating to leave the church and several seeking to worship separately. Johan Bosveld writes about the meeting to discuss this in his book, *Free Reformed Pioneers:*

> *In May 1957 a meeting was held in the house of D. Bosveld on the hill. Many concerned brothers gathered there that evening. They were mainly concerned with*

> the direction of the church council. After a long discussion, and summing it all up at the end of the evening, they decided "to give the church council of Armadale a final ultimatum to change direction and admit mistakes, otherwise they felt compelled to withdraw from the Church, and worship separately."
>
> There were some 20 brothers present. Not just a storm in a teacup. But then, suddenly, everybody was taken by surprise. Brother C. Kleijn, who hardly ever spoke a word in public, asked to speak. He simply said: "Brothers, I don't think that God wills this."
>
> Stunned silence. Not a word was spoken in reply. This one sentence from Brother Kleijn undid all the planning of the whole evening. The long list of objections against Armadale church council shrivelled. "I don't think that God wills this." No arguments, no considerations, no substantiations. Just a short statement.
>
> And all the brothers understood that what they willed was not what God willed. "A man's heart plans his way, but the Lord directs his steps." (Proverbs 16:9) The Lord had something better in store for Armadale than fragmentation. He demanded repentance and humility.[88]

Despite not taking the drastic step of separation, the divisions remained, and the consistory had decided to censure a number of people. This led to more unrest and counter accusations. In an attempt to seek some way forward the consistory asked Reverend P. van Gurp from the Albany Free Reformed Church and Reverend G. van Rongen from the Launceston Free Reformed Church for assistance and for them to visit together and see whether they might be able to arbitrate in the situation. The two pastors agreed to travel to Armadale and devoted a whole week of August 1957 to this undertaking, working from the manse on Robin Hood Avenue. They interviewed nearly all the church members, especially those that felt aggrieved, as well as consistory members. At the conclusion of this they wrote an extensive report with recommendations for the consistory.

Speaking to Reverend van Gurp in 2017, he said that they concluded that the consistory had, in a number of cases, wrongly censured individuals. Their inexperience in matters of church discipline was evident and they had acted unscripturally and not in a church orderly way. This needed to be corrected by withdrawing their censure and apologising to those affected. This was difficult for the consistory to accept, but nevertheless, according to Rev. van Gurp, the majority eventually agreed, and apologies were given. Peace was, however, not totally restored. Rev. van Gurp relates how accusations and counter-accusations continued and, from time to time, he was urgently called to Armadale to further arbitrate in disputes as they flared up.

In the meantime, the Armadale consistory remained active in seeking a pastor and, in May 1958, they extended a call to Reverend M.J.C. Blok who was serving in the Reformed Church Liberated in Utrecht, in the Netherlands. The appeal from the Armadale church members to him was so strong and compelling that, while he could not immediately accept the call, he felt moved to ask his consistory for six months leave so he could serve for that time in Armadale. This they agreed to, so on the 8th of September 1958 Rev. Blok arrived at the Perth Airport to serve Armadale as their teacher and pastor for six months. He had to leave his wife and five children behind in the Netherlands.

According to Rev. van Gurp, it was through his powerful preaching, leadership and counselling that some resemblance of peace was restored amongst the members of the Armadale Free Reformed Church. As a visiting minister, Rev. Blok was able to preach, without fear or favour, the full message of scripture. He provided clear biblical leadership that compelled members to sit up and take notice. "How can you continue to sit in the church benches and consider yourselves Christians if you will not reconcile with your brother or sister?" he asked.

He used the fortnightly church bulletin to reinforce the message of the need to repent without delay. He gave sound leadership in all areas of life and his impact in just those six months was miraculous. God blessed his work and many church members humbled themselves and sought forgiveness and reconciliation where there had been division. The 1951-1974 commemoration booklet of the Free Reformed Church of Armadale refers to this time as "the beginning of the restoration of church life." Rev. Blok left to join his family again in the Netherlands on the 4th March 1959.

When Rev. Blok was in Armadale, Dad had just retired from the consistory. He was finally able to experience peace and thankfulness with the powerful opening of the scriptures by Rev. Blok and the resultant changes it brought in lives and attitudes. No doubt, Dad also had to engage in some self-reflection on many of the stands he had taken during that difficult period and acknowledge that things could have been handled differently. The prolific letter writing, accusations and counter accusations did so little to build the community of saints. Speaking to Mum in 2001, she certainly acknowledged that but for the grace of God there would have been no church in Armadale today. There is no room for human pride when reflecting on the past. Human weakness and inexperience were so prominent in those early years, yet, despite that, the Lord continued to build His church in Armadale and used those 'weak vessels' as His instruments.

In 1959 Dad, after only a year's break, was again nominated for and voted into the consistory – this time as a deacon. The total membership of the Free Reformed Church of Armadale had by that time reached 428.

46. The Union Struggle

"Left-wing zealots have often been prepared to ride roughshod over due process and basic considerations of fairness when they think they can get away with it. For them the end always seems to justify the means. That is precisely how their predecessors came to create the gulag."
~Margaret Thatcher

Besides the struggle and stress associated with being in the consistory during the years of 1954 to 1958, Dad had another challenge to cope with and that was his job security. The Cardup Brickworks had a closed union membership policy, so any prospective employee had to be a member of the union. Initially, that did not worry Dad or other new migrants seeking work. Not being familiar with the language and being assured that it was similar to the trade organisations that were in the Netherlands, of which many had been members, they really didn't give the matter much serious thought. The difference was, however, that in the Netherlands there had been Christian organisations that represented both the worker and the employer. There were no underlying tones of militant class struggle in those organisations as was so rampant in the ethos of Australian Unions.

The Armadale Church Consistory as well as the Immigration Committee had, without hesitation, recommended new migrants to seek work at either the Armadale or the Cardup brickworks, despite the fact that working there meant joining the union. Both businesses were expanding to meet the growing demand in the building scene and so were always on the lookout to recruit new staff. Migrants saw the work there as something to take on for the short term, until they had mastered the language and were then able to seek work in their area of expertise and interest.

That had also been Dad's intention when he initially started work at the Cardup Brickworks in June 1952. He had very reluctantly taken a role there with a view to getting back into his trade as soon as possible. However, as related earlier, he tried this in March 1953 but decided to go back to the Cardup Brickworks after just four weeks. Then, in 1956, he was offered a job at the dairy farm of Tom Cunningham, where his son Niek was working at the time. This was back before the house in Kelmscott was built and so he was happy that with the job came a house, free milk and meat and the opportunity to walk to work and to be home for lunch with an afternoon break. It all sounded wonderful. So, relocation of the family to the farm house was arranged. This house was also on Rowley Road, just one kilometre from Fallon's Place. While it was a more modern house with electricity and flushing toilets, it was a lot smaller, with just three bedrooms and no outbuildings. For the children, the house was a real disappointment.

The hours Dad had to work at the Cunningham farm were long, with a 4.00 a.m. start every morning. His boss was a hard taskmaster and sought value for the money that he paid to his employees. Dad came home exhausted every night. On top of that, in Dad's eyes the farmer seemed to have little empathy for his animals, treating them harshly and cruelly. In the

Netherlands, farmers treated their cows with care and respect and Dad, who had grown up on a farm, found the whole environment difficult to comprehend or appreciate. He also had the additional challenge of being on the Church Consistory that, as related earlier, involved attending many - and long - evening meetings. After just one week, he realised he had made a terrible mistake. But what now? He had even moved the whole family for this job to live free in the house supplied.

Fortunately, he had a good relationship with his former boss at the Cardup Brickworks so, without too much delay, he went to see him about returning. This was no problem at all, so it was all arranged that after just four weeks in the more modern, but smaller house, we all moved back into Fallon's Place and Dad recommenced work at the Brickworks. It appears that Dad, after his initial disappointment and reluctance to work in a 'factory' (Cardup Brickworks) had, after this second setback, concluded that the work in the 'factory' was maybe better than most other options for him. He was not inclined to make another move in a hurry and had to just be content. However, with increasing awareness of the union culture and the ultimate need he felt to withdraw membership from it, meant that this time his tenure at the Cardup Brickworks would be short lived.

The concern about being members of Union organisations in Australia was first expressed publicly by Mr. Klaas Salomons, member of the Free Reformed Church of Launceston and founder and editor of the church federation's magazine, the Una Sancta. In the 9th January 1954 issue (just three months after the founding of the *Una Sancta*), he devoted an article to it in response to the news that, in New South Wales, legislation had just been passed that made membership of unions compulsory. While he wrote that he did not have a full grasp on the legislation or on unions - and asked readers to forward to him any constitutions or rules from unions if they are in possession of them so he can further analyse the situation, he nevertheless suggests that the unions he is familiar with demand total allegiance from its members, and henceforth members could be called on to behave in ways that contravene Scriptural norms. "It is clearly evident," he wrote, "that there are unions where membership would mean having to submit to an authority that does not recognise God's commandments and more than not likely to go directly against God's ordinances."[89]

The next warning about union membership was furnished by the hand of Mr. H. Plug in Albany. Between April and August of 1954 he published a series of six articles outlining the historic background of the Australian unions and came to a clear conclusion. He wrote: "I hope I have made it at least clear in this series of articles that we cannot for principle reasons become members of the Australian Unions."[90]

In his last article, he referred to a court case in Sydney where a conscientious objector challenged the union in the courts against the compulsory membership and where the court ruled that:

> *It accords with the principles of human decency that a man whose religious beliefs prevent him from joining a Trade Union should be permitted to earn his daily bread in his own chosen vocation. The NSW compulsory Unionism Law, which came into force late last year, provides clarity for any employer who takes on an employee who is not a union member, unless he has obtained exemption as a conscientious objector.*[91]

This he suggested, also gave hope to members of the Free Reformed Church who need to object to becoming members.

They should be able to legally apply for an exemption.

The 1950s were the high point for the Australian Union movement. Never before, or since, have they enjoyed such a high participation rate, with over 60% of all adult workers being a member of a union. (By 2020, it had sunk down to 14%). In the 50s, they were closely allied to the Labor Party and when the party was in power in WA – as was the case from February 1953 to April 1959 – their influence and control was indisputable. So, while laws making union membership compulsory were not yet introduced in WA as they had been in NSW, nevertheless the WA Government supported legislation for compulsory preference to Trade Union members in many workplaces and gave the unions free reign in pursuing their goals. Major enterprises like the Armadale and Cardup Brickworks were closed shops and no non-union members could have access to those workplaces. If my Dad and others chose to resign their union membership, it would mean immediate dismissal. Even with a legal exemption, the unions would make sure that such a person's work life would become impossible. Intimidation and standover tactics, even threats of violence, were not foreign to the union culture.

When Rev. van Gurp arrived to take on the position of pastor and teacher in the Free Reformed Church of Albany in June 1955, he very quickly became involved in the union membership debate. The Free Reformed Church of Albany had already experienced the sting of the unions in October 1954, when one of its members was taken to Court by the union, demanding fee payment. Rev. van Gurp immediately saw the issue as one of obedience to Scripture and set about explaining and giving guidance on the issue. Between September 1955 and December 1955, he published a series of articles in the *Una Sancta* explaining and clarifying the need to break from the Trade Unions. Then, on the 22nd November 1956, the Albany consistory provided its members with a declaration regarding union membership. It stated:

> *That there is no place for members of our churches in such organisations, as the Lord calls us to separate ourselves from Babylon (Revelation 18:4) and not associate with her (2 Corinthians 6:14. Revelation 13: 16,17), but on the contrary, fight against her (Genesis 3:15, Revelation 12:7).*
> *That membership of these organisations is therefore incompatible with membership of the Church. The consistory therefore admonishes the members of the Church, for the sake of the Lord and his Word, to distance themselves from such organisations.*[92]

The Armadale consistory was not yet, at this stage, able to make a unanimous decision on this. There was disagreement and, with Rev. Pels leaving in April 1957, there was a lack of leadership. However, remarkably, Rev. van Gurp was able to fill that vacuum and used every opportunity, when in Armadale, to drive the point home that church members needed to break away from the unions. This was especially difficult for Armadale Church as the consistory and the Immigration Committee had encouraged members to take on jobs that involved becoming members of the unions. However, Rev. van Gurp maintained his stance – he saw it simply as a matter of obedience to God and was uncompromising in his approach. In November 1957, just a year after Albany Church, the Armadale Consistory also made a declaration regarding membership of unions and published the following statement in the church bulletin that month:

> *After a discussion about the Trade Unions, joined with the ACTU and the AWU, consistory made the following conclusions:*
>
> *It has become clear to consistory that, considering their foundational principles and, at times, their malpractices, these unions do not act according to Scriptures.*
>
> *Consistory acknowledges, and confesses before the Lord, that they have sinned against the commandment of the Lord that requires from consistory to reject everything that is incompatible with God's Word both in doctrine and life. This applies, in particular, to the position members of the congregation had been placed in.*
>
> *Consistory appreciates that the insight they have obtained regarding this matter will be shared by all brothers and sisters and that this will result in a severing of ties with the Trade Unions.*
>
> *It is the intention of consistory to discuss, at a few meetings, this matter with the congregation so that it will be clear to us what is pleasing to the Lord.*

Many follow up meetings were held. Unions became a topic that was discussed at every opportunity, whether it be in the homes, or at social visits, birthday gatherings and club meetings. By early 1958, it became clear that members meant to abide by the principles espoused in the Consistory's declaration and the first moves were made by individuals to withdraw membership from unions.

Mr. A. Hordyk and Mr. A. van der Plas, both working at the Armadale Brickworks, tendered their resignations on the 14th February 1958 giving three months' notice as per the rules. On the 14th May 1958, Mr. C. Heerema, Mr. J. Hollebrandse and Dad, all working at the Cardup Brickworks, also tendered their resignations from the Union. The end result was that all five men lost their jobs.

This was in spite the State Arbitration Court making an order that the dismissal of Hordyk and van der Plas should be withdrawn. The Labor State Government with the union were quick to lodge an appeal and using their power and influence, the decision was overturned within a week.

The media picked up on the story and over the next few months, dozens of letters to the editor appeared, as well as a few opinion pieces. *The West Australian* ran a supportive editorial on 3rd June 1958 under the heading "*Freedom of Conscience is Endangered in WA.*" Most commentaries and letters supported the sacked men. The unions had displayed their heavy controlling hand and most people didn't like it. It didn't sit well with the Australian culture of fairness and 'a fair go'.

The West Australian also came to visit Dad at Fallon's Place to do a story on him after he was sacked. A father of 13 children now without work because of undue union pressure seemed like quite a story. They came all the way from their Perth office with a reporter and photographer. However, they were rather disappointed. Dad was not experienced with the media and did not see the opportunity to use this to his advantage. He refused to have a photo taken, much to the chagrin of the photographer. Dad also did not show any anxiety when questioned and simply said that he trusted in the Lord and that he was part of a community that would care for each other. There were no accusations or anger which is what they would have been looking for.

Nevertheless, there was still a lot of publicity over the next number of months. It gave Rev. van Gurp and the recently formed Reformed Social Association (later the CPSA – Calvinistic Political and Social Association) as well as others in the church, the opportunity to witness and have their statements published in the media. The Free Reformed Church and their strong Scriptural stance against unionism became well known amongst the Western Australian public. This stance received a lot of empathy amongst the general population and became a point of debate in Parliament. It has been suggested that this issue was one of the reasons that the Labor Government lost the next election held on 2nd April 1959 when the public instead voted in a Liberal team under the leadership of David Brand. This Government, shortly after, introduced exemption clauses, which gave conscientious objectors the opportunity to apply for exemption, provided they paid the equivalent of the union fee to a charity of their choice. Many Church members would make use of this exemption opportunity over the years.

The Liberal Coalition Government, led by Premier Brand, stayed in government for 12 years until 1971, when they lost power to the Labor Party under the leadership of John Tonkin. My parents, and most of the early Dutch reformed migrants, strongly opposed socialism and had been, in the main, supportive of the policies put forward by the Liberal Coalition. As the Labor Party seemed so patently intertwined with the union movement, they were now concerned for their personal freedoms and employment choices under a Labor Government. The Liberal Government, on the other hand had given them full cooperation when they sought exemptions from union membership if that became an issue in the workplace.

47. New Directions

*"When we walk with the Lord
in the light of his word,
what a glory he sheds on our way!
While we do his good will,
he abides with us still,
and with all who will trust and obey."*
~ *John H. Sammis (1887)*

Dad was very sorry to be leaving the Cardup Brickworks. He had thoroughly enjoyed the work that he had been doing for the last few years and fostered a good relationship with the manager, Mr. D. Robinson, who had supported and encouraged him during the six years he had been there. Twice he had left to try something else and both times when that hadn't worked out, Robinson had welcomed him back without hesitation. For the past few years he had been the train driver, transporting coal needed for the brick furnaces, which gave him autonomy and a lot of freedom. Also, during his last year, Robinson had allowed him to go through the brick dump each evening and collect some 20,000 bricks that were suitable for the house he was building.

Robinson was very apologetic when he had to dismiss Dad. It was not something he wanted to do, but he knew that if he didn't the workers would make trouble and possibly go on strike, as they had done at the Armadale Brickworks to force the sacking of Messrs. Hordijk and van der Plas. As the manager responsible for the efficient running of the operation, he could not risk that.

Dad finished at the Brickworks on the 18th August 1958. He had been there since 13th June 1952. Mr. Robinson furnished Dad with a good reference, despite the fact that it untruthfully claimed that he left of his own accord.

It was during this time that Dad had commissioned Mr. Bijl to build the family home. With that, also came a substantial loan from the bank that had to be serviced and paid off over eight years. Dad was under significant pressure to maintain a regular and reasonably well-paid job.

To tide Dad over for a few months Robinson offered Dad a job on his farm near Byford. They were just going into the harvesting season and he could do with an extra hand for a few months. This would allow Dad time to seek another job. Dad happily accepted this offer as he wanted to avoid any lost time without income.

There is evidence that Dad did apply for a number of jobs prior to leaving the Brickyards, but it appears nothing came of them so, when his dismissal became a fact, he had nowhere to go. One of his application letters has survived and was found amongst his papers. Dated 28th May 1958 it reads:

> *Dear Sir,*
> *Today I saw your advertisement in the West for a man on a poultry and pig farm.*
> *As I'm interested in such a job, because I'm looking for something else, I would like to hear some more particulars about it. Enclosed you will find a stamped envelope, so if I'm not asking too much, please send*

> *some details.*
> *At present I'm working at Cardup Brickyards Byford, so if you would like to enquire about me, just ask particulars about "Corney."*
> *With Kind regards*
> *Yours Faithfully*
> *C. Kleijn.*

He was confident that Cardup Brickworks would give him a good reference. He had developed a sound reputation there for being a reliable and conscientious worker. Interestingly, his name Cornelis was somehow Australianised into 'Corney.'

After leaving Cardup, Dad enjoyed working for his former boss, Mr. Robinson, on his farm for a few months until, on the 5th January 1960, he was successful in gaining a permanent position working in a small goods manufacturing business, Watsonia in Spearwood. A fellow church member worked there and had introduced him to the opportunity when the vacancy came up. Watsonia was a family company established in 1909 and had become a leader in the dairy and small goods industry, producing a range of food products. Dad worked in the butter section and spent most of his time in the cool room, packing and storing butter.

For Dad, this seemed a step back, working in a factory, something that he had loathed in the Netherlands. Now here he was in 1960, at 47 years of age, eight years after migrating, back into a similar type of employment. However, while he didn't enjoy the work, he was taking it far more in his stride than years earlier when working in Dutch factories. He had really loathed the work then and it became one of the primary reasons for him to emigrate. When he had just arrived in Australia, and it was suggested to him to seek work at the

Cardup Brickworks, he exclaimed, "I didn't come to Australia to work in a factory!" Nevertheless, he had ended up working there for six years. Still, he fervently yearned to be self-employed again and be independent. However, the question remained: how to begin when there were always pressing financial demands. He had a large family to support, church and school commitments, and now as well, a substantial mortgage that needed repayment in eight years. Regular and reliable income was essential.

It wasn't long before Dad was not feeling well. He spent a lot of time in the cool rooms and it was starting to affect his health. The 27-kilometre journey to work on a motor bike each day was also starting to bother him especially in the winter months. He was suffering from constant kidney infections which were aggravated by the cold. He wrote to his sister Marie in March 1960 that with the house just finished, he is not able to fund the purchase of a car, so had to persevere for the time being with the motor bike. He did own a car, a 1936 Dodge sedan, bought a few years previous for the sole purpose of taking the family to church. It was a large spacious car in which at least 12 people could be squeezed in for the six-kilometre ride to church. However, it was an old and expensive car to run and totally unsuitable for the 55-kilometre daily round trip to work.

In June 1961, after nearly 18 months working at Watsonia, Dad suffered from a hernia caused by heavy lifting at work. He was often required to move heavy cartons of butter and load them onto transport vehicles. To improve the situation, he was operated on, spent 10 days in hospital and was told by his doctor that he cannot return to work for three months. As the hernia happened at work, he received 80% of his salary paid for this period. He wrote to his adopted mother, Miek in July

1961, about a month after the operation, that he was now feeling well and has the opportunity to catch up on church work that he had previously found difficult to keep up with. He was still in consistory as a deacon, but had the additional role of being the church treasurer. He was also on the committee and treasurer of an association that organises Bible study activities for the youth of the church.

Dad was now writing in a very positive way about church life, in contrast to the letters he'd written three years earlier when he was describing his time in consistory as the most stressful period in his life. Now he related how they enjoyed the preaching and teaching of their new pastor, Reverend Kornelius Bruning, who had arrived with wife and seven children on the 11th May 1960. Ordained as pastor in March 1950, he had previously served in two places in the Netherlands: the Reformed Church Liberated of Mildam and the Reformed Church Liberated of Rijnsburg. When called by the Free Reformed Church of Armadale he was overwhelmed by the letters and communication he received from the Armadale church members. Everyone seemed at pains to make it clear how much need there was for a teacher and pastor in the congregation. The joy and thankfulness to God knew no bounds when the Armadale congregation received a telegram from Rev. Bruning on the 29th December 1959 that said 'Call accepted in faith'.

The school, the need of which had been talked about since the first arrival of migrants in the early 1950s, had also now become a reality. Dad had been very supportive of this drive to start a school and had served on the initial committee formed in September 1953 that looked at the feasibility of starting a Christian school. Their report recommended the formation of a focused school association that had a mandate to establish a reformed Christian school for the children of the church as soon as possible. This association was formed at a meeting held on the 20th December 1954, with a membership of 31 all agreeing to pay one pound a week. Mr. H. Terpstra was appointed as the inaugural chairman. After only three years, on the 2nd December 1957, the John Calvin School located on Robin Hood Avenue, Armadale, opened its doors to 70 children from the Free Reformed Church of Armadale. The two teachers, principal Mr. L. Bolhuis and Miss H. Rozema, had both arrived from the Netherlands some months earlier.

My parents saw this development as a real blessing. Five of us children were able to be part of the first group of students there: myself - Harry (Grade 7), Mieke (Grade 5), Willy (Grade 4), Kees (Grade 2) and Arthur (Grade 1). The school was housed in two classrooms, one with grades 4-7 with Mr. Bolhuis and the other grades 1-3 with Miss Rozema.

After three months, in September 1961, Dad returned back to work at Watsonia. He had enjoyed the break, especially the last period when he had been relatively healthy but still not declared fit enough to work. While recovering he had been able to get involved with the family, get all his church commitments up to date and, generally, have a stress-free time. He didn't enjoy his work and was not looking forward to it, especially with the constant health problems he had previously been experiencing.

After only a month back he again suffered extreme kidney pains and even had problems with eating. He was forced to take a week sick leave and visit the Doctor who told him to find another job as the work in the cool room was just not agreeing with him and his situation would only get worse. This really forced his hand. Some time before, he had been offered work in a bakery for a member of the church - Mr. H. B.

Terpstra, who had bought the Spearwood Bakery in partnership with Daan Bosveld, the oldest son of the Bosvelds. Dad was initially reluctant to take on the position but now, following the advice from his doctor, he decided to see Mr. Terpstra to take up his offer of employment.

48. Towards Self-employment

"One father is more than a hundred Schoolmasters."
~ *George Herbert*

On the 8th October 1961 my parents celebrated their 25th wedding anniversary. While things were still extremely tight financially, they, nevertheless, felt extremely blessed by the Lord. They had 13 healthy children, two of whom were married and now also one grandchild, daughter of Peter and Zwannie, Tina Wilhelmina, born on 15th May 1961, just five months before my parents silver wedding anniversary.

The Church, and serving the Lord, meant everything to my parents and, after so many years of church struggles, they were finally experiencing unity and sound Biblical leadership provided by Rev. Bruning. They just loved the Sunday worship services and his preaching, as well as all the other activities that developed within the church during those years. Especially for their children's sake they felt blessed to have a Christian school, youth Bible study clubs and catechism instruction by Rev. Bruning.

There was a good mix of ages and young people so all of their children had no problem finding friends and future partners amongst the church community. But what was paramount for my parents was that their maturing children all sought to serve the Lord, with the married couples being faithful members of the church and, the next three, Niek (21), Janet (20) and Mappie (18), all attending pre-confession classes with a view towards doing their Public Profession of Faith in the church in due time. With these many blessings my parents were very happy and content.

It was with this very positive frame of mind that they could celebrate their silver wedding anniversary. The evening of celebration was organised by their grown-up children, who all went out of their way to make it a memorable event. A wide range of church friends had been invited, including Rev. Bruning and his wife, who were active participants and made a substantial contribution to the entertainment. A number of speeches and skits were recorded on a cassette tape and have been preserved. They reflect a very positive atmosphere of celebration and joy. From listening to the tapes, it is evident my parents were respected and entrenched in the church community. After nine years in Australia it appeared that they were starting to get a sense that this was now home. The fact that all communication with each other and in the church community, including Sunday worship services, was in the Dutch mother tongue certainly assisted them in this feeling.

However, the family back in the Netherlands was missed – Mum had four brothers and two sisters, while Dad had two sisters. Mum's father had died at the age of 87, just six months earlier on the 7th December 1960. Since his wife had died three years earlier, he had moved from the family home in Brandwijk to live with his youngest daughter in Sliedrecht. Without any obvious illness, he died suddenly while sitting in his chair, peeling potatoes for the family. Again, as when her mother died, Mum had to grieve this loss without the opportunity of being present with the family.

For the anniversary, Mum's brothers and sisters in the

Netherlands all got together and spoke on a tape recorder, which was then sent to Armadale in time for the celebration. On the tape they reflected on the past, particularly the positive memory of mother and father Schutte and their life of humble faith and example. They also spoke of the hardships my parents had experienced in their married life like the mobilisation, the war, the hunger and enforced separations. They encouraged my parents and us all to remain faithful in our service to God and to always trust in Him alone. At the end they sang together a few of the family's favourite psalms and hymns that had, for them all, special meaning and memories. Finally, they finished off with the Dutch national anthem. Before singing it, they suggested that it would remind my parents of their Dutch heritage which they claimed they would never lose, despite living in faraway Australia.

It was a moving and special tape, treasured and valued by my parents. For us children it gave some indication of the warm bonds that there were with family in the Netherlands and how much of that contact had been sacrificed when migrating. For example, as children, we had to grow up without the privilege of grandparents, uncles, aunties and cousins.

One of Mum's brothers cheekily suggested that maybe we had left the Netherlands too early as, within a year of us leaving, the country had started experiencing a tremendous boom in construction and rebuilding which was still going on after all those years. Workers were in short supply and a lot of foreign people had to be recruited to ensure the necessary development continued. "If you were here now Kees (my Dad), you would pick up work straight away," he claimed. It was, after all, the lack of reliable employment opportunity that had finally driven my parents to migrate.

Both my parents and the Dutch relatives marvelled at the

technology of being able to record their voices and then for that to be heard and listened to by relatives on the other side of the world. "Who would have dreamt 9 years ago that we could hear each other's voices in this way?" one of Mum's sisters said. When the tape was received in Australia, our family reciprocated by also all speaking on a tape and sending that back to them.

Very good contact was maintained with the family in the Netherlands predominantly with the letter writing of my parents. Even us children were often coached to send a letter to one of our *'ooms'* or *'tantes'*, especially on the occasion of their birthdays. The Dutch relatives were also very generous in sending parcels containing gifts, which could include Dutch delicacies, as well as clothes and other useful items. Dad's sister Marie, who was single, was particularly generous in regularly sending parcels. She had obviously worked out that money was tight and that with a large family there was always some need. All these parcels were warmly welcomed by everyone in the family, as there were often things in there that could be shared - like books, toys, clothes and even lollies. Mum never had to buy material for sewing as it all came to her via those parcels.

The silver wedding anniversary was certainly a highlight that was discussed and talked about for some time. Both Mum and Dad wrote about it in glowing terms to relatives and friends in the Netherlands. Mum wrote to her sister Marie: "The children all put a lot of effort into the day and then surprised us with a gift of an organ. It was a lovely evening that we will not soon forget. The Lord has richly blessed us." Dad wrote to his sister, Marie, that the children organised everything for the evening – "they picked us up by car at 8.00 p.m. and drove us to the Buffalo Hall that the children had hired for the evening." Besides relatives, some 40 guests had been invited. But, Dad wrote, "it was such a pity that my own siblings could not be there. In the circumstances we are thankful for the church community, many of whom have become our extended family."

A few months after the celebration, in November 1961, Dad commenced working with Mr. Terpstra in the Spearwood bakery. It was a busy and growing enterprise, especially with Spearwood at the time settled by scores of new Yugoslavian migrants, many working in and developing market gardens. To cater for this growing Yugoslavian clientele, the bakery started producing European style crusty breads and loaves which became very popular and sought after by the Yugoslavian community. From the day Dad started working there, he noticed demand for the goods baked by the Spearwood bakery was strong and increasingly so.

Dad was now working with a fellow church member. There was a good working atmosphere and there was optimism for the future of the business. It was a real family business with Mr. Terpstra's wife involved with the shopkeeping, and their 16-year-old son Steve working as an apprentice baker. Besides that, their eldest daughter, Tran, left school when she turned 14 in 1961 to also work in the bakery. A year later daughter Helen also left school at age 14 to help in the family business.

Mr. Terpstra had little capital or expertise in business or financial management and was relying on his partner in the business Daan Bosveld jnr., to provide that for him. He was happy to do the work, manage the business and produce the products to meet customer demand, but looked to his partner for capital, business planning and advice.

This partnership came to a tragic end when in February 1962, Mr. Daan Bosveld was involved in a serious car accident and was grievously injured. He had been on his way home from one of his building projects in the north of Western Australia with a fellow workman behind the wheel when they hit a bridge, seriously injuring Daan. He never recovered. Because of severe head injuries he was unable to communicate or care for himself. He became totally dependent on care, which his parents were eventually able to give him after he was released from hospital and transported to be with them in Tasmania. He died eight years later in 1970 at the age of 41. He had been an enthusiastic and driven entrepreneur who had touched the lives of many and who had, without hesitation, employed many of the early Dutch Free Reformed migrants, who had not always found it easy to procure jobs elsewhere, particularly in areas where there was union control.

His accident had a major impact on the Terpstra business and family and, in turn, also on my Dad. The growing business needed additional capital to buy more equipment and upgrade machinery. It needed an astute businessperson to give advice and plan the best way forward. Now, with this tragic turn of events the Spearwood bakery had lost a valuable business partner and, with that, lost access to capital and business acumen. The Terpstras were now called upon to find money to pay out to Mr. Bosveld's attorney what was his rightful share in the business. And the business plan that had been developed with Mr. Bosveld, only some six months earlier, could no longer be rolled out.

Consequently, the working hours were increased and the Terpstra family, including the children, were called upon to work unbelievably long hours to keep the business going. Dad had a more regular routine. Except for special days like Christmas or Easter, where shifts of 24 hours were common, normal working times for him were: Monday, starting at 1.00

a.m.; Tuesdays to Thursdays at 2.00 a.m.; and Fridays at 10.00 p.m. On weekdays he took the youngest Terpstra children, Janet and later, Sandra, to the John Calvin School, dropping them off in Armadale on his way home each morning. This meant it was necessary he finish and leave the bakery about 8.00 a.m. each morning. Only on Saturday morning would he work longer.

Tran and Helen recalled in 2019 how they, from the age of 14, started work at 4.00 a.m. each morning and then worked right through to about 3.00 p.m. in the afternoon. The work for the family was relentless with never a break. They both recall my Dad with fondness, remembering him as an extremely hard worker, who was always calm and considerate. He also maintained a certain sense of decorum - always wearing long white trousers, a white apron and a tall baker's hat. They appreciated Dad intervening at times when he felt their Dad was being unreasonable or short tempered towards them as young children. They would be asked to leave and then my Dad would address Mr. Terpstra on the issue in their absence. According to Tran and Helen, their father had respect for my Dad and would take notice.

They also remembered lots of humorous and memorable times in the bakery. Helen would work alongside Dad on one of the two ovens they had. Mr. Terpstra and his son Steve would work on the other oven. The equipment was old and not the most efficient and a lot of the bread, especially the Italian loaves, had to be made by hand. It was hard and hot work, but no one complained, and everyone adapted themselves to what was needed. Despite the hardship, Tran still says it was a unique family time of working together.

As an employee, Dad was privileged that he did not carry the worries of the business and could leave when his work of baking was done. The packaging, distribution and running of the shop as well as the accounts and finances of the Spearwood bakery was something the Terpstra family, as owners of the business, carried responsibility for. Dad did, however, have other commitments in life, including in the Church consistory and being a father of a large family. He was often away at night, attending consistory meetings or making home visits to families of the church. To be able to do this, he had to make sure he got a bit of sleep during the day because he had to leave at 1.00 a.m. in the morning to go to work. These were not ideal hours when you had extensive family and church commitments.

Tran and Helen remember their younger sisters, Janet and Sandra, relating how Dad, on his way to dropping them off at school, would have difficulty staying awake. They would have to keep talking or singing all the way to stop him from falling asleep. There were lots of close calls but, in November 1968, it became a reality when he nodded off and the car left the road and rolled. While the car (which was a 1946 Ford Prefect) was a write-off, miraculously nobody was seriously hurt and, within a few days, Dad purchased a Suzuki Holden and was back behind the wheel again.

Dad had never given up the idea of becoming self-employed again. He loved the idea of being independent and not having a boss to answer to. After all, this was how he started when he got married back in 1936, independent and running his own business. He still had such fond memories of those early years and the dream of being self-employed again never left him. By the mid-1960s the idea of starting a pig farm was forming in his mind. Since 1954, he had always kept a pig or two for fattening and slaughtering to meet the family needs. In 1964 I had purchased 30 piglets for fattening and sold them six months later at the market in West Perth. At the time I worked on a mixed poultry and pig farm just across the road from where we lived and so was able to relate to Dad the economics of it all. My eldest brother, Peter, was in the building trade and he agreed to help build some of the sheds Dad needed.

While Dad's hours were not the most desirable, it allowed him to do quite a few things during the day, providing he didn't spend too much time trying to catch up on sleep. So, he allowed himself to be sleep-deprived and instead, worked on setting up a pig farm. His sister, Marie, asked him in a letter why he is so thin and Dad wrote in return: "Well, that is easily answered. I have been far too busy the last period, working in the bakery at night and during the day trying to build up a piggery business so that eventually I can work full time from home."

Early in 1968 Dad bought his first lot of 70 pigs. He had calculated that he needed to build this up to at least 300 pigs to have a viable business. More sheds and facilities were built over the next two years. He was now working to a deadline in realising this dream, as he started to see that he may soon need to look for another job.

Dad recognised the situation at the Terpstra Spearwood Bakery as reaching a crisis. The hours of unrelenting work put in by the whole family was just not sustainable and eventually something had to give. Not having a business mind and lacking the capital since losing the founding partner, Daan Bosveld, continued to have a negative effect, despite occurring many years earlier. After eight years of working together, Dad had grown very close to them and, no doubt would have had some discussion with Mr. Terpstra about the best way forward. He was personally concerned about their wellbeing and saw that, particularly for the Terpstra children, the relentless work did not allow them to live normally balanced lives as maturing young adults.

By the end of 1968 Mr. Terpstra decided to try and sell the business. His wife was particularly keen to not only get away from the business, but also move back to the Netherlands. By Easter 1969 the business was sold and the Terpstra family, minus their eldest son, Steve, and two eldest daughters, Tran and Helen, moved back to the Netherlands.

Unfortunately, Dad was not quite ready to start working from home so he found temporary employment with another bakery. More sheds and facilities needed to be built to accommodate the 300 pigs he considered necessary. It took nearly another 12 months before he could finally and confidently become self-employed and start his own piggery business working from home. His long-cherished dream finally became a reality in February 1970. He was 56 years of age and it had been 17 years since he arrived in Australia in 1952.

49. Changing Dynamics in the Family

"Rejoice with your family in the beautiful land of life."

~Albert Einstein

In the passage of time from when Dad started work in the Terpstra bakery, just after my parents 25th wedding anniversary in October 1961, to when he started working at home in his piggery business in February 1970, a lot changed for my parents and their family. At the time of their silver wedding anniversary the two eldest were married and they had one granddaughter. By February 1970, another five of their children had married and they had been blessed with a total of 20 grandchildren.

Five months after the anniversary on the 28th March 1962, Niek left by train to go to Tasmania to be with his girlfriend, Ina Bosveld. They got to know each other while the Bosveld family lived in Armadale and had kept up correspondence since they had left for Tasmania in 1957. Less than a year later, on the 1st February 1963, Niek and Ina were married in Tasmania and decided to make that their home. Niek worked as a builder with his father-in-law, while also working towards setting up his own farm.

CHANGING DYNAMICS IN THE FAMILY

The following year on the 3rd April 1964 Mappie married Herbert Strating, a recently-arrived Dutch immigrant who worked as a draftsman at Cockburn Cement. They settled in Armadale. Mappie, who finished her junior certificate, the first in the family to do so, had for several years been working as an office clerk with an office supply company, Lamson Paragon in Perth.

A year later, on the 23rd April 1965, Janet married Eddy Schoof, a nursery man who came with his family from Tasmania in 1962. They also settled in Armadale. Janet had worked at home with Mum from when she was 14 but when Reverend Bruning and his family arrived in April 1960, she started working full time helping Mrs. Bruning.

On the 19th March 1966, I married Maria Jacoba Schoof, a younger sister of Eddy. For a number of years she had worked at the Boans store in Perth in the accounts department, on a ledger machine. I left school in 1962 after completing my Junior certificate (Year 10) to work at George Wood's Poultry and Pig farm, which was just across the road from our house. While there, I completed the Leaving Certificate (Year 12), studying at night and went back full time to the Perth Technical College to study Architecture. A year later, about six weeks before marrying, I started work as a quantity surveyor with the building company, Karlson Construction. We settled in Armadale.

Four years later, on the 3rd March 1970 Willy married Reinhard van der Laan. He worked in the building industry as a roof carpenter. Willy had for some time been working in an office, also in Perth. They too, settled in Armadale.

Three months earlier, on the 21st November 1969 Jenny and Jan Hollebrandse, with their three adopted children, had decided to return to the Netherlands. Jan had an ageing mother and was keen to introduce his family to her and his siblings that he had left behind when he migrated in 1952. They were unsure how long they might stay in the Netherlands, but there was some expectation it could be a while.

So, by April 1970, of the 13 children in the Kleyn household, one had moved to Tasmania, one to the Netherlands, the other five married ones all lived within 10 kilometres of the family home and six were still at home. These were: Mieke (22), Kees (19), Arthur (17), Mary (16), Susan (14) and Margaret (13). The married children had, by now, a total of 20 children between them all.

In May 1968 the number of grandchildren for my parents jumped by three when Mappie gave birth to triplets. It was a first for the Armadale Maternity Hospital and so created a lot of excitement and publicity for the town. When they finally came home (all healthy after some weeks in incubators at the King Edward Memorial Hospital to which they had been transferred), the work for Mappie was relentless and impossible on her own. It was decided that Mieke, who at the time was working as a home helper for the Egberts family, would go and move in with the Strating family and help there full time. She did this for eight months before returning to the Egberts family.

During this time Mum went without an assistant in the home. However, this really became too much for her. The demands for washing, cleaning and cooking for the grown up family never seemed to lessen. On top of that, there were always a lot of visitors to care for and, over the weekends, dinner tables of at least 20 was the usual to cook for. The teenage girls also attracted lots of potential suitors who came visiting. Besides this, Mum still kept in close touch with many families in the congregation that had special needs and it was not uncommon for a number of boarders to be taken up for weeks on end, to give their parents a break. Mum maintained her ethos to always be ready to help others. As children we were also roped in with that quest and had to make sure we would invite over, for a Sunday or evening visit, those who might have special needs and were not naturally able to develop friendships. I was regularly requested to invite over and entertain a blind boy in the congregation, Jacob Heerema, who was about my age.

Mum was always ready to offer one of her daughters to help out when she became aware of a need in a family. She would make a unilateral decision on behalf of her daughters and then relate to her daughter what she had arranged. My sisters simply had to comply and devote their energy and time to the family that Mum had made the arrangement with. All of them remember working in other households for varying periods of time, depending on the circumstances. Sometimes it might have been just a few days to help out, in other cases it involved longer periods, even up to a year.

When Mary finished her Junior Certificate (Year 10) at the end of 1969, she was asked to leave school and help in the household and so fill the gap left by her older sister. She had planned to do her Leaving Certificate but was told she would have to try and achieve that through night school. By that time, the piggery was going and the arrangement was made that Mary would help Dad one day a week in the piggery and, on the other days, assist Mum. In the afternoon she would get a few hours free to attend to her studies.

Mary related in 2019 how she enjoyed both the farm work and working for Mum which she did till she went nursing in September 1972. She does, however, recall the sheer amount of housework that the household demanded, and the way things were done, especially the washing where everything was still washed and rinsed the old fashion way. Mum was slow to adapt to new ways. In 2019 my sister still clearly remembered the routine - Monday washing, Tuesday ironing and cleaning the bedrooms, Wednesday baking, Thursday washing again and Friday cleaning all the living areas.

Until Dad came home to work on the piggery, his time with the children individually was very restricted. His life was always so busy. Except for the one-year break given to the elders and deacons after a term of four years was served, Dad was always in consistory. He was also very conscientious in attending all other arranged meetings for church members - like those for the school, for the youth clubs, for political and social study and the fortnightly men's Bible study group. With the evenings often tied up with meetings of all kinds, as well as the required visits to families as an elder or deacon, he was forced to find some time during the day to sleep and so had little spare time when the children were around.

With courting couples and growing children, it was Mum who bore the bulk of the load of communicating and coaching the children during this period. It was always Mum who was there to see her children off in the morning, whether to school or work and to be there to welcome them back home. Any of the children going out in the evening could expect Mum to be waiting for them, no matter what time they came home. She simply could not go to bed until she had welcomed everyone back home.

While working for Terpstra's bakery, Dad enjoyed normal annual leave but that was usually taken up by working at home. Only twice in those years did he actually take a week off with Mum and they were not lavish affairs, once being in Yanchep and another time in Coogee. In December 1963, my parents had a week's holiday at Coogee and for the first time ever took some of the younger children that were still at home. This was a rare experience for everyone, and it had never happened before. The older children who were married or working by that time, had never experienced a holiday time with their parents. There had just not been the opportunity nor the money. Then, during the last few years working at the Spearwood Bakery, Dad used all his spare time trying to set up the Piggery business, so, again, any leave was not used for holidaying but to work at home.

Until the late 1960s money was always tight. A baker's salary was not particularly generous, and Dad needed additional income from other family members to make ends meet. It was customary in our family for the working children to pay 50% of their salary to our parents. This was considered quite normal amongst migrant families – children contributing to the family coffers. In fact, many parents even insisted on receiving 100% of the children's salary and then only giving back to their children some pocket money that might be needed for their miscellaneous expenses. So only paying 50% seemed like a reasonable arrangement.

In my case I had started full time work in August 1962. This was six months after Niek left to go to Tasmania and we all knew that his leaving left a hole in the family budget. I was receiving a salary of 14 pounds per week and gave 7 pounds of that to my parents, which was a welcome relief. In today's value the seven pounds would be worth $206. Two years later, my salary had jumped to 20 pounds, so my parents received 10 pounds per week ($285 in today's value). Mum wrote to Marie, Dad's sister, in November 1962 that I had started working, "which was a big relief for the finances."

Towards the end of the 1960s the financial pressure eased

somewhat as the loan on the house had, by that time, been paid off. This gave Dad a bit more flexibility to start spending money on developing his piggery business and a bit more confidence in being able to take a risk. Having a debt free home and property allowed him to arrange a line of credit to fund the infrastructure needed for housing at least 300 pigs and the capital to buy the initial stock of pigs.

Speaking to my younger siblings, Mary and Susan, in 2019, they do not recall experiencing any financial hardship in their youth. They found Dad generous with gifts and special treats and, at no time, did they sense there was any financial stress. This is such a contrast to what the older children in the family experienced, especially those that had grown up in the war years and those first years after immigration. After all, my eldest sibling was born in November 1937 and my youngest in May 1957, nearly 20 years later. When my eldest brother Peter got married in 1960, my youngest sister Margaret was only three years old.

50. The Dutch Family

"Blood is thicker than water."
~German Proverb

Due to the tyranny of distance, my parents really missed the siblings they had left behind when immigrating and would have loved it if one of them came over to visit them. Mum was a prolific letter writer and, each week, she would write an average of five to ten letters to send to family and friends in the Netherlands. When the mailman came past each day, about mid-morning, there would be an immediate rush to collect the mail. If there was no letter from the Netherlands there would be disappointment but, if there was one, everything else in the household could wait until the letter was read. How she missed her family and how she would love it if some of them came over to Australia to visit. "We have the space and would love to welcome you and show you around," she wrote. In the early 1960s Mum still had four brothers and two sisters, and Dad's two sisters were also still alive.

While both Dad and Mum's parents had passed away, Dad's foster mother, Miek Verhoef, was then still living. Born in 1879 she had lost her husband Pieter in 1936, just a few weeks before my parents were married. Miek meant a lot to my Dad as she and her husband had reached out to him when, as a youngster, he had undergone such a traumatic experience in respect to his parents. While Dad had grown up at his grandfather's place, Pieter and Miek had always extended their hospitality and, when Dad's grandfather passed away, Dad, at 19 years of age, had moved into their home where he stayed till he got married, four years later. His sister, Marie, had been fostered by Pieter and Miek after the death of their mum in 1919 so, whenever Dad was there, he was also in the company of his sister, which he really appreciated.

After immigrating my parents regularly corresponded with Miek and she, in turn, showed genuine interest in the weal and woe of the family by reciprocal correspondence. This was one Dutch relative that we as children definitely needed to write to for her birthday. She was always interested in what everyone was doing and how we were going. When Rev. Bruning went to the Netherlands for three months in 1965 he, to the delight of my parents, visited Miek to pass on their greetings and best wishes. As they, themselves, could not visit her this meant a lot to them.

In 1966 Miek, who had been a widow for nearly 30 years, was, at 87 years of age, becoming frail and weak. She had difficulty moving about and really needed someone to assist her in her daily needs. Dad's sister, Marie, decided to take leave from her midwifery practice in Amsterdam and move in with her in Brandwijk. Miek was her foster mother and Marie was prepared to do anything for her, including providing the best possible care. She put her own needs and work on hold for this.

In May 1966 Dad wrote Miek a personal and moving farewell letter. In it, he expresses regret that he cannot come over to visit her, but tells her that his thoughts and prayers are constantly with her. "We believe that the Lord will give you what is necessary in the circumstances," he wrote, "and may you experience the peace, that trust in Christ will give you." He then went on to thank her for what she had all done for him over the many years both before and after his marriage, and for the support and encouragement she had given when they had migrated. She was one of the few in the family who, in those early planning times of migration, had understood and given total and unconditional support. Dad had been blessed to have such a loving, caring and Christian couple - and later widow - involved in his life at the most critical times.

Miek died on the 12th May 1966. Dad's letter had arrived just a few days earlier. Dad's sister, Marie, confirmed she was able to read it out to her and that Miek had still been able to understand it. Miek and Pieter never had children of their own and had always treated my Dad's sister as their own daughter. For Dad also they had been like parents. It was painful for my parents, particularly for Dad, to be so far away when she was ailing and nearing death. They were however comforted to know that she had died in faith and that she was now with the Lord. She had always been a powerful Christian witness and example for Dad.

The death of Miek hit Marie particularly hard. It brought back into sharp focus the tragic death of her mother, when she was only three. While Dad had tried to block the event out of his mind and not even talk about it, Marie had constantly tried to understand and come to terms with the event. She had often visited her dad after he was institutionalised. While my parents heard little from her over the next few months after Mieks death, they sensed that she was not coping well. My Mum appealed to her to come to Australia to be with the family here. In September 1966 she wrote:

I have already written it in the last letter for you to

come here but now I emphasise it again, please do come here. I firmly believe you should get totally away from your current situation. Being here and being involved in completely new experiences will act like mental therapy and could be the best opportunity for you to move forward. This is not a frivolous invitation Marie; I really mean it. Don't ponder over it too long - <u>Just come</u>!

Furthermore, we can only point you to the revealed Word of God. He is the Father of orphans. Haven't the three of you (Dad and his two sisters) experienced that in your whole life? Don't ever forget that. The Lord gives strength to carry our burdens. He gives to the weary courage. Trust in Him in all things.

Despite more appeals and overtures to Marie to come to Australia, it was not till December 1969, more than three years later, that Marie finally made the decision to come to Perth and visit the family. Attempts had been made to also have her sister, Lijsje, come with her but, while she would have loved to come, her husband did not support the idea. He had always been totally opposed to the immigration undertaken by my parents and still had not come to terms with it. So, for his wife to leave for a month to visit was out of the question.

All the family - except Niek and Ina who were in Tasmania and Jenny and Jan, who had just left two weeks earlier to return to the Netherlands - were there to greet Marie when she arrived at the Perth Airport on the 10th December 1969. She had a lot to catch up on. When we left the Netherlands in 1952 my parents had nine children. Now they had 13, six married and between those, 20 grandchildren.

She stayed for six weeks and, during that time, really

endeared herself to everyone. She was an enthusiastic and energetic lady with a wide set of interests. Having run a midwife clinic in Amsterdam, she also could relate lots of interesting experiences. She was the contact with our past that we had all missed, so she was treated with respect and love by everyone. Day outings were organised, including a day on Rottnest Island with the whole family, as well as a family dinner held at our parents' place. Dad had just resigned from his temporary job at the bakery, so he could be free for the whole time his sister was in Australia. After she left, his plan was to work full time on the piggery.

During her six week stay, Marie arranged plane tickets for herself and my parents to visit Tasmania for ten days to see Niek and Ina and their family. While Niek had been to Western Australia twice since he had left eight years earlier, my parents had never, as yet, had the opportunity to go to Tasmania. By this time, Niek and Ina had four children and were living on a property they had bought, with the intention of developing it into a productive beef farm. Their busy life was put on hold for a few days so they could provide hospitality to both the parents and the Auntie from the Netherlands. It was a special time of bonding and sharing and the contact with Marie and the Tasmanian family, that was then established, would always remain strong.

It is understandable that Marie would want to talk a lot with my parents about the tragedy of her parents. She had struggled with it all her life and brought it up often with my parents during her stay in Australia. This was a problem as Dad's coping mechanism was to try and suppress the whole event and not talk about it. My parents had also decided, when leaving the Netherlands 17 years ago, that the children would be protected and not told about the terrible circumstances surrounding the death of Dad's parents.

Only Jenny had been told by Mum while they still lived in the Netherlands but on immigrating, my parents had made a conscious decision to not speak about it to anyone anymore. Jenny was asked to not share the story with her siblings. In 1952 Australia seemed so remote and far away from the Netherlands so they thought the knowledge of the family tragedy that had occurred in the Netherlands back in 1919 didn't need to be carried forward to Australia. They wished to protect their children from the horror of it all and any possible stigma that may result.

Mum told me later that it did cause some strain with Marie when she was in Australia that first time. Dad had real difficulty talking about his parents and yet his sister often wanted to bring it up. My parents were also very sensitive about the children learning about it somehow, through overhearing conversations or simply because Marie had no compunctions about discussing it and sharing the story. After all, her coping mechanism was to talk about it – the exact opposite of her brother. They would have confided to Marie that they had decided not to tell their children about the event and that they wished that to remain like that. No doubt she would have disagreed but would have been careful not to mention anything while the children were present.

After six weeks, on the 21st January 1970, the whole family was back at the Perth Airport to farewell Marie before she travelled back to the Netherlands. For everyone it had been a memorable time and, for most of my siblings, it was the start of a journey of regular correspondence to the one Auntie they had now met and formed a strong bond with.

51. Working from Home: A Dream Realised

"Agriculture for an honorable and highminded man, is the best of all occupations or arts by which men procure the means of living."
~ *Xenophon (430-354 B.C.)*

After Dad's sister left to go back to the Netherlands following a six week stay, Dad focused his time and energy on making a success of his piggery business. From having only some 60 pigs when he'd started in early 1968, he now had capacity for over 300. With the assistance of his oldest son Peter, he built one large shed which boosted the capacity to about 150 and two slightly smaller sheds with a capacity of 100 each. The interior of the sheds was divided into separate pens, with each pen holding about 15 pigs. The floors were concrete and could be washed out easily with a high-pressure hose. All the debris would then run into drains from which it then flowed into a large open pit outside. This pit was emptied daily by a sprinkler system that operated across the 5-acre property. This waste, in turn, provided good compost for the grass that helped feed the six or so young beef cattle that Dad reared each year.

Drinking water for the pigs came from automatic watering systems. The pelleted food had to be dished out twice a day.

The piggery was set up as a new modern way of rearing pigs for slaughter. They were kept clean on washed concrete floors, not given any waste food, and kept on a strict diet of pellets. Many piggeries in those days were relying on waste foods from restaurants and kitchens so this was a bold step, relying on expensive pelleted food as their only supply.

It did mean, however, that it was a relatively clean business: the health of the pigs could be better controlled and if one became sick it could be quickly quarantined. The stock could be inspected, fed, and cared for from a central corridor that ran through all the sheds. Cleanliness and hygiene were of utmost importance and each time a batch of pigs left, the pens had to be thoroughly cleaned and disinfected. Pigs are very susceptible to disease, so prevention of a possible outbreak was always a priority.

The business model was simple – Dad bought the pigs from the market as weaners when they were about six weeks old and then sold them back into the market three months later as porkers. The difference in purchase price and sale price had to be sufficient to cover all his costs and then to provide a reasonable income. It was simple mathematics to work out what the profit was each time he sold a batch of pigs.

Nearly every week, on Tuesday, some 30 pigs would be picked up by a transport contractor to be offered for sale at the Midland Markets. Dad would also go to the market and if prices and stock looked right, he would purchase another batch of about the same number. The pigs he bought would then arrive via the contractor late in the afternoon. With between 300-400 pigs on hand most of the time, his weekly turnover would be between 30-40 pigs. The record number he ever had was just below 600.

Dad was highly successful in caring for and farming the

pigs. His stock rarely suffered from disease as he was absolutely fastidious in his focus on cleanliness and oversight. He was exacting by nature and paid great attention to detail so could easily spot any pig that needed special attention or a preventive injection. Due to his outstanding care, the quality of his pigs on the market was always excellent and often he was listed in the Farmers Weekly as having achieved top prices in his category. This was always a moment of pride for him which he would proudly share with his family.

In a way, it was an idyllic lifestyle for him. He worked from home, had breakfast, morning coffee and lunch with his wife and whoever was home at the time, and then, after an afternoon siesta with his wife, he would get back at 3.00 p.m. for about a two hour shift feeding and cleaning. It was only on market day that the workday was long and hectic. However, it was a seven-day a week cycle of care and attention so having a holiday break, even a short one, was difficult. Nevertheless, Dad was very appreciative and thankful for this time at home working in the piggery and later would often refer to it as the best period of his working life.

Something that he could not control, however, were the market prices that he received. The pig market was notoriously fickle, and prices could fluctuate enormously from season to season. Dad's pigs were sought after for their quality by the buyers but that did not protect him from an overall drop in pig prices. In 1970, when he started full time, he was getting an average of $30 per porker but by 1973 this had dropped to below $20, a drop of 30%. At those prices there was simply no profit left for him.

My youngest sister, Margaret, left school after completing Year 10 in November 1972 to work at home, helping Dad with the pigs and Mum in the house. She spent about half her time helping out with the pigs and became quite proficient in the task, which she enjoyed. Margaret recalled in 2020 how she helped Dad each morning and afternoon with the feeding, and, on market days, would go with him to the Midland Markets.

One memory that stands out in her mind was the time, about four months after she started work, in May 1973, that she was left in charge of the pigs while Dad and Mum took a week's break in Geraldton. During that week, a whole pen of pigs became sick and two died. She remembers how frantic the situation was and how she, with her sister Susan, had to bury those dead pigs in pouring rain and in soaking wet soil. She certainly was pleased to see her parents back home again. After Dad came home a further two pigs from that pen had to be euthanised as they were too far gone. For Dad it highlighted the fact that it was difficult to get away for a break or vacation. He was amazingly attuned to the health of his pigs and would often intervene with injections and medication before any virus got out of control. This type of care was hard to delegate to his 16-year-old daughter.

Margaret also clearly recalls how incredibly difficult it was in 1973/74 for Dad to make a living from the pigs. The prices were far too low to make a profit and she recalls feeling really concerned for her parents, who, now heading for retirement, were still struggling to make ends meet. Besides the costs of running the business, each month they also had to meet the interest payments of the loan they had taken out to set up the piggery. During this time Dad had to engage in some part time work to supplement the income and Margaret also felt the need to seek employment to help with the family budget. In August 1974 she was successful in finding a full-time job at a local childcare centre. Mum wrote in her diary in August 1974 that the piggery had to be subsidised by over $100 per week due to the low prices – "That is just not sustainable, so Dad is now supplementing his income by contract work cleaning newly constructed houses," she wrote.

Relief was not far away, however. Sir Charles Court was elected premier of Western Australia in April 1974. He was a dynamic entrepreneurial type of leader who drove the development and economy of the state. Mines and support industries were being opened up, with the resultant jobs and economic growth. There was general optimism that affected prices and business everywhere. Overseas migration to Australia in 1974 was more than double the previous year from 8,910 to 19,700.[93] This in turn increased the demand for consumables and this, no doubt, would have filtered down to the increased demand for pig meat. Also, with the very low prices experienced during the previous 1972-1973 years, many piggeries had either folded up or diversified into something else. This meant for Dad that there was less competition in the field.

Whatever the reason, by late 1974 and early 1975 the market for pigs changed and prices for Dad's porkers more than doubled from the previous low of $20 to an average of $45. What a difference that made. It gave them the financial ability to now seriously plan for that long-desired trip back to the Netherlands.

52. Reunification with the Old Country and Barriers in the New

"If we spoke a different language, we would perceive a somewhat different world."
~ *Ludwig Wittgenstein*

It was 23 years since my parents had migrated. Despite Dad's sister Marie having visited twice they longed to catch up with all their siblings, some of whom were not in good health. They also had the added incentive that three of their children now also lived in the Netherlands: Jenny and Jan Hollebrandse with their three children, Kees, who had left in 1972 to study for the Ministry at the Theological college in Kampen and Mieke who, at 27 and single, had also decided to move to the Netherlands in 1974.

If they were to go, it was decided that they would need at least three months to catch up with all the family and friends. To be away for that period of time, Dad would have to sell all his pig stock. He had learnt from previous short stays away that you cannot delegate the care, nor leave that responsibility of so many pigs to others. Dad did the sums and found that selling all the pigs at the current high market price would leave them able to pay off their bank loan and have enough left to pay for the trip and meet living expenses for the period required before income would be available again.

The family situation was now different with only the three youngest daughters, Mary (21), Susan (20), and Margaret (18) still at home. Both Mary and Susan were nursing and generally only home on the weekends. Arthur (23) had married Hilde Bruning on the 3rd August 1974 and Susan was engaged to be married to Martin Bijl, a building contractor and son of the Bijls who had migrated from the Netherlands in 1952 on the same boat as us.

Dad booked to leave for the Netherlands on the 25th April 1975 and return 24th July 1975. Mum wrote in her diary on 26th December 1974: *"We are looking more and more forward to this trip to the Netherlands. Each night we dream about it and we find it hard not to talk about it all the time."* Her excitement shines through the words. Finally, after so many years, to be back in her home country, amongst family and old friends. On the day they left for Holland Mum wrote in her diary, *"What a blessing that the Lord makes this possible and that we still have the health to do this."*

The trip met all their expectations and some more. Already after the first day, on meeting all of Mum's siblings who came together for the occasion, Mum wrote:

> *"We had a marvellous time with all the family. Something we will never forget. Just this get together is enough for us never to have any regret in making this trip. We felt so at home and a sense of belonging. The 23 years of separation just fell away. It was from all sides an experience of thankfulness and happiness to be able to meet each other again."*

The trip was an outstanding success for them. They had great times with their children as well as with their own family and friends. The three months passed by very quickly for them. They were also thankful to be there to farewell Mum's oldest brother, Aart, who died of cancer while they were there.

Looking at the photos taken of them during that period, their joy and happiness were evident. I remember my siblings looking at those photos saying at the time, "We have never seen Mum like that – such exuberance and spontaneous laughter." We knew her as always being so serious and restrained. It appeared to us that the burden of migration had weighed heavily on her and had affected her personality and demeanour.

One of those burdens that with time became increasingly problematic was her lack of English. She had not mastered it, despite many attempts. Before moving to Australia she had lessons and achieved what she thought at the time was some success. At various times in Australia, she made arrangements for lessons, but there had never been the possibility of following through. She realised the necessity of mastering the English language. In 1973 she wrote in her diary: "I do believe that as you get older and the English language is spoken by all the younger people that you will become lonely if you can no longer understand them." She was very aware of her own future predicament if she was unable to master the language. She wrote about making a firm commitment to master the language and to get her youngest daughter Margaret, who was home at the time, to assist her. Speaking to Margaret in 2020, she could not recall ever being asked by Mum at any time to assist her in learning the English language.

Already by 1975, with the growing number of grandchildren, most of whom could not speak Dutch, it was becoming a real problem for her. She did not have the confidence to talk in the best English she could muster, nor did she have the disposition to laugh or joke about this handicap as some other migrants might do. It remained a challenge that she never overcame. As a consequence, her communication with her growing number of grandchildren became stilted and difficult. For her, it was a heavy burden for she loved all her grandchildren and had such a wish to be able to freely talk with them. For Dad, it was a lot easier, as he had picked up the language at work.

This would have possibly been the primary reason why the three month stay in the Netherlands was so relaxing and enjoyable for her. No longer hindered by the stress of trying to understand and communicate, she could go shopping with confidence, communicate with her three grandchildren there and could follow the Dutch sermons.

Coming back to Australia, the reality of English-speaking grandchildren and an English-speaking community hit hard. It was not only her grandchildren but also her children who would communicate amongst each other in English. At the regular family get-togethers or birthday parties, all the children would be chatting in English and only those sitting next to my parents would be communicating with them in Dutch. They could not participate in the group discussions. It was a sad situation.

53. Towards Retirement

"Nothing is better for a man than that he should eat and drink, an that his soul should enjoy good in his labour. This also, I saw, was from the hand of God."
~ Ecclesiastes 2:24 (NKJV)

On returning from the Netherlands, Dad wasted no time in re-establishing his piggery. It took him just over a month to relaunch and build the stock up again to over 300 pigs. The prices were stable, and he was confident of being able to get a reasonable income. He was also well rested and enthused to be back working from home again.

Just a month after returning, on the 23rd August 1975 Susan and Martin Bijl got married. This left just two daughters still at home - Mary, who was working as a nurse and youngest daughter, Margaret, who was working in a childcare centre.

The three youngest daughters, Mary, Susan and Margaret, had all at one time or other, worked in the piggery helping Dad, so with that experience they provided a good backstop whenever my parents wanted to have a break. During the time of running the piggery my parents tried to have regular breaks, but they avoided going for lengthy periods, generally limiting it to one week. They also timed their breaks to coincide with the holidays of their daughters, so they could then be available to manage the piggery.

Even when working full time, my sisters were often called to help out if they were home, especially weekends, so Dad could have it easier at least one day a week. Margaret remembers how she was taught to milk the cow in 1971 so she could do that, as well as feed the pigs, every second Sunday morning so Dad could have a sleep-in. The milk cow had been sold just prior to their departure to the Netherlands, thus ending a family tradition maintained since 1953.

But his daughters were growing up and starting to live their own lives. Margaret, for years the main backstop for the piggery, became engaged on the 23rd October 1976 to Hans Vermeulen, a building tradesman from Albany. A week later, Margaret moved to Albany to be close to her husband-to-be, whom she married on the 9th April 1977. A few days after Margaret moved to Albany, Mary, then 22, left to live for a time in the Netherlands to join her brother and two sisters there. At ages 63 and 61 my parents were finally empty nesters. Four of their children were back in the Netherlands, one was in Tasmania, one in Albany and the other seven all lived within a half an hour drive from their Kelmscott home.

Dad still needed assistance from time to time in the piggery, especially on market days. Susan was able to help out most market days and, from 1977, one of their grandsons, Henry Strating, who was 12 at the time, came over regularly on Saturdays to help. By mid-1977 Dad started planning his exit from the piggery. He was due to turn 65 on the 5th November 1978 but, besides this, there was pressure from the local council for Dad to close the piggery, due to residential development plans in the area. Each year he had to renew the piggery licence so it was fortuitous that this pressure to close coincided with his season of retirement.

The pig prices had stayed strong since he had re-started after the trip to the Netherlands so, financially, they had been reasonably comfortable. It had become a sound business with ample profits each year. Dad could finish his working life in a positive frame, clearing his debts with a little nest egg to assist him in his retirement. In September and October 1978, he began progressively to sell his pig stock without buying replacements. The last 46 were sold on Tuesday the 25th October 1978. Dad demolished some of the sheds and cleared the area. The era of the piggery was finished. He was extremely grateful to God for having had the opportunity, so late in his working life, to have been self-employed again and now, after 8 years of operation, to wind the business up in a satisfactory way to coincide with his retirement.

This was also the year that Dad came to the end of his term as elder in the church. It was to be the last time he would serve in the office. The language barrier was becoming increasingly more difficult for him, with many young people in the church now no longer able to understand Dutch. While Dad could converse in English, he certainly was not fluent and over the last few years as he was working from home and talking less English his mastery over the language had diminished.

More than 25 years since institution, the Free Reformed Church of Armadale was slowly moving to using English more regularly. Up to 1964 all services had been in Dutch, then it went from one Dutch and one English service until finally in 1975, both services were held in English. To cater for some of the early migrants who had not been able to master the English language a separate Dutch service was held for them. This continued into the 1990s.

When my parents arrived in Armadale in 1952 membership was about 130. When Dad retired as elder in 1978 church membership had grown to 991. Plans were in place to build a second church in Kelmscott and, later that year, Reverend S.G. Hur from the Presbyterian Church of Korea was ordained as the second pastor for the Free Reformed Church of Armadale. He worked together with Rev. Bruning until the institution of the Free Reformed Church of Kelmscott which occurred on the 31st December 1980. Rev. Hur than served in Kelmscott while Rev. Bruning continued to serve in Armadale.

My parents were positive and thankful to God for the church life they could contribute to and be part of. Dad was able to serve 3 four-year terms as elder and 2 four-year terms as deacon since he was first elected in 1954. It was only in the first few years that he had found it extremely stressful and draining but after that 'dark' period he was just pleased at the unity and faithfulness to Scripture. In correspondence sent to his sisters in the Netherlands, he often referred to the leadership and faithful preaching of Rev. Bruning and how grateful they were to have him as their pastor.

Now, at the end of 1978, he no longer had the responsibility of the office of elder nor did he have the responsibility of running the piggery. Together with his wife, they were now entering a new phase in their lives devoid of the daily pressures and responsibilities they had lived with over so many years.

54. Sickness and Death

"To everything there is a season,
A time for every purpose under heaven:
A time to be born,
And a time to die;…
A time to weep,
And a time to laugh;
A time to mourn,
And a time to dance…"

~ Ecclesiastes 3:1,2 & 4
(NKJV)

When Dad started the piggery business in 1970 my parents had been married nearly 35 years and been blessed with all healthy children and grandchildren. With 13 children and 20 grandchildren at the time, that was remarkable. Mum's mother had lost five children at an early age and Dad had lost both of his parents before he was married, so they did not take their blessings for granted. However, over the next few years they would be confronted with the frailty of life amongst their own children and grandchildren. This would test their resilience and faith.

Willy, born in 1949 and married to Reinhard van der Laan, gave birth on the 29th July 1971 to a daughter who was still-born. Willy had not been feeling well for a few days and that day was attending a birthday celebration of one of her sisters-in-law when she became quite sick. My parents, present at the birthday celebration, insisted they drive her home and after about an hour they took her to the Armadale Maternity Hospital. They both sensed that something was not right. Several hours later their foreboding was confirmed when they were called back to the hospital with the message that the baby was stillborn, but that Willy was okay.

Four days later the baby, who they named Rhonda, was buried at the Fremantle Cemetery. Rev. Bruning officiated at the funeral. Willy, who was still in hospital fighting infections, was released for a few hours to attend the funeral.

After this birth Willy had ongoing health problems. She suffered from constant fatigue, sore joints, and patchy skin, and despite regular visits to the doctor no diagnosis could be given. She struggled on, but it was obvious that something was wrong. Willy had always been strong and determined and not one to complain unnecessarily. Fourteen months later on the 8th September 1972 Willy again gave birth to a still-born baby boy, who they named Michael. This time her life was in serious danger. She suffered chronic kidney disorder and for three days was placed in intensive care. She was to spend three weeks in hospital. Willy was too ill to attend the funeral. Mum wrote in her diary:

> *We are all thankful that the Lord spared Willy's life. We often don't give it much thought when a healthy baby is born, and everything goes well but this time we have been reminded very clearly. It is a gift from God who gives life.*

The kidney infection had been severe and affected Willy's ongoing health. Specialists tried to diagnose what was really wrong but could not come to any conclusive decision. She was just advised to rest and take it easy. They prescribed various medications to try and improve her condition but, despite suffering lots of side effects, they gave little relief. Because of her sore joints and stiff fingers, the doctors thought she might have some form of rheumatism, so they prescribed tablets for that. Willy got so disenchanted with doctors that she tried to avoid seeing them.

Nine months later, in June 1973, she suffered a miscarriage after only two months gestation. My parents became increasingly concerned about her health. Coming home from hospital she had difficulty walking, was all stiff and generally looked very run-down and unhealthy. She tried to take a holiday with her husband Reinhard but, after only two days, had to rush back to the hospital because of severe pain in one arm that had swelled up. The doctor thought it was thrombosis. Her life became a constant struggle with unexplained pains and skin disorders showing up at random intervals. By the end of the year she could hardly walk and was mostly confined to bed.

It was during this time, on the 7th August 1973, while they were dealing with the deteriorating condition of Willy, that they got a disturbing call from their son Niek in Tasmania. He delivered the sad news that his 20-month-old son, Peter, had drowned in the creek behind the house. Niek and Ina lived on a rural property in Lapoinya, a small agricultural centre located on the north west coast of Tasmania. They were slowly improving the property to develop it into a beef cattle farm but, in the meantime, Niek was working as a builder specialising in the construction of farm shed buildings. During the week he was often away for a number of days at a time as his work was all over Tasmania.

On that day, he had been in Launceston on a building project. Back at home the children were, as usual, happily playing outside behind the house, riding around on their little bicycles. About 40 metres behind the house the land sloped down to a creek which in summer just had a trickle of water, but due to recent heavy rains was now a roaring torrent. Inadvertently young Peter had sped down the slope on the bank towards the creek on his little bike, slipped and ended up in the water and was swept away. He was playing with two of his brothers, and one immediately went to call his mum, while the other tried to see if he could reach Peter.

On hearing her son relate what had happened, Ina ran to the creek and leapt into the water to try and rescue her son. However, she could not swim, the water had a strong current, and she had to hold on to overhanging branches to avoid being washed away herself. Frantically she continued the search for Peter, but had to eventually conclude that she needed help. She called the local police who, with the aid of a boat, were able to retrieve Peter's lifeless body from the water. Soon after, Niek got a call from Ina and drove the 180 kilometres home to be with his wife and family.

When Dad and Mum heard the sad news from Niek they decided to leave for Tasmania to be with him and Ina in this time of grief. They had never seen Peter nor the twin boys, Rodney and Stephen, who were now three months old. The last time my parents were in Tasmania was when Dad's sister Marie was in Australia and that was now nearly four years ago.

They spent 10 days in Tasmania and were able to attend the funeral of Peter who was buried in the Wynyard cemetery. It was the third time in three years that they attended a funeral of a grandchild.

Returning home, they were immediately confronted with the serious situation of Willy. Life for her had become a daily struggle.

On New Year's Eve 1973 her condition deteriorated with high fever, constant vomiting and increasing skin discolouring to the extent that her husband decided to take her into Armadale Hospital. The doctor in Armadale saw her condition and thought it best if she went straight to Perth to the Shenton Park Hospital. There they recognised her condition as serious and were committed to find a diagnosis. After a number of days of extensive testing and observations they concluded that she had a rare blood disease known as Systemic Lupus Erythematosus. It is a chronic disease that causes inflammation of joints, rashes and impaired kidney functions. There is no cure, but treatment can be given to minimise the impacts.

For Willy, however, the disease had now developed to a critical stage. Since her first baby was born in 1971 the disease, which had until then been dormant, flared up and never abated, becoming worse with each subsequent pregnancy. Now her body was racked with the disease and worn out after two years of struggle. Despite the doctor's constant care, her condition deteriorated. She could no longer walk, often had bouts of vomiting and had difficulty breathing. The doctors at Shenton Park Hospital decided they no longer had the facilities to take proper care of her. She needed oxygen and both her kidneys and heart were starting to fail. Four weeks after being admitted to Shenton Park, on the 30th January she was transferred, now extremely sick and in a critical condition, to the Royal Perth Hospital and placed in an intensive care unit.

For my parents, this was an immensely stressful time. Reinhard was now predominantly domiciled at my parents' place so they could between them organise visiting times.

Willy was in a protected isolation unit at the hospital to guard against infection, and visits to her were restricted to afternoons only with just one visitor at a time, limited to my parents and Reinhard. When my parents first saw her in the intensive care unit they were shocked at the sight – she looked so frail and tiny and was engulfed with tubes and wires that were connected to machines that kept her vital organs going. She also had a tube down her throat to give her oxygen, but that made it difficult for her to talk. During one visit with my Mum, Willy frustratingly pulled it out so she could at least say a few words.

Each day my parents tried to see her, but it would be each one individually and then only for a few minutes. Being in the Intensive Care Unit, there was a constant presence of nurses and doctors, but they could give little assurance as to Willy's condition and prospects. 'While there is life there is hope,' they told my parents. There was so little known at the time about the disease and it appeared there was a lot of medical experimentation going on and that the doctors themselves just didn't know the outcomes of their treatments.

For three long weeks, Willy lingered between life and death. At times she was not conscious but there were times when my parents could communicate and give words of comfort. On Friday the 22nd February 1974, her body finally gave up the struggle. Her life on earth was finished; the Lord called her home and she was relieved from further suffering. It was three weeks before her 25th birthday.

Four days later she was buried in the same grave as her two still-born children at the Fremantle cemetery with Rev. Bruning officiating. Some 200 people came to witness her funeral and to share in the grief of the family. The gravestone later placed on the grave had inscribed on it:

'Together now in peace before God's Throne.'

My parents, particularly my mum, went through a long period of grieving. Witnessing her daughter suffer and being incapable of reaching out and helping in any way, had deeply affected her. Despite the tremendous support they got from family, friends and church members and the knowledge that Willy was now in a better place, she nevertheless had to process the intense pain and sorrow at losing her beloved daughter. That was going to take time. While my parents did not at any time demonstrate any favouritism with their children, there is also no doubt Willy had a special place in their hearts. She was named after Mum and had a lot of Mum's characteristics and interests.

When son Arthur got married six months later, she found it difficult to be joyful for the event and even had suggested to Arthur to delay the wedding. With her grieving, it was a difficult time for all those that were still at home as there seemed little room for joy or happiness. Youngest sister, Margaret, related how it struck her that when Mum returned from the Netherlands from their first trip there, some fifteen months after the death of Willy, she noticed that Mum was laughing again, something she had not witnessed since Willy had died. It appears as if that wonderful trip to the Netherlands finally brought that long grieving process for Willy to an end.

55. The Early Years of Retirement

"I want to paint the way a bird sings."
~ *Claude Monet*

When Dad moved into retirement after his 65th birthday in November 1978 it was just over 26 years since he had migrated from the Netherlands. While he started his married life in 1936 being self-employed, since emigrating to Australia, with the exception of the last eight years in his own piggery, he had been an employee with just average income potential. Nevertheless, he seemed to develop a certain contentment after the many disappointments experienced during the war and subsequent years in the Netherlands. He came to Australia with high hopes and initially said that under no circumstance would he go and work in a factory. Nevertheless he'd ended up accepting a job at the Cardup Brickworks where he worked for six years. If it had not been for the union issues, he, no doubt, would have stayed much longer. Having a secure and reliable job to go to each day was so important for him to provide for his family. He had learned to accept what he received with thankfulness to God, even if the situation did not meet his personal aspirations.

He could look back at those 26 years in Australia with a

great deal of satisfaction and gratitude. Family life, church life and the freedom and opportunities that Australia offered to his children and grandchildren were all things he treasured deeply. There was no doubt that migration had disrupted the lives of some of his children – their education was cut short, they had grown up with no extended family and they had to make the necessary adjustments. But, despite all of that, my parents could reflect on the fact that their children and grandchildren lacked nothing, they always seemed to have work and have the ability to purchase their own homes and provide for their families. What was most important for my parents was that they had all done their public confession of faith in the church and were all, in their own ways, active in church and community life. Now in retirement, my parents could devote their time to staying in touch with this ever-expanding family. With four children living in the Netherlands they had an additional incentive to visit their homeland from time to time.

In those 26 years Australia, and Armadale, had gone through remarkable changes. The 1400 homes in the district in 1952 had grown to 10,756 homes by 1979, the year Armadale was declared a Town.[94] In the 10 years prior to 1968 the Armadale District had the highest growth rate in Australia, doubling its population in just five years. With this came a comparable growth in infrastructure and services including additional schools, shopping centres and sporting facilities. Armadale was no longer the small country town but now a sub-regional centre of the Perth Metropolitan district with plans for massive future growth.[95]

With this growth, services to its residents also improved. A lot of gravel roads were sealed including Third Avenue, Kelmscott, where my parents lived. In 1973 my parents were connected to scheme water, so they no longer needed to rely on rain and well water. In 1967 Armadale built its own sewerage plant and over the next few years converted most of its residences from septic to sewerage. With the clay soils septic tanks did not drain well and proper sewerage was seen by the council as a necessary service for the growing town.[96]

With all this growth and pressure to acquire subdivisible land by developers, a lot of orchards, wineries and other rural industries disappeared. Armadale lost its status as the food bowl of Perth and many orchardists and farmers had to move out of the district to continue elsewhere. However, for others this growth and expansion provided work and business opportunities; so, for many migrants the district gave plenty of scope for builders and entrepreneurs. Many first and second-generation migrants, including members of my family, became builders and tradesmen in this expanding economy.

When Dad retired, Western Australia was still run by the dynamic and energetic premier Sir Charles Court. He would remain premier till 1982 and is credited with initiating the major industrial and mining development that the State experienced during this time. While Armadale had experienced major changes since 1952, so had Western Australia. In those 26 years the state population more than doubled from 600,000 to 1,227,851.[97] This growth was particularly evident in outer suburbs like Armadale where open vacant land could be easily subdivided and developed. The city of Perth had also experienced a renaissance in high story office blocks and service buildings. Mining companies were establishing offices in Perth from which to run their remote mining sites. The late sixties and seventies was a period when Perth demolished many of its heritage buildings to make way for modern skyscrapers. Perth was slowly being transformed into a major city with the appropriate infrastructures and services.

It was not long before my parents were planning another trip to the Netherlands. One of their sons, Kees, was due to graduate from his theological studies at the seminary in Kampen after which, on the 1st July 1979, he was to be ordained as the minister of the Reformed Church Liberated in Zevenbergen. Just a week earlier, on the 21st June 1979, he was to marry Nellie Jonker, a nurse, whom he met in the Netherlands. Also in the Netherlands to visit were daughters Jenny, with husband Jan and their three children, as well as daughters Mieke and Mary. And of course, their own siblings and friends. They had plenty of reasons to visit their mother country once again.

This time they did not need to rush so they decided to go for seven months, from the 3rd March to the 4th October 1979.

Again, for them it was a marvellous time. They could witness the ordination and marriage of their son. They could spend relaxing times with their three daughters as well as renew bonds with siblings and friends. And they did not need to speak English and could converse comfortably in their mother tongue. What joy!

"*The Lord blessed us and gave us such special and memorable times,*" Mum wrote in her diary. She kept a daily diary of the whole trip, the text of which ran into 75 pages of typed script. In it, she detailed all the many visits and experiences they encountered. With this extensive diary she would later recall and relive those special times they could have.

When they arrived back at Perth Airport, most of the family was there to welcome them back. As part of their welcoming back gesture, the family had given their house and gardens a complete makeover, so everything looked clean and fresh. Mum wrote in her diary "*What joy to meet the whole family at the airport. When we came home the house was all decorated, there were vases full of fresh flowers as well as pot plants placed around. The house was totally set up for us with bread, groceries and even cakes. It was overwhelming."*

After initially catching up with everyone, including the many friends that came over during their first weeks back, they could settle down into the routine of retired life. In his spare time, Dad was keen to experiment with oil painting and bought some equipment to get started. Since a child he'd always had an interest in painting, but never had the opportunity or time to take it further. Now, he thought, with more time he could finally immerse himself in this hobby. He enrolled for some lessons and, with the equipment now in hand, he was ready to go.

Time, however, was not so readily available. Besides having a large property and garden to maintain, which he did fastidiously, there were lots of contacts and visits to maintain. Reading through the letters and diaries of these years it is evident that life revolved around church and family life commitments. The early migrants were getting older and, as a consequence, were starting to suffer ailments as well as the loss of loved ones. My parents paid regular visits to the sick and those that had lost a loved one. The bond between the first migrants that arrived in the 1950s was strong, and they reached out to support each other whenever the need arose. They formed an 'Over 60 Club' and got together every fortnight for a few hours. The morning could involve a guest speaker or simply playing games and having interesting conversations – all in Dutch. Every few months they might organise a bus trip and go out for a day. Araluen, Churchman's Brook, Serpentine Dam, Yanchep and El Caballo Blanco were a few of their favourite places to go. About 20-30 would attend each fortnight and with this they developed a great camaraderie and support network.

Then there was the growing family. When they returned from the Netherlands in 1979 my parents had 38 grandchildren. The children would visit once a week, most of them either on Thursdays or Saturday mornings. Birthdays were always seen as a special day of celebration, so families would get together on those occasions. My parents would try and visit whenever one of the family was celebrating a birthday, including any of the grandchildren.

Then there was the ongoing contact with children and family in the Netherlands. Besides her siblings and friends in the Netherlands, Mum wrote weekly letters to her children. With five children living away as well as siblings and friends to keep up with, she would have needed to write between 8 to 12 letters each week.

The Dutch children also visited from the Netherlands on a regular basis. During those visits, my parents would put everything on hold to give priority to their visiting children.

The bottom line was that, in retirement, Dad and Mum had a busy and fulfilling life and, after a period of trying to take on the hobby of painting, Dad had to admit he just could not find the time. There was always too much to do.

56. More Travel, Celebrations, and Visitors

"The past is not a package one can lay away."
~ Emily Dickinson

Six months after their seven-months stay in the Netherlands, my parents headed back again on May 2nd 1980. This time it was for a seven-week holidays. Their daughter Mary, a nurse, who left in 1976 to live in the Netherlands was engaged to Martin van Haeften, a political researcher. They witnessed the wedding – the twelfth child to get married – on the 2nd June 1980 and again caught up with their Dutch children, grandchildren, siblings, and friends. The wedding was special as it was officiated by their son, who was now Reverend C. Kleijn.

On returning it would be another five years before my parents ventured back to the Netherlands, just one more time. In the interim, the Dutch family were making regular trips to visit the family in Australia. In July 1980 their oldest daughter Jenny, with husband Jan and three children, visited for five weeks. In December of the same year, the newly married couple, Mary and Martin van Haeften, came for six weeks. The following year, in October 1981, daughter Mieke visited for five weeks. In September 1982 son Kees, with wife Nellie and their two young children, came for four weeks.

Then in October 1983, Mum's sister, Marie, with husband Henk Smit, came to visit for six weeks. This would be Mum's first and only sibling to ever visit. They had an additional incentive because one of their sons, Jaap, lived in Western Australia. They connected well with the Kleijn family, who were all delighted to meet and catch up with an Uncle and Auntie from the Netherlands.

In 1984 there were three visits made from the Netherlands – in January Mieke came for four weeks; in July, Mary and husband Martin, with two young children came for four weeks while in August, Jenny and husband Jan and daughter Cora came for six weeks.

My parents still enjoyed relatively good health and were able to easily accommodate these visitors in their spacious family home. However, by early 1985 they started thinking about selling their property. The burden of looking after the large house, gardens and five acres of land was getting too much. The property had been zoned for a future Technical School site so any buyer would have to take that into account. This did complicate things as it was then not suitable for a buyer considering long term occupation. This caused some drop in value, but the Government was prepared to compensate for this.

With these conditions a potential sale did fall through but eventually in August they were able to finalise a sale with a buyer. It had been a property that served them well for nearly 26 years, but they had come to the realisation that the time had come to downsize and buy something a bit more manageable. They were successful in acquiring a house in central Armadale, on Selkirk Road, which was located opposite the Armadale train station. A bonus was that their daughter Mappie and family lived in the same street, just across the road. The house was a simple three-bedroom, one-bathroom affair on a quarter-acre block. The attraction for my parents was that there was a large outbuilding in the back yard that could function as an independent accommodation unit. They were still thinking about and planning to host visiting family.

Upon selling their house, it was an opportune time to take another trip to the Netherlands. Their children arranged to move everything for them into the new house and have it all set up by the time they returned from the Netherlands. So, on the 3rd September 1985 my parents took their fourth and last trip to the Netherlands – for nine weeks. Each visit gave them great joy but to now watch their own son preaching on a regular basis was, for them, part of what made this particular trip so special.

Arriving back home they moved straight into their new home. As arranged, the children had moved everything for them while they had been away. This house on Selkirk Road suited them well. Its central location meant that it was conveniently close to church and shops and they found that both family and friends would more easily, and often spontaneously, drop by.

On the 8th October 1986, a year after returning from their holiday and settling into their new home, they could celebrate their 50th wedding anniversary – and what a celebration it became. For the first time in 25 years all the children came together, also those from the Netherlands and Tasmania. It was a major family reunion. My parents had, besides their own children, 59 grandchildren and three great-grandchildren. Eleven of their grandchildren were married.

Most of those that came from overseas stayed for a number of weeks, so there was a constant flow of family outings and get-togethers. Besides these outings, the formal celebrations for the 50th anniversary consisted of a dinner for my parents and their children at our home, a dinner including the grandchildren at a local Armadale restaurant, the Gypsy Baron, and a reception for friends and extended family in the Armadale St John Ambulance hall at which about 165 guests attended. It was all an overwhelming time of joy for my parents. Mum wrote in her diary, *"Praise the Lord for his many blessings. How great it was to be all together in total harmony, happiness, and thankfulness."*

In his speech to his children at the anniversary dinner, Dad made a rare reference to his youth.

> *What a blessing to have so many children, grandchildren and even great-grandchildren. They could all receive the sign and seal of God's covenant with baptism and our children seek to walk in the ways of the Lord and have also taken over the task in church and school from us seniors. God's Grace is amazing. We have to confess that our work, also the upbringing of our children, was done with many shortcomings. I lost my parents early in life and then was so often jealous of those children that still had both their parents. If you miss something you really get to appreciate it. It was therefore often difficult for me to understand why children could sometimes be so difficult towards their parents. We have sometimes not taken enough effort to understand you sufficiently. I hope that you can forgive us. We all need forgiveness.*

He otherwise had never spoken of his youth and the tragic circumstances of his parents' death. From his own admission it still affected him, especially when one of his children had become difficult and argumentative. He did not have the understanding or means to deal with that and thought that children that grew up with loving and caring parents should also be able to show some appreciation for this. At this, his 50th anniversary, he put it on the table as an issue he had struggled with and, in so doing, sought forgiveness for the times that his temper might have got the better of him. They had been rare occasions, and often with good reason, but he, on reflection, accepted that he had sometimes dealt with situations in an inappropriate or harsh manner.

Despite Dad's reference to losing his parents, the tragic events remained unspoken. Only those children that decided to live in the Netherlands had been taken into confidence by my Mum, prior to them leaving. She figured that once they lived in the Netherlands, they would hear from other family members anyway; she thought it better to prepare them for that. However, she told them that under no circumstances should they talk to Dad about it. It appeared as if she was trying to protect him from a situation he simply could not deal with. His coping mechanism was to try and forget and bury it somewhere in his subconscious.

57. A Wedding – More Visitors and a Move

*"Now also when I am old and grayheaded,
O God, do not forsake me,
Until I declare Your strength to this generation,
Your power to everyone who is to come."*

Psalm 71:18 (NKJV)

Seven months after their 50th wedding anniversary, my parents were overjoyed with news of the impending marriage of their daughter, Mieke. She had lived in the Netherlands since 1974, worked in aged care, and had met a Dutch resident, Harm Snip, a factory worker. On the 7th of May 1987 they committed to each other in marriage. Mieke was 39. My parents were no longer comfortable taking the long trip to the Netherlands, so had to be content with listening to - and experiencing - the event via tapes, video and photos.

Nevertheless, Mieke had a good Kleijn representation at her wedding. Besides her brother Kees, who officiated the wedding, she had sisters Jenny, Janet and Mary as well as brother Harry present, together with their spouses. Her wedding reception was like a Dutch family reunion with many uncles, aunties and cousins in attendance. With the four extensive trips taken to the Netherlands by my parents, and four children domiciled there, the contact between all the extended family had remained strong. Mum's consistent letter writing also played a big role in maintaining that connection.

In October of the following year, Mieke, husband Harm Snip and their eight-month-old daughter, Wilma, travelled to Australia to visit my parents and family. It would be the first time they met Harm and their grandchild.

The Kleijn children living away continued to visit the family and parents as opportunities arose. Niek and Ina drove from Tasmania in a bus with ten children in June/July 1988 for a 3-week stay. One of their children lived in Western Australia so that was, for them, an additional incentive to come over.

In January 1990, son Kees with wife Nellie and their four children came for three weeks when on their way to Legana, Tasmania, where Kees had accepted a call to minister in the church there. His Dutch-speaking children were a delight for my parents. On the 4th February 1990 Kees was ordained as minister of Legana.

In December of the same year daughter, Mary and husband Martin and two of their children came from the Netherlands for a four-week holiday. Then in 1991 oldest daughter Jenny, with husband Jan, came for three months. So, my parents virtually had a visit from one of their overseas children every year.

Dad's sister, Auntie Marie, came in November 1993 for a 12-month stay spending six months in Tasmania with Niek and Ina. The highlight was when Dad's other sister, Auntie Lijsje, came for three weeks in January 1994. Her husband, Uncle Dirk had died in December 1991 and she had always dearly wished to come. At 82 years of age and never having been in a plane before, she took the bold step to fly all the way to Australia to visit her brother and his family, and to visit while her sister was there. On the trip she was accompanied by

Jenny's son and daughter-in-law, Alec and Gerda Hollebrandse.

With their common shared experience as children they had a special bond that had remained with them all their lives. Dad and his two sisters were inseparable during those three weeks they were together. Auntie Lijsje was so pleased to have been able to make this trip and later often spoke about the joy she experienced in seeing her brother and his family in the Australian environment.

As my parents were getting older they experienced, on the one hand, the joy of the younger generation, of grandchildren doing their public profession of faith, of them marrying and receiving children while, on the other side, they began losing older family members and friends to the final enemy - death. By early 1995 Mum was 80 and Dad 82. They were both still relatively healthy and appreciated each day they could still be together. However, by this time many of their compatriots that had arrived in Australia in the 1950s had either died or were seriously ill. The Over-60s club which had given so much pleasure to early migrants had dwindling numbers.

Reading through correspondence and diaries of this period it's clear that visiting the sick and funeral attendance was a regular occurrence. They were constantly confronted with the frailty of life and were just so thankful for every day. However, with age, they also started developing ailments. In October 1993 Dad was diagnosed with prostate cancer. The initial prognosis was that it had already spread and was evident in his bones. Treatment was initiated via some medication and a monthly injection. Miraculously, the disease seemed to slow down and, in time, became dormant and no longer life-threatening.

However, Dad was getting progressively weaker and short of breath and was starting to find even simple tasks difficult. In

February 1995 he was diagnosed with emphysema, a disease of deteriorating lung capacity often developed by smokers. Dad had been a smoker. The prognosis was not good. It was predicted that he would gradually worsen to the stage where he would need the assistance of oxygen to breathe.

Looking after the house and garden became too much for Dad so they started planning to move into the Fair Haven Village, a Free Reformed facility set up for the aged within the church. Launched in June 1985, the facility comprised a 9-bed hostel that could provide high care as necessary and was surrounded by individual units that were suited for those that could still care for themselves. The units were basic; most had two bedrooms, a lounge area with an adjoining kitchen area. Gardens were generally cared for by Fair Haven staff, and, if any help was needed, the hostel was close by.

By March 1996, my parents had successfully sold their house and moved into a unit at the Fair Haven complex. With the downsizing they had to get rid of lots of their belongings and spent a number of months clearing things out, including throwing away or destroying many of their memorabilia and letters. I caught them in the middle of it once and vociferously appealed to them not to destroy these things but to keep all their old letters, memorabilia and diaries together and give them to someone who would value and care for them. After all, they had been pioneers, and future generations should be able to learn about those times. Some days later, my parents came past my home and dropped off all the diaries and scrapbooks for me to take care of. However, Mum insisted that all her letters to her mum and from her mum would be destroyed. She just considered them too personal. So, while I was gifted with lots of the letters she had received from her siblings and others, those from her own parents disappeared.

58. Serious Illnesses

"Therefore we do not lose heart. Even though our outward man is perishing, yet the inward man is being renewed day by day. For our light affliction, which is but for a moment, is working for us a far more exceeding and eternal weight of glory."
~ 2 Corinthians 4:16-17 (NKJV)

My oldest brother, Peter, had married Zwannie Zuidema in 1960. By 1994 they had been married 34 years, and received six children and six grandchildren. Zwannie had always been an active person, both in the family and community. Early in 1994, however, she started showing signs of inattention and confusion. What was wrong with her? Her personality had changed – she was just not her normal self anymore. Did she have the same disease as her brother John who died five years earlier in 1990, at just 52 years of age, from a form of Alzheimer's Disease?

Unfortunately, this proved to be the case. After various diagnostic attempts, she was finally diagnosed with Alzheimer's in January 1995. Tragically, she could not come to understand her own situation and resisted attempts at restricting her. She was just 56 years of age, a young person to be struck down by such a disease. She was taken up by a number of specialised hospitals to determine how best to provide the appropriate medication and care. She was admitted to the Fair Haven Hostel in August 1996. Sadly, by the time she was admitted to Fair Haven she had lost the art of speech and gave little sign of recognition or understanding.

(Zwannie's condition continued to deteriorate, and she became more and more silent and withdrawn. In May 2003, seven years after being admitted to Fair Haven she was taken home by the Lord. She was 63).

On New Year's Eve 1995, nearly 12 months after Zwannie had been diagnosed with Alzheimer's, sister Janet had a serious brain haemorrhage. She was 53 and had eight children and five grandchildren. Four of the children were married. The youngest four, aged 20, 18, 15 and 12, were still at home.

She suffered the stroke when at home, serving coffee on Sunday morning. She was taken by ambulance first to Armadale Hospital, but then rushed to Perth Sir Charles Gairdner Hospital, where she went through an emergency operation to try and relieve the pressure on her brain. The initial prognosis was not encouraging. She spent the first two weeks in intensive care on life support until she could breathe without assistance but remained in a coma. After three weeks she was transferred to the Shenton Park Rehabilitation Hospital. For weeks she made little progress and the doctors were saying that she could possibly be brain dead. But, after two months, Janet slowly started to respond. Every week there was a little progress in her movement and awareness and eventually she was also able to talk a little. However, physically, her left side was completely paralysed and even her other side had limitations. She was going to need a lot of patience and therapy to make progress.

After eight months in the Shenton Park Rehabilitation

Hospital she was transferred to Fair Haven, early in September 1996. What joy to be close to her loved ones and to be cared for by her own community members. From the initial prognosis by the doctors, Janet had come a long way. However, she still needed high-level care and could do little herself. She was able to read a little and her talking had improved considerably, although still very soft.

Of course, these serious family events had a major impact on my parents. They prayed fervently for healing and relief both for Zwannie and Janet and made regular visits. When both were eventually transferred to Fair Haven, my parents were thankful that they also now lived on the premises and could easily visit them on a regular basis.

Mum wrote in her diary:

> *We must continue praying and hoping for healing but only if we can say "Your will be done." We do not know what the Lord's ways are with Zwannie and Janet. We have had many good years as a family. Now have come setbacks with serious illnesses. Now the Lord asks the same from us as when we had everything going well. These are trials for us in which we have to be able to demonstrate that our faith in God, the Son and Spirit is steadfast in good and bad days.*

On 8 October 1996, six months after moving into their Fair Haven unit, my parents could celebrate their 60th wedding anniversary. We celebrated the occasion with a family dinner held at Peter's place. The fact that his wife was in Fair Haven suffering Alzheimer's, and could not attend, cast a shadow over the evening's festivities. She had always contributed so much to these types of events.

Janet was able to attend and was driven from Fair Haven in an especially adapted vehicle. The three daughters from the Netherlands, Jenny, Mieke, and Mary had come for the occasion. Son Kees from Tasmania, with his wife Nellie, were also able to attend. This time none of my visiting siblings could lodge at my parent's place so they were all shared out amongst the family. Having visiting children being able to stay at their home had always been a special treat for my parents and they had been able to maintain that until they had moved into their Fair Haven unit.

The following evening a dinner was organised in the Armadale church hall for all the children, grandchildren, and great-grandchildren. Since the 50th wedding anniversary the family had grown considerably. Twenty three grandchildren had by now married. My parents now had 67 grandchildren and 52 great-grandchildren. While a number were absent due to living in America, the Netherlands and Tasmania, the dinner party was well attended.

My parents felt incredibly blessed to still be together at their age and to be surrounded by so many of their children, grandchildren, and great-grandchildren while celebrating this special milestone. During the weeks following the occasion, there were the painful farewells, as children returned back to their own homes. It would be back to weekly letter writing.

Janet attending the family anniversary dinner had been her first outing since her stroke. She was slowly making more progress. With therapy and coaching, and with the help of her sisters Mappie and Susan, Janet got to the stage where she could be cared for by her husband. She remained wheelchair-bound, but developed some strength in one leg and arm as well as the ability to independently eat and drink. She also gained writing skills so she could write letters and cards to family and friends. It had been a long hard journey, but in November 1999, four years after her stroke and more than three years since moving to Fair Haven she could go home and be cared for by her husband, Eddy Schoof. What joy for her to be in her own home again.

Two and a half years after the 60th wedding anniversary my parents received news of their eldest son in law, Jan Hollebrandse. He had married my oldest sister Jenny in 1958 and, in 1969, they moved back to the Netherlands. In recent years, Jan had been battling various health issues and had twice been operated on and given hip replacements. In April 1999, while undertaking a hip operation, doctors discovered he had cancer. It had already reached a critical stage having spread throughout his body. There was little they could do. In May, he was released from hospital so his wife, Jenny, who was a trained nurse, could provide him with palliative care. He lingered on for four months, during which time he suffered enormously, but was nevertheless happy to be home and cared for by his wife. On the 7th July 1999 he was taken up by the Lord. He was 74.

59. Dad's Final Weeks

*"Children's children are the crown of old men,
And the glory of children is their father."*
~ *Proverbs 17:6 (NKJV)*

Just under two years after the 60th wedding anniversary, son Kees came with his family to visit in June 1998 from Tasmania. He had accepted a call to the Free Reformed Church of Pretoria in South Africa and, on his way there, stayed a week in Armadale to farewell family. My parents could catch up with their extended family again and a Kleijn get together luncheon was organised in the Armadale Church hall. About 90 Kleijn children, grandchildren and great-grandchildren were in attendance.

By this time Dad was becoming increasingly frail. His lungs were progressively deteriorating, causing him constant shortness of breath. After just short walks he needed a puffer to assist in getting his breath back. As a couple, they were becoming more house bound. To be able to catch up with their growing family on the occasion of their son moving to South Africa, was though, for them a unique opportunity.

On the 29th June 1998 Dad wrote a letter to his sister Marie. Besides giving updates on family and health he also wrote about Fair Haven and church. It highlights how dear church and community life was for him.

> *The Fair Haven Hostel is extending again with an additional five rooms. In August they hope to have them finished which then gives them a capacity of 14 rooms. The first migrants that are still living are now all over 80 years of age.*
>
> *In Byford a school is being built which D.V. will open in February. We now have schools in Armadale, Kelmscott, Rockingham and then also in Byford. A lot of growth in just 40 years.*
>
> *Besides Armadale, churches have now also been established in Kelmscott, where they have already split and have four services every Sunday, Bedfordale, Byford, and Rockingham. Both Albany and Tasmania also now have two churches each. Lots of activities and growth. May the Lord give His blessing to it all.*

In August 1998 Mr. and Mrs. Bijl moved into a unit directly across from my parents. They had been friends since they met each other on the boat coming to Australia in 1952. Close contact had been maintained over the years. Their son Martin had married sister Susan. It was very special for both couples, that in their twilight years they could live in close proximity to each other, making mutual visits and support possible.

By early 1999, Dad's lungs had deteriorated to the extent that he now had to be permanently connected to an oxygen bottle. The puffer was not helping with his lack of breath anymore. He was no longer driving and could rarely attend church. Any slight cold caused him lots of hardship. The children took action to help with the household, cleaning, washing and shopping. Mum devoted a lot of her time to assisting Dad.

In September 1999 Mum wrote to her daughter Mary that

she looks back, with Dad, on their conjoined lives with joy and thankfulness:

> *We have had a blessed life – even now. God be praised that we may still be together and support each other. The children all care well for us. For the rest, our time is in God's hands. He knows what is good for us.*

In early December 1999 Dad wrote a letter to his sister Marie, replying to her letter sent on the occasion of Dad's 86th birthday on the 5th November. He wrote that all the children had visited on the day, but, as they could no longer cope with all the grandchildren and great-grandchildren visiting, they had been encouraged to send letters or cards. Further he wrote:

> *Every morning one of our daughters or daughters-in-law come in to help with whatever is needed. Wim (Mum) has severe back problems and has difficulty walking and needs a stick to avoid falling over. Every day that we are still together is a special blessing from the Lord. Every day we give thanks to God for that.*

On the 9th December 1999, just a few days after writing to his sister, Dad suffered a stroke. After her morning shower Mum found him on the floor. He had difficulty talking and one side was paralysed. The doctor's prognosis was not encouraging. He did not expect him to live much longer than 24 hours. All the children were notified. My eldest sister, Jenny, who had lost her husband just five months earlier, had already booked to come to Australia for a three month stay and was due to arrive on the 12th December. Brother Kees, now living in South Africa, on hearing the news, booked immediately to arrive in Perth on the 11th December. A few days later, on the 14th December sister Mieke, with husband Harm, also arrived in Perth from the Netherlands.

Meanwhile, to the surprise of the doctor, Dad's condition improved slightly. He was able to regain some movement on his paralysed side and was, at times able to communicate, although with difficulty. It was hard to determine his level of understanding.

He was, nevertheless, an extremely sick man. Two people were needed around the clock to assist him. Mum was determined that he would be cared for at home. She sat by his bedside with steely determination. Amongst Dad's daughters there was enough nursing experience. Eldest daughter, Jenny, as well as Susan, were experienced nurses. Mieke had spent years in aged care. So, these three, together with sister Mappie, set out a plan of how to care for Dad on a full-time basis. They virtually took over the house from Mum, made schedules and timetables and, in pairs, were always there. Other members of the family came to assist in other ways, like cleaning and cooking. Mappie's husband, Herbert, gave a daily email summary of progress so all the broader family could stay informed.

My parents' unit, which was known as the Kleijn headquarters, now lived up to the name with family members constantly filing in and out. While Dad's condition had improved somewhat, the prognosis by the doctor was still the same – his condition was terminal. Grandchildren were invited over to say their farewells. During this period, many evenings were spent together in the lounge room of the unit with siblings, together with married partners, reminiscing about times past. It became a special time of family bonding. Reverend van Rietschoten, who was the relieving pastor for the

DAD'S FINAL WEEKS

Free Reformed Church of Armadale (because their own Pastor, Rev. Huizinga, was on a sabbatical), often dropped by to give words of comfort. He was conversant in the Dutch language, which for my parents was so important and appreciated.

On the 23rd December, brother Kees, who had come over on his own, had to fly back to South Africa to attend to his work as minister in his congregation over the festive period.

Herbert, in his regular brief, wrote that day:

> *Today it is exactly two weeks ago that Dad had a stroke. Since then quite a few things have happened. All our human calculations of how long this will last have come to nought. It is the Lord who "switches off people's lives" at his time! No second earlier! Today was no different to the last few days. Tired in the morning and bright on occasions during the day..... Throughout all this Moeke faithfully discharges her duty as Dad's wife by remaining alongside the man she married more than 63 years ago.*

Eight days later, on the 31st December at 10.45 p.m., Dad was taken to glory. Mum was sitting at his bedside. She wrote in her diary that he died very peacefully, with his breathing becoming intermittent and then stopping.

On the 7th of January, Herbert wrote his final instalment for the benefit of the overseas family. In this report he detailed the events as they happened after Dad's death.

> *This is then the last instalment of the happenings around Dad's death on the 31/12/99 at 10.45 p.m. and subsequent funeral on Friday 7th January 2000. The time between Dad's death and the night before the*

funeral was a busy time for all the children. It started already on Saturday morning being New Year's Day when the funeral had to be arranged etc. Mary and husband, Martin, arrived from the Netherlands on Tuesday, Kees and wife Nellie arrived from South Africa on Wednesday, Niek from Tasmania arrived on Wednesday and Margaret and Hans from Albany arrived on Thursday. (All the Kleijn children were now in Armadale). Tonight, the evening before the funeral was a special evening where Dad could be viewed in the funeral home by all the children, grandchildren and great-grandchildren, followed by a gathering in the Armadale Church hall building. The viewing was between 7.00-8.00 p.m. and most of the children, grandchildren and great-grandchildren saw Dad's body.

The evening in the Church hall commenced at 8.30 p.m. Oldest son Peter called the gathering to order and welcomed everyone present. On behalf of Mum he thanked all the children and grandchildren and great-grandchildren for their attendance and also thanked the daughters on behalf of Mum who looked after Dad during the last three weeks on this earth. Peter also mentioned the catering service by children and grandchildren which all in turn made sure that the carers and Mum did not have to cook dinners etc. during the last three to four weeks. Natalie Kleijn then read a poem made by granddaughter Willemien from South Africa in remembrance of Opa. This was followed by some words of comfort by Reverend van Rietschoten. He said that, as a pastor for Armadale in the absence of Reverend Huizinga, he had visited all the

people in the Fair Haven complex, so also Dad and Mum, and he had noted a childlike faith and trust in God with them, and after the stroke also found this unity of faith with the family. He read from Revelation and explained what he read. We were all encouraged by the talk. The evening was also an opportunity to "reacquaint each other with each other," to talk to Oma and meeting the visitors from overseas. Out of 166 children, grandchildren, and great-grandchildren about 100 were present. The gathering finished at 10.00 p.m.
Friday the 7th January – the day of the funeral.
All the family gathered at the Armadale Church hall before the service and then entered together with about 100 family members the Armadale church building through a side door to all take a seat in the reserved section of the church. Husband of Janet, Eddy Schoof, played the organ. The church was full. Reverend van Rietschoten led the service. His text for the meditation was Psalm 68 verses 19 and 20:
Blessed be the Lord
Who daily loads us with benefits,
The God of our salvation
Our God is the God of Salvation
And to God the Lord belong escapes from death.

The Reverend's meditation was very comforting. He had translated it in Dutch for Mum, which was very thoughtful of him.
The pallbearers were the five brothers - Peter, Niek, Harry, Kees and Arthur, together with son-in-law Herbert. The pallbearers walked next to the hearse from the gate of the cemetery to the grave – quite a

> distance. There was one stretch limousine in which Mum travelled together with Jenny, Harm and Mieke. After the funeral there was time for condolences in the Armadale Church hall. The Armadale Auxiliary took care of all the refreshments and a light lunch.
>
> I hope that our contribution over the past four weeks in keeping you all up to date with the happenings leading up to the funeral has given you also a feeling of belonging to us here in Australia. Jenny hopes to stay in Australia for a few more months and stay with Oma in her own unit. It gives Oma an opportunity to adapt to a new phase in her life.

The poem made by granddaughter Willemien Kleijn from South Africa, and read by granddaughter Natalie Kleijn, summarised so well the thoughts of so many of the descendants of Dad Kleijn.

> *Although Opa has left his earthly tent,*
> *Which had become all worn and rent,*
> *We, who are left behind,*
> *Will never forget this man, so gentle and kind.*
> *He was always seeking to enrich someone's life.*
> *Never looking for discord or strife.*
> *Always peaceful, always calm,*
> *never seeking anybody's harm.*
> *And when he sinned, he always knew,*
> *That Christ had died for his sins too.*
> *And for this his thankfulness did show,*
> *So that we, the next generation, too should know*
> *This heavenly Lord and King*
> *And his praises should learn to sing.*

Now he would not wish for us to be grieving,
At the loss, due to his leaving.
For that which causes us pain,
For him is eternal gain.
For there, in heaven above,
He is now with the One who bought him in His love.
And there one day we too shall be,
From all pain and sorrow forever free.

60. Postscript

"[He] who will also confirm you to the end, that you may be blameless in the day of our Lord Jesus Christ. God is faithful, by whom you were called into the fellowship of His Son, Jesus Christ our Lord."
~1 Corinthians 1:8-9 (NKJV)

After Dad's death, Jenny stayed with Mum in the Fair Haven unit for another five months till 22nd May 2000, when she returned to join her family in the Netherlands. Mum missed Dad enormously and would often talk to him as if he were there. A year after Dad's death she wrote in her diary:

> *Being at home every day when Dad was there was fine. But now going out on my own I so miss him. It is already nearly a year since he has been with the Lord. It seems so recent. I really hope it does not take years before the Lord also calls me to himself.*

After a few falls in late 2001 she moved out of her unit into the Fair Haven Hostel. Here she received full care. She remained fragile, however, and as she experienced bouts of dizziness, she was a candidate for unexpected falls. Despite being in the hostel the falls continued causing bruising and cuts. On the 6th December 2002 she had a fall with a more serious consequence – a broken hip. This put her in the Fremantle Hospital where she underwent an operation. There, despite initially recovering well from the operation, she had a sudden bad turn and was taken to the Lord in the early hours of the 14th December 2002. It was, within a few weeks, three years since she had lost her husband.

At the funeral service oldest brother Peter gave a talk in memory of 'Moeke'. In part, he said:

> *After father's death on New Year's Eve, three years ago, Moeke stayed in the unit until a year ago when she moved to room 16 in the Fair Haven Hostel. Where she was very happy and said "ik ben hier tot rust gekomen" (I have found my rest here). She no longer had to worry about things around the house, the plants etc. She was content with the care she received. She kept herself busy by writing letters, sending cards to all the grandchildren and great-grandchildren for their birthdays, profession of faith and any special occasion. And there were many of them 67 grandchildren and 96 great-grandchildren. Also knitting was an activity she took up again.*
>
> *The last few months she had a few falls. After her second last fall she was very sore and bruised, even cracked a little bone and her health was deteriorating as well. She was just picking up when she had another fall and broke her hip. She had a half hip replacement operation in the Fremantle Hospital which was successful, and she seemed to be doing very well at first. However, as time progressed things did not go so well, she was feeling sick and was so very tired, too*

tired to go and have the physio she needed. Last Friday December the 13th I visited her in the afternoon. She was so sick and was saying she wanted to be with Father.

In the early hours of Saturday morning December 14 at 3.15 am the Lord took her home. We as children are thankful to the Lord, who gave her as our Mother, as our Moeke.

References

Chapter 3

[1] De Kok, H. (2007). *Boer en Boerderij in de Alblasserwaard en de Vijfheerenlanden.* Boerderij & Erf. Alblasserwaard-Vijfheerenlanden. Nederland. Vol 3. p. 249

[2] Algra, A. & H.(1983). Dispereert Niet. *Twintig Eeuwen Historie van de Nederlanden.* Wever,T. Franeker. Nederland. Vol 3. p. 379.

[3] Ibid. p. 384.

Chapter 7

[4] Koers, M. (2013). *Gezin of Gesticht? Onderzoek naar gezinsverpleging voor geesteszieken in Nederland 1900-1940.* Masterscriptie Geschiedenis. Amsterdam.

[5] Slangen, J. (2011). *Van Koningsplein naar Lazarusklap.* Eburon. Delft, The Netherlands.

[6] Ibid.

[7] Ibid.

[8] Ibid.

[9] Van de Peppel, L.P.J., Van der Pols P.A. & Stolk, C. (1988). *Verwarring en Verwondering. Terugblik 100 Jaar Gereformeede Kerk Molenaarsgraaf-Brandwijk.* Molenaarsgraaf.

Chapter 13

[10] Van de Peppel, L.P.J., Van der Pols P.A. & Stolk, C. (1988). *Verwarring en Verwondering.Terug blik 100 Jaar Gereformeede Kerk Molenaarsgraaf-Brandwijk.* Molenaarsgraaf.

[11] Amelink, A.(2003). *De Gereformeerden.* Amsterdam The Netherlands. Bert Bakker.

[12] Deenick, J.W. (1991). *A Church en Route. 40 Years Reformed Churches of Australia.* Geelong Victoria. Reformed Churches Publishing House.

[13] Van de Peppel, L.P.J., Van der Pols P.A. & Stolk, C. (1988). *Verwarring en Verwondering.Terug blik 100 Jaar Gereformeede Kerk Molenaarsgraaf-Brandwijk.* Molenaarsgraaf.

Chapter 16

[14] Van der Velden, H. (1996). The Dutch health services before compulsory health insurance, 1900-1941.

Chapter 18

[15] Kennedy, J.R. (1977). Dutch Defensive Preparations. 1933-1940. United States Military Academy. Kansas, USA.

Chapter 19

[16] Kennedy, J.R. (1977). Dutch Defensive Preparations. 1933-1940. United States Military Academy. Kansas, USA.

[17] Algra, A. & Algra, H. (1971).*Dispereert niet. Twintig eeuwen historie van de Nederlanden* Derde Deel . T Wever, Franeker, The Netherlands

[18] Kennedy, J.R. (1977). Dutch Defensive Preparations. 1933-1940. United States Military Academy. Kansas, USA

[19] Ibid.

[20] Wilhelmina. (1959). *Eenzaam Maar Niet Alleen.* W. Ten Have. Amsterdam. The Netherlands. Translated by G.J. Kleyn.

[21] Couvee, D.H.(1960), *De Mei Dagen* van '40. Bert Bakker. Den Haag, The Netherlands.

[22] Kennedy, J.R. (1977). Dutch Defensive Preparations. 1933-1940. United States Military Academy. Kansas, USA.

[23] Ibid.

[24] Jongeling, P., De Vries, J.P., & Douma, J. (1979). *Het Vuur Blijft Branden.* J.H. Kok. Kampen, The Netherlands.

Chapter 20

[25] Bredewold, H. & Zwaan, J. (1975). 1940 de Mei-Oorlog. Buijten & Schipperheijn. Amsterdam, The Netherlands.

[26] Couvee, D.H. (1960), *De Mei Dagen van '40.* Bert Bakker. Den Haag, The Netherlands.

Chapter 22

[27] Werkman, E., de Keizer, M.& van Setten, G.J. (1980). *Dat kan ons niet gebeuren.* De Bezige Bij. Amsterdam, The Netherlands.

[28] Ibid.

[29] Algra, A. & Algra, H. (1971). *Dispereert niet. Twintig eeuwen historie van de Nederlanden.* Vijfde deel. T. Wever, Franeker, The Netherlands. (Translated by H. Kleyn).

[30] Werkman, E., de Keizer, M.& van Setten, G.J. (1980). *Dat kan ons niet gebeuren.* De Bezige Bij. Amsterdam, The Netherlands.

[31] Ibid.

[32] Ibid.

Chapter 23

[33] Werkman, E., de Keizer, M. & van Setten, G.J. (1980). *Dat kan ons niet gebeuren.* De Bezige Bij. Amsterdam, The Netherlands.

[34] Ibid.

[35] Korpel, A. (1984). *De Waard in Oorlogstijd.* De Klareon. Alblasserdam, The Netherlands.

Chapter 24

[36] Werkman, E., de Keizer, M. & van Setten, G.J. (1980). *Dat kan ons niet gebeuren.* De Bezige Bij. Amsterdam, The Netherlands.

[37] Norel, K., De Vries, A., & De Zwerver,F. (1947). *Den Vijand Wederstaan.* Zomer & Keuning. Wageningen, The Netherlands.

[38] Werkman, E., de Keizer, M. & van Setten, G.J. (1980). *Dat kan ons niet gebeuren.* De Bezige Bij. Amsterdam, The Netherlands.

Chapter 26

[39] George Duncan's Lesser-Known facts of World War II. Retrieved from; http://members.iinet.com.au/~gduncan/index.html

[40] Korpel, A. (1984). *De Waard in Oorlogstijd.* De Klareon. Alblasserdam, The Netherlands.

[41] Ibid.

Chapter 27

[42] Biesbosch.nu. Retrieved from: http://www.biesbosch.nu/historiepagina.php?code=19

[43] Werkman, E., de Keizer, M. & van Setten, G.J. (1980). *Dat kan ons niet gebeuren.* De Bezige Bij. Amsterdam, The Netherlands.

[44] Dando-Collins, S. (2015). *Operation Chowhound.* Palgrave MacMillan. Fifth Avenue, New York.

Chapter 28

[45] Verzets Museum. Dodenaantal Tweede Wereldoorlog. Retrieved from: https://www.verzetsmuseum.org/jongeren/inval/doden_wo2

[46] Ibid.

[47] Ibid.

[48] Nationale Bibliotheek. Oranje bitter, Nederland Bevrijd. Retrieved from: https://www.kb.nl/themas/geschiedenis-en-cultuur/tweede-wereldoorlog/oranje-bitter-nederland-bevrijd

[49] De Dokwerker. Ter dood veroordeelden. Retrieved from: http://www.dedokwerker.nl/terdoodveroordeeld.html

[50] Algra, A. & Algra, H. (1971). *Dispereert niet. Twintig eeuwen historie van de nederlanden* Vijfde deel. T. Wever, Franeker, The Netherlands. (Translated from Dutch by H. Kleyn)

[51] Ibid.

Chapter 30

[52] Norel, K., De Vries, A., & De Zwerver, F. (1947) *Den Vijand Wederstaan.* Zomer & Keuning. Wageningen. The Netherlands.

[53] Jongeling, P., De Vries, J.P., & Douma, J. (1979). *Het Vuur Blijft Branden.* J.H. Kok. Kampen, The Netherlands.

[54] Van de Peppel, L.P.J., Van der Pols P.A. & Stolk, C. (1988). *Verwarring en Verwondering.Terugblik 100 Jaar Gereformeede Kerk Molenaarsgraaf-Brandwijk*

[55] Ibid

[56] Jongeling, P., De Vries, J.P., & Douma, J. (1979). *Het Vuur Blijft Branden.* J.H. Kok. Kampen, The Netherlands.

[57] Van Tongeren, H.(1965). *Mandate maintained. The 'Vrijmaking' in a nutshell.* American Reformed Church. Grand Rapids, United States of America.

Chapter 31

[58] Veldman. H. (2019). *De Vrijmaking van 1944. Hoe de start in Den Haag doorwerkte in Noord Nederland.* Veldman en Gort. Zuidhorn/Grijpskerk. Nederland.

[59] *Hoe een kleine kerk Kerk Bleef ; Bergschenhoek 1941-1945.* De Raad van de Gereformeerde Kerk te Bergschenhoek.

[60] Deddens, D. & te Velde, M. (1994). *Vrijmaking – Wederkeer. Vijftig jaar Vrijmaking in beeld gebracht. 1944-1994.* De Vuurbaak, Barneveld, Nederland.

[61] *Hoe een kleine kerk Kerk Bleef; Bergschenhoek 1941-1945.* De Raad van de Gereformeerde Kerk te Bergschenhoek.

[62] Kok, J.,& Van Der Waal, C. (1971). *Van Strijd en Zegepraal*. Oosterbaan & Le Cointre. Goes. The Netherlands.

Chapter 33

[63] Peters, N. (2006). *The Dutch Down Under. 1606-2006*. UWA Press. Crawley, Western Australia.

[64] Een Nieuwe Toekomst. Australia and New Zealand Bank Limited. London, England.

Chapter 34

[65] Museum Victoria. Retrieved from: https://collections.museumvictoria.com.au/articles/15587

[66] Peters, N. (2006). *The Dutch Down Under. 1606-2006*. UWA Press. Crawley, Western Australia.

Chapter 35

[67] Peters. N. (2001). *Milk and Honey-but No Gold*. University of Western Australia Press. Crawley, Western Australia.

[68] Peters, N. (2006). *The Dutch Down Under 1606-2006*. University of Western Australia Press. Crawley. Western Australia.

[69] Zubrzycki, J. (1995). Arthur Calwell and the origin of Post war immigration. Bureau of Immigration, Multicultural and Population research. Canberra, Australia. retrieved from: http://www.multiculturalaustralia.edu.au/doc/zubrzycki_1.pdf

[70] Peters. N. (2001). *Milk and Honey-but No Gold*. University of Western Australia Press. Crawley, Western Australia. p.18.

[71] Parliamentary Library. Migration to Australia since Federation: a guide to statistics. Retrieved from: https://www.aph.gov.au/binaries/library/pubs/bn/sp/migrationpopulation.pdf

[72] South African History Online. Retrieved from: https://www.sahistory.org.za/topic/women-children-white-concentration-camps-during-anglo-boer-war-1900-1902

[73] Little, R.J. (1954). Statistical Register of Western Australia for 1951-52. By Authority William H. Wyatt. Government Printer. Perth, Western Australia.

[74] Carter, J. & B. (2011). *Settlement of a City. A history of the Armadale district and its people*. City of Armadale. Armadale, Western Australia.

[75] Bosveld, G.J. (2008). *Free Reformed Pioneers*. Pro Ecclesia Publishers. Armadale, Western Australia.

[76] South Western Advertiser. 19th July, 1951.

Chapter 36

[77] Minutes Immigration Committee Meeting. Reformed Church Armadale. 10th January 1952.

[78] Ibid.

[79] Bosveld, G.J. (2008). *Free Reformed Pioneers*. Pro Ecclesia Publishers. Armadale ,Western Australia

[80] *South-Western Advertiser*. 22nd May 1952.

[81] *South-Western Advertiser*. 12th June 1952.

Chapter 38

[82] Buirchell, A.W. (1998) *Only One Oakford. A History of Oakford Primary School 1923-1998*. Oakford Primary School. Oakford, Western Australia.

Chapter 40

[83] Una Sancta. Vol.2. No.26. 17th September 1955. p. 12.

Chapter 41

[84] Dutch Dikes. Retrieved from: http://dutchdikes.net/

[85] Van Rees, H.J. (1994). *Eenheid en Scheiding. Historische Schetsen van Molenaarsgraaf en Brandwijk*. De Groot Drukkerij Goudriaan. The Netherlands.

[86] Delta Works Flood Protection, Rhine-Meuse-Scheldt Delta, Netherlands. Retrieved from: https://www.water-technology.net/projects/delta-works-flood-netherlands/

[87] Watersnoodramp (1953). Een Rampzalige stormvloed. Retrieved from https://historiek.net/watersnoodramp-1953/6913/

Chapter 45

[88] Bosveld, G.J. (2008). *Free Reformed Pioneers*. Pro Ecclesia Publishers. Armadale Western Australia. p. 299.

Chapter 46

[89] Salomons, K. Varia. *Una Sancta* Vol. 1 no. 8. 9th January 1954.

[90] Plug, H. The Australian Unions. *Una Sancta* Vol. 1. no. 22. 24th July 1954.

[91] Plug, H. The Australian Unions. *Una Sancta* Vol. 1. no. 23. 7th August 1954.

[92] Van Gurp, P. Uit de Kerkeraad's Vergaderingen. *Una Sancta* Vol. 4. no. 8. 19th January 1957.

Chapter 51

[93] Australian Bureau of Statistics. 1367.5 – Western Australian Statistical Indicators, September 2001: Feature article – A century of Population Change in Western Australia.

Chapter 55

[94] Popman, D. (1980) *First Stage South: A History of the Armadale-Kelmscott District, Western Australia*. The Town of Armadale. Armadale, Western Australia.

[95] Carter, J. & B. (2011) *Settlement to City: A History of the Armadale districts and its people*. City of Armadale. Armadale, Western Australia.

[96] Ibid.

[97] Australian Bureau of Statistics. 1367.5 – Western Australian Statistical Indicators, September 2001: Feature article – A century of Population Change in Western Australia.

Bibliography

Algra, A & H. (1983). *Dispereert Niet. Twintig Eeuwen Historie van de Nederlanden*.Franeker. Nederland. T. Wever.

Amelink, A.(2003). *De Gereformeerden*. Amsterdam, The Netherlands. Bert Bakker.

Australia and New Zealand Bank Limited. (1951). *Een Nieuwe Toekomst. Gids voor Europeanen die belangstelling hebben voor een nieuwe toekomst in Australia en Nieuw-Zeeland*. London, England.

Baardman, C. (1946). *Een Lied van den Biesbosch*. Den Haag, The Netherlands. J.N. Voorhoeve.

Batenburg, J.A. (1994). *Sliedrecht in Oorlogstijd. 1940-1945*. Sliedrecht, The Netherlands. J.A. Batenburg.

Bos, I.W. (1970). *Sliedrecht zoals het was 1890-1940*. Den Haag, The Netherlands. Rijkhoek.

Bosveld, G.J. (2008). *Free Reformed Pioneers*. Armadale, Western Australia. Pro Ecclesia Publishers.

Boxma, W. (1970). *De Alblasserwaard. Nederland in Miniaturen*. Nijkerk, The Netherlands. G.F. Callenbach.

Bredewold, H. & Zwaan, J. (1975). *1940 de Mei-Oorlog*. Amsterdam, The Netherlands. Buijten & Schipperheijn.

Buirchell, A.W. (1998) *Only One Oakford. A History of Oakford Primary School 1923-1998*. Oakford, Western Australia. Oakford Primary School.

Carter, J. & B. (2011). *Settlement of a City. A History of the Armadale District and its People*. Armadale, Western Australia. City of Armadale.

Couvee, D.H. (1960). *De Mei Dagen van '40*. Den Haag, The Netherlands. Bert Bakker.

Dando-Collins, S. (2015). *Operation Chowhound*. Fifth Avenue, New York. Palgrave MacMillan.

Deddens, D. & te Velde, M. (1994). *Vrijmaking – Wederkeer. Vijftig jaar Vrijmaking in beeld gebracht. 1944-1994*. Barneveld, Nederland. De Vuurbaak.

Deenick, J.W. (1991). *A Church en Route. 40 Years Reformed Churches of Australia.* Geelong, Victoria. Reformed Churches Publishing House.

De Kok, H. (2007). *Boer en Boerderij in de Alblasserwaard en de Vijfheerenlanden.* Alblasserwaard-Vijfheerenlanden, Nederland. Boerderij & Erf.

De Raad van de Gereformeerde Kerk te Bergschenhoek. *Hoe een kleine kerk Kerk Bleef; Bergschenhoek 1941-1945*

De Vries, W.G. (1977). *K Schilder als gevangene en onderduiker.* Groningen. The Netherlands. De Vuurbaak.

Harinck, G. (2005). *Tussen Lijdelijheid en Verzet. Gereformeerden in Bezettingstijd.* Barneveld, The Netherlands. De Vuurbaak.

Jongeling, P., De Vries, J.P., & Douma, J. (1979). *Het Vuur Blijft Branden.* Kampen, The Netherlands. J.H. Kok.

Kennedy, J.R. (1977). *Dutch Defensive Preparations. 1933-1940.* Kansas, USA. United States Military Academy.

Kerkwijk, P.A. (1968). *Alblasserwaard en Vijfheerenlanden. Een stukje historisch en groen Holland tussen Lek en Merwede.* Ameide, The Netherlands. Crezee Ameide.

Knoop, H. (1945). *Een Theater in Dachau.* Goes, The Netherlands. Oosterbaan & Le Cointre.

Koers, M. (2013). *Gezin of Gesticht? Onderzoek naar gezinsverpleging voor geesteszieken in Nederland 1900-1940.* Amsterdam, The Netherlands. Masterscriptie Geschiedenis.

Kok, J., & Van Der Waal, C. (1971). *Van Strijd en Zegepraal.* Goes, The Netherlands. Oosterbaan & Le Cointre.

Korpel, A. (1984). *De Waard in Oorlogstijd.* Alblasserdam, The Netherlands. De Klareon.

Norel, K., De Vries, A., & De Zwerver, F. (1947). *Den Vijand Wederstaan.* Wageningen, The Netherlands. Zomer & Keuning.

Norel, K & De Man, H. (1949). *Mannen van Sliedrecht.* Nijkerk, The Netherlands. G.F. Callenbach.

Ooms, J.W. (1985). *De Alblasserwaard in vroeger Tijd.* Kampen, The Netherlands. De Groot Goudriaan.

Peters, N. (2006). *The Dutch Down Under. 1606-2006.* Crawley, Western Australia. UWA Press.

Peters. N. (2001). *Milk and Honey-but No Gold.* Crawley, Western Australia. University of Western Australia Press

Popman, D. (1980). *First Stage South: A History of the Armadale-Kelmscott District, Western Australia.* Armadale, Western Australia. The Town of Armadale.

Schakel, M.W. (1993). *De Waard onder Water. De Alblasserwaard in woord en Beeld Tijdens de Watersnood in 1953.* Molenaarsgraaf. The Netherlands. Stichting Publicaties Binnenwaard.

Schilder, K. (1945). *Bezet Bezit.* Goes. The Netherlands. Oosterbaan & Le Cointre.

Slangen, J. (2011). *Van Koningsplein naar Lazarusklap.* Delft, The Netherlands. Eburon.

ter Laak, P.J. (1982). *Sliedrecht in de goede oude tijd.* Sliedrecht, The Netherlands. Wijngaarden.

Van de Peppel, L.P.J., Van der Pols P.A. & Stolk, C. (1988). *Verwarring en Verwondering. Terugblik 100 Jaar Gereformeede Kerk, Molenaarsgraaf - Brandwijk.*

Vandersmissen, H. (1986*). Ophogen en Uitdiepen. Tien Eeuwen Nederlands Baggerbedrijf.* Den Haag, The Netherlands. Smits.

Van Der Toorn, J. (2014). *Tabak in de Tuin. Mijn Jeugd in de Oorlog.* Houten, The Netherlands. J Van Der Toorn.

Van der Zwan, J. (1970). *De Dag dat het Manna Viel.* Den Haag, The Netherlands. J.N. Voorhoeve.

Van Dooren. G. (1986). *And We Escaped.* Burlington, Canada. Golden Jubilee Committee.

Van Rees, H.J. (1994). *Eenheid en Scheiding. Historische Schetsen van Molenaarsgraaf en Brandwijk.* Goudriaan, The Netherlands. De Groot Drukkerij.

Van Tongeren, H. (1965). *Mandate Maintained. The 'Vrijmaking' in a Nutshell.* Grand Rapids, United States of America. American Reformed Church.

Veldman. H. (2019). *De Vrijmaking van 1944. Hoe de start in Den Haag doorwerkte in Noord Nederland.* Zuidhorn/Grijpskerk, Nederland. Veldman en Gort.

Verburg, G. (1955). *Storm over Nederland.* Nijkerk, The Netherlands. G.F Callenbach.

Werkman, E., de Keizer, M. & van Setten, G.J. (1980). *Dat kan ons niet gebeuren.* Amsterdam, The Netherlands. De Bezige Bij.

Wilhelmina. (1959). *Eenzaam Maar Niet Alleen.* Amsterdam. The Netherlands. W. Ten Have.

www.ingramcontent.com/pod-product-compliance
Lightning Source LLC
Chambersburg PA
CBHW070728020526
44107CB00077B/2081